FRIEDRICH MEINECKE
AND GERMAN POLITICS IN THE
TWENTIETH CENTURY

Friedrich Meinecke
and German Politics in the
Twentieth Century

ROBERT A. POIS

UNIVERSITY OF CALIFORNIA PRESS
BERKELEY   LOS ANGELES   LONDON
1972

University of California Press
Berkeley and Los Angeles, California
University of California Press, Ltd.
London, England
Copyright © 1972 by The Regents of the University of California
ISBN: 0-520-02045-6
Library of Congress Catalog Card Number: 70-157818
Designed by W. H. Snyder

To my parents

Preface

IN CONSIDERING Hamilton Fish's position in President Grant's somewhat tainted administration, some wag of that age referred to him as "the jewel on the head of a toad." Critical reviewers, if they indeed bother at all to read prefaces, must certainly view their positions relative to the books they introduce in a similar fashion, for it is in the preface that the author exhibits both modesty and gratitude, two qualities he then proceeds to eschew in the body of his work. Furthermore, it is in the preface that the author often acknowledges that the thesis or theses presented in the work might very well not be valid until the end of time and that, indeed, *error,* in one form or another, might very well have crept into his work. Keeping my eye on the casuistry involved in the process, and being somewhat conservative in matters of style, I would like to affirm my adherence to this pleasant tradition.

This book began as a doctoral dissertation under the direction of Dr. George L. Mosse of the University of Wisconsin. Besides supervising my work on the dissertation, Dr. Mosse has been the single most important intellectual influence on my life, and the gratitude that I owe him is without measure. Several of my colleagues at the University of Colorado have been of immense help in assisting me in the clarification of some of the ideas presented in this book. Here, I must mention Dr. David Gross, Dr. Daniel M. Smith, and Dr. Robert A. Skotheim. Dr. and Mrs. Robert G. Athearn were of incalculable value in helping me to translate my work from that peculiar sort of Low German characteristic of young professors suffering from an overexposure to German philosophy, into English. Furthermore, a correspondence with Dr. Georg G. Iggers of the State University of New York at Buffalo was of great value. Grants provided in 1966, 1967, 1969, and 1970 by the Council on Research and Creative Work of the University of Colorado allowed me to do necessary research, the grant for the summer of 1969, in fact enabling me to go to Germany. The staffs of the *Preussischer Geheimes Staatsarchiv* in Berlin, the *Institut für Zeitgeschichte* in Munich, and the *Bundesarchiv* in Koblenz were all immensely helpful and courteous. The secretaries of the Department of History of the University of Colorado have displayed both energy and patience in dealing with me and with my manuscript. The final copy was typed by Mrs. Barbara Nielson of Boulder. My thanks go to all of them. Finally, for encouragement and support in often trying times, I must express a deep sense of gratitude to A. M., whose presence has meant so much.

R. A. P.

Contents

1
Introduction, 1

2
Friedrich Naumann and Friedrich Meinecke, 4

3
Statism Triumphant, 12

4
Nach der Revolution, 26

5
The Clash between Power and *Kultur*, 49

6
Friedrich Meinecke and the Weimar Republic, 86

7
The Rejection of Power, 131

8
The Rejection of Politics, 138

9
Summary, 144

Postscript, 148

Bibliography, 157

Index, 161

1

Introduction

IT IS DOUBTFUL if there is a more significant period of history than that spanned by the life of Friedrich Meinecke (1862–1954). For this reason he had the opportunity to observe and react to events of awesome splendor and terror, events that made his Germany synonymous with both heroism and horror. His well-known statism of earlier years was put to the monstrous tests engendered by two German catastrophes. The naked state egoism he implicitly praised in *Cosmopolitanism and the National State* (*Weltbürgertum und Nationalstaat*, 1907) failed to meet these tests, and Meinecke's subsequent rejections of it in favor of a superpolitical cosmopolitanism have been described by Walther Hofer, Richard Sterling, and, in his *Consciousness and Society*, by H. Stuart Hughes. These works have been concerned primarily with the ethical and, in the case of Walther Hofer, methodological ramifications of Meinecke's troubled journey on the road from statism to cosmopolitanism.

However, Meinecke's reactions to Germany's history in the twentieth century in purely political terms have never been subject to study in any great detail. Except insofar as he has been traditionally considered an eloquent defender of the Weimar Republic during its fifteen-year history, Meinecke, as a commentator on German internal politics, has been largely ignored. For this reason, I feel many questions of considerable importance have been left unanswered: What were the political implications of Meinecke's turning away from the naked machiavellism of *Weltbürgertum und Nationalstaat*? What was Meinecke's understanding of Nazism and the forces that underlay its coming into being? What was the significance—if any—of his devotion to the political ideas of Friedrich Naumann? The purpose of this essay is to attempt to provide at least partial answers to these questions and in so doing to point out why Meinecke's supposed eventual rejection of statism created more problems than it solved. I also hope to show how this rejection served to make it extremely difficult, if not impossible, for him to arrive at any real understanding of the basic needs and perversions that drove his ill-starred countrymen from abyss to abyss.

The course of Meinecke's political thinking has often been described as one conditioned by a gradual but inexorable rejection of the naked power politics rationalized in his first great work, *Weltbürgertum und Nationalstaat* (1907). Meinecke's post-World War I and post-World War II works, *Die Idee der Staatsräson,* 1924 (translated by Scott as *Machiavellism*) and *The German Catastrophe* (*Die deutsche Katastrophe,* 1946), do point to a strong reaction against the moral casuistry necessitated by unconditional state worship. However, I feel that Meinecke's eventual turning toward the Goethean cosmopolitanism he had once rejected indicated either an avoidance of, or an inability to comprehend, the basic issue of twentieth-century German history: the politicalization, in terms of *mass* politics, of certain aspects of German *Kultur.* By the end of World War II, Meinecke had, in effect, rejected politics in the name of *Kultur,* thus implicitly indicating that he thought a qualitative difference between politics and *Kultur* indeed existed. Through his rather parochial definition and application of *Kultur* to historical investigation, Meinecke thus tended to divorce cause from effect in divorcing politics from the societal and cultural framework(s) within which politics must develop. This process allowed him to draw fairly close—particularly during the Weimar period—to elements we have come to recognize as being salient to German right-wing political thinking. He thus flirted with corporatism and with a romantic-organic view of the state and the *Volk*'s role in the state without ever fully appreciating the role these elements played in the maximalist ideologies that at first threatened and then took over Germany.

Meinecke's rejection of the naked statism inherent in *Weltbürgertum und Nationalstaat* combined with vestigial elements of this statism (this to be seen in his rather narrow view of the role of Nazism vis-à-vis the state and in his lifelong adherence to the national-socialist ideas of Friedrich Naumann) prevented him from gaining an appreciation of the forces that destroyed the spiritual integrity of the German nation.

Of course, when we consider Meinecke's political writings during the Weimar period, we must bear in mind that he did indeed stand to the left of much of the middle class. Those who belonged to the German People's party (DVP) never forswore allegiance to the monarchy. Also, if one considers the German National People's party (DNVP), which espoused anti-Semitism within the party program itself, Meinecke must be seen as representing a center of cool reason. Furthermore, when we finally consider his *The German Catastrophe* of 1946, we must bear in mind that this work was written by a man who was 84 years old and half blind to boot. However, the fact that Meinecke, during the Weimar period, was a part of the more enlightened element of Germany's *Bildungsbürgertum* serves simply to give the history of this period more poignant, if not tragic, overtones. Moreover, the obvious deficiencies and oversights of *The German Catastrophe* were not merely the results of the ravages of old age, unless we view Meinecke's entire post-World War I life as being a prolonged battle with senility. The weaknesses of Meinecke's post-World War II reaction to Nazism had substantial rooting in the whole course of his intellectual development after World War I, as well as that of the *Bildungsbürgertum* of which he was a member.

Of particular importance here was Meinecke's tendency to reach for the "nonpolitical," or at least superpolitical, solution. Like so many of his class, Meinecke apparently viewed mundane political affairs with contempt. To a degree, this may be attributed to the legacy of Leopold von Ranke who, as we shall see, felt that politics was legitimately the concern only of the unified *state*, in a word, that *foreign policy* stood above the concerns of interest groups and factions. Meinecke, like his intellectual mentor Ranke and very much like Thomas Mann of the World War I period, eschewed the pluralism of the, to him, vulgar and self-centered interest groups. For Meinecke, even when he supported the German Democratic party during the Weimar years, the politics that mattered were the politics of state; and, throughout his life, he never rejected that attitude which eschews political conflict in favor of the stasis hypothetically provided by a unified state. Whether Meinecke was a monarchist or a republican, whether he was attacking the apparent chaos of the Weimar Republic or the Nazis, his attitudes were determined, at least in the political arena, by a fundamental commitment to the unified *Volksstaat*, one in which mundane politics had to have been subordinated to, if not displaced by, the interests of the whole.

Because of the nature of this work, most of Meinecke's methodological essays and works—except those that bear at least a tangential relationship to his political evolution (e.g., *Die Idee der Staatsräson* and *Die Entstehung des Historismus*)—have not been considered. This work is concerned with Meinecke as a political commentator upon German internal politics during the twentieth century. Considerations of ethics and methodology—although obviously not of *Weltanschauung*—are thus left to the treatments of Walther Hofer and Richard Sterling. The almost exclusive concern of this essay with politics is not to be taken as being directed against any of the approaches of Meinecke's previous critics. I merely hope to point out certain aspects of Meinecke's political thinking which, in a grimly quiet fashion, provide their own commentary on the German tragedy of the twentieth century.

2

Friedrich Naumann and Friedrich Meinecke

As THE GERMAN NATION stood at the brink of World War I, largely preoccupied with external threats to its security and increasingly concerned with the prospects of enhancing its position among the family of nations, it was also faced with the continuing problem of breaking the dominance of aristocratic power over national political life. Since the formation of the empire in 1871, the fate of its people had been largely determined by a combination of the traditional Junker military class and powerful bourgeois interests that sought to emulate the imperious qualities of the Junkers. However, around the turn of the century a curious challenge to this powerful, if unlikely, alliance began to emerge. Its most arresting characteristic was the demand for social and political reform in the name of the state.

At its inception the leaders of the movement were regarded as no more than ephemeral "armchair" radicals, but by the eve of the war their ideas had gained some recognition by at least one existing political party, the newly refurbished (1910) Progressives.

This particular challenge to the ruling Junker clique was posed by a group of bourgeois intellectuals. This group drew its strength from the left wing of the National Liberal party and from the ranks of the Progressive party, and it revolved around the political ideas of two prominent German intellectuals, Max Weber and Friedrich Naumann. The latter figure exercised an almost charismatic influence upon Friedrich Meinecke, one that would persist even after the latter had consigned state worship to the dustbin of history. For this reason, it is useful to take a close look at Naumann and his particular variety of statism.

The story of Friedrich Naumann's political thinking is somewhat similar to that of Friedrich Meinecke's in that it is one of a nineteenth-century nationalist attempting to come to terms with the twentieth century. Nevertheless, Naumann differed from Meinecke; he approached the age of mass man in a positive, or at least more hopeful fashion. Naumann's first major public activity was his association with the vitriolic and anti-Semitic Pastor Adolf Stöcker in forming the Union of German Students (*Verein Deutsche Studenten*) in 1881. This group was significant as one of the first Volkishly oriented youth movements in post-unification Germany.[1] However, Naumann's association with the group was tenuous, and, by the end of the decade, he had turned his efforts toward broader horizons.[2] Although Naumann rejected the anti-Semitism of the Union of German Students, its naïve conception of Christian social justice impressed him deeply and, as early as 1890, he was calling on the stodgy liberals of Imperial Germany to infuse their programs with a sense of social justice and thus to provide for a firm bridge between liberals and Social Democrats.[3]

In 1895, Naumann attended Max Weber's inaugural address at the University of Freiburg. He was deeply impressed by Weber's emphasis upon power and the state and upon the predominance of foreign policy goals in determining the tenor of national life.

From this point on, we can detect a rather interesting shift in Naumann's approach. Under the strong influence of Weber, Naumann began to emphasize power over ethics as the primary justification for a program of social justice and the integration of the masses into the state. One year after Naumann had been exposed to the almost quaint—as it must appear now—statism of Weber, he established the National Social Union (*National-Sozialen Verein*), dedicated to the fusion of national bourgeois and proletarian socialist ideals into a cohesive national whole, in a word, to the task of bringing the masses to the state. The anti-Semitism of Naumann's formative years was missing from the party's program. So was the emphasis upon Christian social justice, although Weber still found enough traces of it to call for a mild rebuke on his part.[4] Naumann's rather esoteric group lasted only seven years; Naumann himself dissolved it in 1903. However, the political philosophy informing it became a prominent feature of the pre-World War I political philosophy of Friedrich Meinecke.

For Naumann and, as we shall see, for Meinecke also, the primary problem that confronted the German state around the turn of the cen-

1. George L. Mosse, *The Crisis of German Ideology* (New York, 1964), p. 193
2. Koppel S. Pinson, *Modern Germany: Its History and Civilization* (New York, 1954), pp. 170–172; Hans Kohn, *The Mind of Germany, The Education of a Nation* (New York, 1960), p. 281.
3. Pinson, *op. cit.*, p. 171.
4. See "Gründung einer National-Sozialen Partei," in Max Weber's *Gesammelte Politische Schriften* (2d ed., ed. Johannes Winckelmann; Tübingen, 1958), p. 27.

tury was anachronism, "the dressing of the industrial *Volk* in the political clothes of the agrarian state."[5] Naumann felt that this problem could be solved in part by utilizing certain basic features of German industrial development as bases for a new state structure that combined constitutionalism with social and economic improvements. Naumann thought that the industrial syndicates of Germany could serve as corporate agencies which represented and embodied the wishes and interests of manager, capitalist, and worker. This process could be linked with an overthrow of such time-hallowed institutions as the three class voting system (*Dreiklassenwahlrecht*) in Prussia. However, Naumann did not feel that an overthrow of the Hohenzollern Dynasty would be necessary, or even desirable. Indeed, in *Democracy and Empire* (*Demokratie und Kaisertum*), first published in 1900, he saw an important role for the monarchy. After all, according to Naumann, it was the Kaiser, rather than the Reichstag, who was pointing the way to future German greatness. In his concern for a strong navy and in his role vis-à-vis the army, Wilhelm II was displaying far greater foresight than the hidebound parliamentarians who seemed to be concerned with stricturing Germany's role in the world rather than with enhancing it.[6]

In this regard, we must confront a rather interesting aspect of Naumann's thinking: his tendency to link together democracy and power. There can be no doubt that Naumann wanted to increase the power of the Reichstag and provide social justice for the working man. However, he displayed a tendency that had been prominent in German political thought since the early writings of Ranke: the subordination of internal affairs to the broader interests of foreign policy. In *Democracy and Empire,* Naumann pointed out that internal and external politics and policies were inextricably intertwined. Nevertheless, the course of foreign policy was fraught with "more serious consequences" than that of internal policy.[7] Internal reform had to be accomplished to strengthen the state and thus to make it more capable of exercising a strong role in the family of nations. Internal reforms and social legislation were dependent upon the course of foreign policy anyway. After all, what good would proletarian betterment do if the state that provided for it were smothered by Cossacks?

Naumann's view of the German state itself was rather interesting inasmuch as he maintained that Empire (*Kaisertum*), democracy, and the new "industrial aristocracy" were really aspects of one and the same

---

5. Friedrich Naumann, *Das Blaue Buch von Vaterland und Freiheit* (Leipzig, 1913), p. 64.
6. Friedrich Naumann, *Demokratie und Kaisertum* (3d ed., enlg.; Berlin, 1904), pp. 187–189.
7. *Ibid.*, p. 178.

thing: the state. In this regard, Naumann pointed out that democracy meant merely the majority principle in legislative matters, while *Kaisertum* embodied the unitary principle of the state. The "industrial aristocracy" was, of course, the economic substance of the developing German state.[8] Thus, the economic and political reforms envisioned by Naumann were not seen by him as being *primarily* of constitutional significance. Certainly, in his eyes, they were not to be interpreted as being part and parcel of a given political doctrine.

It is not liberalism . . . or even less, socialism; but its pressing forward combines liberal and social elements: economic progress and elevation of production through associations, through organizations of work.[9]

The economic aspect of Naumann's program, that is, economic planning and control through functional syndicates, had been, as Naumann saw it, inhibited by the fact that Germany had never really accepted the meaning of the industrial age. It had tended, as Max Weber also pointed out, to stricture its socioeconomic development in the Procrustean bed of an archaic adherence to the once heroic form of *Junkertum*.[10] Naumann saw this fact as the primary reason Germany needed so many state regulatory agencies and so many laws: "because our industrial government is so underdeveloped." [11] Naumann went further in pointing out that there was a need for labor unions, management, and the various associations of Germany's capitalists (*Unternehmerverbände*) to work together to give the "protection and freedom of movement necessary for the working class . . . in order [for them] to be [come] human." [12]

Basically, Naumann's primary purpose was to increase the state's ability to direct the attention of the German working class to national goals and particularly to those that involved national expansion. "If Germany wants to assume its great role," he maintained, "it will need to clothe itself in new garments to that purpose. The old Prussian clothes are too stiff for that." [13] In other words, for Germany to be assured a place in the sun commensurate with her massive potential, capitalism had to be blended with socialism and the class conflict tran-

8. *Ibid.*, pp. 180–181.
9. *Ibid.*, p. 67.
10. Wolfgang J. Mommsen, *Max Weber und die deutschen Politik: 1890–1920* (Tübingen, 1959), pp. 107–108.
11. Naumann, *Demokratie und Kaisertum*, p. 199.
12. *Ibid.*, p. 205.
13. *Ibid.*, p. 214.

scended. Germany's colonial ambitions and concerns for power had to be protected and *"a great general will to progress upwards must be made alive in the masses."* [14] The key to making this mass will come alive resided in the state's ability to rally the German working class to the standard. Naumann felt they could be rallied with relative ease if the above-mentioned fusion of capitalistic nationalism and quasi-syndicalist reform was implemented. Once the masses had been brought to the state, events would follow apace, for "the German worker movement represents the greatest volunteer militarism [*freiwillige Militarismus*] on earth." [15] For Naumann, the political struggle in which he was engaged was not meant "to raise essentially the human happiness of each individual . . . but to build the state." [16] After all, for this new devotee of the pristine Weberian power state, the source of all human rights was power. Democracy, Naumann maintained, had to be purged of a vitiating "internationalism" and a new "democracy of the Fatherland" (*vaterländische Demokratie*) set up in its place.[17] He was adamant in maintaining that the democrats of Germany could and should never renounce Germany's basic power drives, and he indicated that any group seeking to do so could never sustain itself in Germany. Democracy and naked power were inextricably bound together; and, in an age of mass war, *"Germany's military future depends upon the degree to which its democracy is impregnated with national thought."* [18] Richard Nürnberger points out that, for Naumann, providing men with dignity and arousing in them a feeling "of responsibility for the whole" were really one and the same thing.[19]

As might be expected, war was seen by Naumann as being a necessary if unfortunate ingredient in the lives of states. "As long as there has been a world, only the stronger have had historical justification." [20] If there was to be peace, it could be assured only by the great powers.[21] Indeed, even in his rose-tinted *Central Europe* (*Mitteleuropa,* 1915)—where Naumann envisioned an economic and, to a lesser extent, constitutional unification of Central Europe through German influence—he was careful to point out that though he considered such unification a

14. *Ibid.*, p. 205; emphasis is Naumann's.
15. *Ibid.*
16. Theodor Heuss, *Friedrich Naumann: der Mann, das Werk, die Zeit* (Stuttgart, 1937), p. 173.
17. Naumann, *Demokratie und Kaisertum*, p. 57.
18. *Ibid.*, p. 202; emphasis is Naumann's.
19. Richard Nürnberger, "Imperialismus, Sozialismus und Christentum bei Friedrich Naumann," *Historische Zeitschrift*, Band 170, Heft 3 (1950), p. 545.
20. Naumann, *Demokratic und Kaisertum*, p. 10.
21. *Ibid.*, p. 206.

first step in the direction of a "United States of the World," the proposed bloc would at first have to gird its loins against blocs of other states.[22]

What Naumann in effect had done was to fuse freedom and authority and reform and power in the name of the state. While such an achievement might have appeared an anomalous one in the context of pre-World War I Germany, Naumann was actually drawing his political sustenance from a curiously German permutation of liberal thinking which saw the individual and the state and freedom and authority not as necessarily opposed but indeed complementary, if not identical. The concept of the individual receiving a spiritual mandate of sorts from the collective whole in which he participated is a common one in the history of German political thinking. There can be little doubt that Naumann, perhaps even more so than his political mentor, Max Weber, had become very much a part of this tradition.

Friedrich Meinecke, who was born in 1862, was but two years younger than Naumann. He was thus of Naumann's generation and was confronted with approximately the same problems and issues. He also was concerned about drawing the masses to the state, and he also tended to emphasize external affairs, seeing internal reform as a response to the pressing needs of foreign policy. In this regard, Meinecke had a more impressive intellectual pedigree than did Naumann: Meinecke was a historian and more immediately heir to the impressive tradition of Ranke.

Yet, there were substantial differences between the Saxon Naumann and the Prussian-born Meinecke. The most substantive of these differences was the one of mood and temperament. Naumann, as we have seen, welcomed the industrial age and felt little fear for Germany's future. *Kultur* need not, Naumann presumed, be damaged by the emergence of mass man onto the world stage. Meinecke was of a somewhat different temperament. By his own admission, he was a *Biedermeier*.[23] In a word, he was spiritually rooted in the mid-nineteenth century, in a social world of bric-a-brac and official piety, protected by a divinely

---

22. Friedrich Naumann, *Mitteleuropa* (trans. Christabel Meredith as *Central Europe;* New York, 1917), p. 179.

23. Friedrich Meinecke, *Erinnerungen*, Vol. II, *Strassburg, Freiburg, Berlin, 1901–1919* (Stuttgart, 1949), pp. 261–262. *Biedermeier* originally referred to a variety of interior decoration fashionable between 1815 and 1848 (the period of German history often referred to as *Vormärz*), and which emphasized solid bourgeois comforts and traditional craftsmanship over any variety of radical experimentation. From this time on, *Biedermeier* was often used to depict a "self-satisfied philistine," one who is straightforward to the point of simple-mindedness. In referring to himself as *Biedermeier*, Meinecke probably meant that he was old-fashioned.

sanctioned sword wielded by the few in defense of the few. While Meinecke may well have understood some of the phenomena of the industrial age intellectually, he could hardly suffer it emotionally; and it was this factor that, more than any other, drew him to Naumann.[24] Naumann both understood and appreciated the new age, or at least he spoke and wrote as if he did. Consequently, Nauman would remain the one unshaken political idol for Meinecke, even after the power state which they both once worshipped had been rejected by the latter. Although the story of Meinecke's career after World War I was largely the story of his rejection of power in favor of *Kultur* (that curious word which Walther Rathenau once wrote should be banned from the German language), Naumann's political ideal—the fusion of social justice and interest of state—remained Meinecke's ideal also. The functional state —a hypothetical entity in which each of its members found both fulfillment and meaning without having to disrupt the activities of the whole —remained Meinecke's guiding star until his death. Indeed in his last work, *The German Catastrophe* (*Die deutsche Katastrophe,* 1946), Meinecke would go so far as to say that Naumann's synthesis combined "both the most spiritual and the most practical . . . elements in the German people . . . ", that it achieved at last "that synthesis of classical liberalism" which had thus far eluded not only the Germans, but in fact all European politicians and political philosophers.[25]

It would be most inaccurate, however, to maintain that Meinecke derived his entire political *Weltanschauung* from Naumann. Although the latter was mentioned with plaudits in several of Meinecke's works, Meinecke himself partook of the same spiritual heritage regarding the state as did Naumann. Meinecke's somewhat more esoteric interests merely prevented him from putting his ideas down in the form of a broad political program. In a way, we might say that Naumann existed as the political alter-ego of Meinecke, an alter-ego that spoke aloud those ideas and programs Meinecke the historian had to sublimate in the name of more remote issues.

Yet, Meinecke was a more complex individual than Naumann. Whether Meinecke was made this way by an exposure to the Weimar period, which Naumann's early death (1919) prohibited him from having, or whether he was naturally so can never be known. Nevertheless, Meinecke, particularly after World War I, came to embody several contradictory characteristics: he remained a student of statecraft, yet to save *Kultur* he thought it necessary to overthrow the power/*Kultur* synthesis of which the state was composed. He was bitterly opposed to

24. *Ibid.*
25. Friedrich Meinecke, *Die deutsche Katastrophe* (trans. Sidney Fay as *The German Catastrophe;* Cambridge, Mass., 1950), p. 19.

Nazism yet, perhaps without knowing it, sympathetic to some of the emotionalism behind it. He was a defender of the Weimar Republic, yet he remained almost morbidly suspicious of parliamentary government. In fine, Meinecke was the good, bourgeois German of the post-World War I period, a far more complex individual than Naumann, whose enticing political program he more than once attempted to justify.

The pre-World War I Meinecke was apparently afflicted with few of the dichotomies that would blight him later. If he was somewhat troubled by the problems of industrialism and mass democracy, he yet felt, as did Naumann, that Germany was on the path toward a solution. If he felt that the state should be conscious that it had to maintain and promote power/*Kultur* synthesis of which it was composed, he yet seemed confident that the final step in this synthesis was not far away. Indeed, one might say that Meinecke was approaching the issue of the state on a far broader front than was Naumann, for he was not merely attempting to strengthen it in a mundane, political fashion, but was creating a profound rationalization for it in the intellectual history of his country. *Weltbürgertum und Nationalstaat* (*Cosmopolitanism and the National State*, 1907) was the product of these efforts, and it is to a consideration of this work and the ideational world behind it that we must now turn.

3

*Statism Triumphant:
Meinecke up to November, 1918*

SPIRITUALLY, Meinecke was able to assume a much more sophisticated position concerning the state than was Naumann. While Naumann approached the state tangentially—that is, at first through his concern for Christian social justice—Meinecke was weened on the Rankean statist historiography and served as an archivist in the Prussian State Archives between 1887 and 1901. His mentor there was none other than the Prussian historian Sybel who, along with Dahlmann and Droysen, sought to emphasize the importance of Prussian history and who also emerged as one of the most prominent defenders of Bismarck.[1] In brief, Meinecke had been imbued with the salient principles of the Prussian School of historiography, a "school" that had been, in turn, greatly influenced by the sovereign mind of Leopold von Ranke. Perhaps the most characteristic single tenet of Prussian historiography since Ranke was its emphasis upon the state, not the state of Hegel, which in reality drew its value and meaning from the awesome evolution of Absolute Mind—that is, that comprehensive triad of Art, Religion, and Philosophy—but the state as an independent entity, operating in terms of its own laws. Hegel, in his heroic Idealism, had bound the state, even while exalting its glory, to a higher realm where the great World Spirit moved in profound silence. Ranke had brought the state down to earth by a spiritualizing of power itself. The state now stood on its own feet, in all its earthly glory, to be exalted if not worshipped by a generation of German historians who stood in understandable awe before the creation of Bismarck. Meinecke, while not uncritical of this creation, was yet very much a part of this singular tradition.

His *Life of General Field Marshal Hermann von Boyen* (*Leben des*

1. Hans Kohn, *The Mind of Germany, The Education of a Nation* (New York, 1960), p. 129.

Generalfeldmarschalls Hermann von Boyen, Stuttgart, 1896–1899), had exalted this hero of the Liberation period. Here was a man who had sought to strengthen the state and to preserve its cultural heritage by wedding its inhabitants to it through democratizing the army. He had attempted to do this in the face of traditional Prussian authoritarianism and, in the end, he had been defeated by this tradition.[2] Nevertheless, his cause had been a good one. Meinecke's biography of von Boyen, while massive, is not really of great importance for our considerations. However, it does reveal an interesting aspect of Meinecke's thinking, one that brought him into fairly close proximity to Naumann: his willingness to *sacrifice* traditional institutions and values in order to best strengthen the state. Necessity of state, *Staatsnotwendigkeit,* was the touchstone of Meinecke's political thinking up to the end of World War I.

The magnum opus of Meinecke's statist period, however, was not concerned merely with the doctrine of "reason of state" but rather with the evolution of the state idea (*Staatsidee*) itself. *Cosmopolitanism and the National State* (*Weltbürgertum und Nationalstaat*) appeared in 1907, and this brilliant work established Meinecke as one of the leading German historians of intellectual history. While a work in the history of ideas, *Cosmopolitanism and the National State* also served to rationalize the political thinking of Meinecke during this period (1900–1918). It is important for yet another reason, inasmuch as Meinecke's post-World War I thinking was largely directed *against* the statist rationalizations contained in this book.

The purpose of *Cosmopolitanism and the National State* was to trace the state "Idea" as it developed in nineteenth-century Germany. Thus, it was concerned mainly with describing the politico-philosophical atmosphere that existed in Germany during this time. Briefly, Meinecke felt that two ideas, whose origins he traced back to the period of the Enlightenment, had to be circumscribed in their influences and effects if a truly "national" conception of the state was to be formulated. (This conception had to be based, of course, upon a firm understanding of empirical historical reality.) The two ideas were: (1) the idea of the "Universal" man, the corollary of this idea being the appreciation and demand for a universal and supernational order, and (2) the idea of the importance of the individual and his right to create and to develop himself according to the dictates of his reason. Meinecke claimed that the earlier German Romantics were deeply influenced by these two ideas. However, both of these notions had to be and were abandoned, at least as key principles in political philosophy, during the course of German political evolution.

2. Friedrich Meinecke, *Leben des Generalfeldmarschalls Hermann von Boyen,* Vol. II (Stuttgart, 1896–1899), pp. 390–392.

Succinctly, Meinecke felt that the Romantics (particularly the early Romantics, *Frühromantiker*) had tended either to ignore or to deprecate the political state in their individual pursuits of the Universal. In their eyes, the Universal could find temporal embodiment only in the *Kultur*, that is, the spiritual heritage of a given people (*Volk*). This concept both stemmed from and reinforced the notion that "the German *Reich* and the German nation were two different things; that *Kultur* and the character of the German nation were independent from its political fates . . . ."[3]

Meinecke thought that Johann Gottlieb Fichte (1762–1814) had managed to extricate himself from the Romantic Universalism that up to then had inhibited the emergence of the state idea (*Staatsidee*). However, Fichte's own concept of the "State of Reason" (*Vernunftsstaat*), whereby the state received a mandate of sorts from Universal Reason, also had served to hypothetically inhibit the state's ability to act as a free agent.

According to Meinecke, even the early Prussian patriots and reformers—Stein, Gneisenau, and Scharnhorst—had failed to appreciate the prerogatives to which the Prussian state was entitled simply as a consequence of its being. Concepts of a "United Europe," predicated upon slavish adherence to Universalist principles, prohibited these reformers from appreciating the unconditional nature of the power drives of the state.[4]

Universalism and Romanticism had warped the political views of both the legitimists and the nationalists of the post-Napoleon Restoration period.[5] It took a Leopold von Ranke to appreciate the state as an organic, self-seeking phenomenon which developed in terms of prescribed laws of self-interest. With Ranke, the state had come into its own. Furthermore, he was able, through his limited application of teleology, to fuse the individual phenomenon in history to the general forces of which it was representative. For Ranke, "the nature of the thing and opportunity, genius and good fortune [all] work together."[6] Meinecke pointed out that Ranke had thus been able to avoid the Hegelian tendency to subordinate all individual and national activities to the role of being a mere "play" (*Schauspiel*) of the World Spirit as it searched for fulfillment in self-contemplation.

Ranke had viewed states as being, particularly in their relationships with other states, self-seeking organisms. This led to two primary

3. Friedrich Meinecke, *Weltbürgertum und Nationalstaat* (München. 1908), p. 54.
4. *Ibid.*, p. 154.
5. *Ibid.*, p. 261.
6. *Ibid.*, p. 285.

tendencies in Rankean thought: (1) The tendency to see the state as a "nation-builder" rather than the other way around. A people might have a sense of national identity, but it was only through the "moral energy" (*moralische Energie*) of the state that this people could be infused with a sophisticated awareness of its own being and purpose. According to this view, the nation could only rationalize itself in terms of its being an instrument of the state. (2) The tendency to view internal developments as being subordinate to and indeed *implemented* in response to the overpowering demands of external developments, that is, to the issues that arose as the individual state came in contact with other states. Both of these points were of great importance in determining Meinecke's political attitudes up to the time of Germany's collapse in November 1918. Furthermore, even though Meinecke later turned against statism as such, he was never able to place internal affairs on the same level as foreign affairs.

Meinecke, in *Cosmopolitanism and the National State,* saw the evolution of German political thinking being crowned by the realization that the state was an organic, self-determining entity. Furthermore, at this time he accepted the notion that power and *Kultur* could exist side-by-side within the state framework and that, indeed, *Machtstaat* and *Kulturstaat* were one. Meinecke's purely political writings of the pre-World War I and World War II periods were based upon the presuppositions and conclusions of *Cosmopolitanism and the National State.* The book had extolled the state idea. Now, the very real German state of the twentieth century had to be strengthened. Meinecke's reactions to the course of political events in Germany during the prewar years and to his country's participation in World War I become understandable if we bear in mind that, in the Rankean tradition, he viewed external events as determining domestic developments. Thus, he tended to view internal developments, say, reform, as being dictated largely by the demands of foreign policy. Even if we accept the proposition that Meinecke often did not view internal reforms in terms of their intrinsic value, we must not gainsay the fact that he evinced a thoroughgoing interest in drawing the German masses to the state. This interest drew him into the left-wing of the National Liberal party and, of course, caused him to display considerable interest in the political thinking of Friedrich Naumann. At this time, however, Meinecke did not reject the power-political aspects of Naumann's thinking. While this did not vitiate the sincerity of the former's desire for at least a more constitutional form of monarchy, it does point out that Meinecke, like Naumann, did tend to subordinate considerations of reform to those of power.

Strengthening the German state, to steel it for its growing role in world affairs, necessitated reform. The little group of liberal bourgeoisie of which Meinecke was a member was well aware of this need. By 1912, the Social Democratic party was the largest single party in Germany. The liberals were well aware of it also. Strengthening the state and heading off a suspected stampede to the Left on the part of the German proletariat and its bourgeois sympathizers were merely different sides to the same question. Obviously, that anachronism, the *Junkerstaat,* had to give way to a state of all the German people (*Volksstaat*) if Germany was to be capable of assuming a place in the sun commensurate with its power potential. "Everywhere, a new aristocracy is developing among us," Friedrich Meinecke counseled his countrymen in 1912. "Without . . . agreement, it is developing from the most modern needs as an instinctive adjustment to them." [7] As a Nauman-supporting left-wing National Liberal, Meinecke attacked both the Conservatives and the Catholic Center party, declaring, "The liberals have taken up the task of directing the righteous indignation of these masses, so far as this is possible, onto national paths." [8] Here, Meinecke's conception of the role of liberal reform is clear. The indignation felt by Germany's masses toward their government and toward those parties that were supporting it was justified. However, it was the task of the liberals—one assumes that Meinecke here means the left-wing National Liberals and the Naumann-dominated Progressives—to convert this indignation into an emotional commitment to the state. The liberal bourgeoisie thus had the great task of strengthening the state by drawing the bulk of Germany's population to it. Those elements already committed to the state had to participate in creating a nationally conscious people. Thus it was necessary to end the archaic *Dreiklassenwahlrecht* in Prussia, and to break the fiscal stranglehold that had been maintained by the Junker class since 1879.

To say that Meinecke desired a democratization of the state would be stretching his spirit of reform somewhat thin. Probably, the establishment of a true constitutional monarchy and palpable concessions to republicanism were his ultimate goals. Meinecke's attitude toward politics was revealed in a letter to G. von Below, dated December 22, 1911. Here, Meinecke indicated that Germany needed both conservative and liberal ideologies. However, he himself was more concerned with making " '*Konservativ*' useful again." He admitted that, although he felt free from party pressure, effective reform could not take place without it.[9]

Meinecke's own political activities before World War I were some-

7. Friedrich Meinecke, *Politische Schriften und Reden,* ed. Georg Kotowski (Darmstadt, 1958), p. 50.
8. *Ibid.,* p. 53.
9. Friedrich Meinecke, *Ausgewählter Briefwechsel,* ed. Ludwig Dehio (Stuttgart, 1962), p. 35.

what limited, but they are of interest. In 1912 he and Aschoff were the National Liberal delegates from Freiburg and, in that capacity, attended the National Liberal *Parteitag* in Berlin. Meinecke was not inspired by Bassermann, the party leader at the time, who seemed uncertain as to the position of his party, particularly inasmuch as the conservative right wing, dominated by heavy industry, seemed closer to the Conservatives than to Naumann's Progressives.[10] During the campaign itself, Meinecke did come out strongly for the "new conservatism" he had mentioned previously. In the *Breisgauer Zeitung* of January 11, 1912, he attacked the old Conservative party, as well as the *Reichspartei*, for not recognizing the "true colors of our political life." True conservatism accepted change, and thus the National Liberal party was the only true conservative party left.[11] Old and new had to be synthesized and, throughout 1912, Meinecke was adamant in voicing his belief that the Social Democrats had to be won for the nation.[12] The same was true for Catholics and, in a *Strassburger Post* article of January 10, 1912, Meinecke called upon Catholics to differentiate between "true Catholicism" and that form of antinational political Catholicism which was embodied in the Center party.[13]

Meinecke's call for a new form of conservatism was indicative of his concern for the preservation of the German state in a new world of industry and mass armies. It also led him in the direction of a sort of volkish socialism, and one of the individuals for whom he expressed admiration was the anti-Semitic "state-socialist," Adolf Wagner.[14] Meinecke at this time was not terribly concerned with creating a great, unified party of the bourgeois center; but, he was concerned with the "unlimited unfolding of all the strengths of bourgeois Germany in the service of national unity." [15] Meinecke's interest in this and his concurrent desire for bringing the working classes to the nation put him in the camp of Naumann, if not in the latter's particular party.

The outbreak of World War I served to catalyze Meinecke's thinking on the subject of needed social and political reforms. If Germany was to be able to tap its burgeoning national potential in response to the white heat of total war, an amalgamation of previously disparate groups

10. Friedrich Meinecke, *Erinnerungen*, Vol. II, *Strassburg, Freiburg, Berlin, 1901–1919* (Stuttgart, 1949), p. 130.
11. Stiftung Preussischer Kulturbesitz, Geheimes Staatsarchiv, Rep., 92, Nachlass Meinecke, Nr. 92, *Breisgauer Zeitung,* January 11, 1912.
12. *Ibid.*
13. Stiftung Preussischer Kulturbesitz Geheimes Staatsarchiv, Rep. 92, Nachlass Meinecke, Nr. 92, *Strassburger Post,* January 10, 1912.
14. *Ibid., Breisgauer Zeitung,* January 11, 1912.
15. Geheimes Staatsarchiv, Rep. 92. Nachlass Meinecke, Nr. 92, *Breisgauer Zeitung/Freiburger Neueste,* February 13, 1912.

was dictated by necessity of state (*Staatsnotwendigkeit*), and, for Meinecke, implied a nationalization of all the parties in response to the stress of war. Meinecke, however, seemed to be aware of the danger involved in suddenly infusing nationalist thought into a previously inert and politically immature people. He found it necessary to inhibit the irrational misuse of Nietzschean and Darwinian thinking and to curtail "the fashionable and uncritical racist teachings" [16] in the name of that same *Staatnotwendigkeit* that demanded the strengthening of the German state by drawing ever-increasing numbers of the population to it. In a 1915 article, "Social Democracy and Power Politics" ("Sozialdemokratie und Machtpolitik"), Meinecke wisely pointed out that the influence of "mighty mass action" could and would probably be more detrimental to the cause of peace than "the secret policies of cabinets and diplomats." However, he remained adamant in his demand that Germany advance further on that journey to a true "national community" (*"nationalen Gemeinwesen"*) that had begun in 1813.[17] The German state had to fulfill its historical function of creating a true state of the people (*Volksstaat*). The unified and virile state of *Cosmopolitanism and the National State* had finally to emerge from the shadowy half-life of obscurantist social divisions and meaningless palliatives. Once the war was over, even the Social Democrats and the workers they represented had to be rewarded for their efforts to defend a state into which they had been, unfortunately, only partly integrated.[18] After all, as Meinecke pointed out in 1917, "domestic and foreign politics are narrowly and inextricably intertwined with each other." [19]

Meinecke was cognizant of the fact that the term "necessity of state" could be misused and, on this basis, he fought diligently, as a charter member of the People's League for Freedom and Fatherland (*Volksbund für Freiheit und Vaterland*), against the annexationist war goals of the Fatherland's party (*Vaterlandspartei*). The frightening combination of Pan-German chauvinism and cold Machiavellism displayed by such groups as the latter convinced Meinecke that there was "a grievous lack of real-political sobriety on the part of the larger portion of our educated elements." Nevertheless, he still fought with great determination for the unified *Volksstaat*, one ideally infused with what he called "the specific German sense of citizenship." [20]

16. Meinecke, *Politische Schriften und Reden*, p. 86.
17. Friedrich Meinecke, *Die deutsche Erhebung von 1914* (Stuttgart, 1914), p. 13.
18. Friedrich Meinecke, "Für Welche Güter zog Deutschland 1914 sein Schwert?" *Schützengraben Bücher*, no. 115 (1918).
19. Meinecke, *Politische Schriften und Reden*, p. 215.
20. *Ibid.*, p. 248. Meinecke is never very clear in defining the actual socioeconomic or even political content of the bourgeoisie. However, the

During World War I, the statist form displayed in *Cosmopolitanism and the National State* received statist substance. A rational social and political structure inside would help to assure rational direction of the state's foreign policy. In his *The German Revolt of 1914* (*Die Deutsche Erhebung von 1914*), Meinecke did point out that the Bismarckian state system had lost much of its validity as Europe moved into the age of mass politics and mass war. However, this merely indicated that the state ideal had to be diffused ad infinitum throughout the mass state. In a new world in which the comforting rigidity of secret diplomacy and cavalry leather was of scant importance, "each one of us must have a little of Bismarck . . . ." [21]

What Meinecke desired during the war years was the emergence of the total *Volk* into the state, the creation of a *Volksstaat* in order to best ensure the strengthening of the *Machtstaat*. The superior German freedom, which was characterized by a synthesis of individualism and devotion to the whole, had to infuse the entire *Volk*. Only then would Germany be able to assume that role "assigned to her by history": that of being "a newer, higher type of world people [*Weltvolk*]." [22] In this context, we can again observe Meinecke's allegiance to a basic tenet of post-1848 German liberalism: the reconciliation of freedom with power in favor of power.

We must now recall what we mentioned earlier: Meinecke's inclination to view internal history as being "inextricably intertwined" with the course of external affairs. Of course, such a formulation, even if it begs the question in specific instances, has an obvious heuristic value in historical and political analysis. However, as pointed out before, Meinecke tended to see internal affairs—for example, reforms—as either being subordinate to foreign affairs or, ideally, as responses to the dictates of external necessity. This tendency tarnished somewhat Meinecke's reputation as a liberal, at least during the war years. Both in *The German Revolt of 1914* and in his 1918 contribution to the *Schützengraben Bücher* series (literally, *Trench Book* series), "For What Goals Did Germany Draw its Sword in 1914?" (*Für welche Güter zog Deutschland 1914 sein Schwert?*), themes of political reform were subordinated to

---

qualities he praised as constituting that specific German "citizenship sense" were its combining of freedom of the individual with order and its ability to provide for the harmony and strength of the whole ". . . and so to attain political consequences of the life ideal of our classical poets and thinkers . . . ." This sense of citizenship was obviously a bourgeois phenomenon. Thus we could say that the bourgeoisie in fact represented and/or embodied those elements necessary for the harmonious functioning of state life.

21. Meinecke, *Die deutsche Erhebung von 1914*, p. 29.
22. *Ibid.*, p. 35.

broader, quite machiavellian ones of increasing power. Also, quite idyllic themes—interestingly enough, most prominent in the 1918 work—of a German protected *Mitteleuropa,* free trade areas, and sublime colonial adventures made their appearance. Moreover, Meinecke maintained, a strong Germany was necessary to preserve a "plurality of culture and power within the society of nations" against possible British hegemony.[23] It would not be unfair, then, to maintain that Meinecke gave top priority to state power interests and that he felt that German internal political developments had to be oriented in terms of these interests. It is certainly true that Meinecke disavowed the schemes of such groups as the *Vaterlandspartei.* However, he did so more out of his Clausewitzian sense for war as an instrument of foreign policy, than out of any deep-seated feelings against expansion. Expansion in terms of goals established in a real-political fashion was acceptable, if not laudable. *Expansionism,* that is, expansion as part of an ideology, was quite wrong inasmuch as it violated the most basic canons of *Realpolitik.* Meinecke —as did, of course, Friedrich Naumann—did not choose to recognize extensions of political and economic power into southeastern Europe as constituting expansion. However, all this really proved was Meinecke's basic lack of sympathy for the "raw bestiality of the south Slavs." [24]

As early as November 1914 (in a letter to Alfred Dove), Meinecke indicated that he thought the military situation dictated the necessity for a Hubertusburg-variety peace of reconciliation. ("Hubertusburg Peace" refers to the peace treaty of that name which, in 1762, ended the Austro-Prussian portion of the Seven Years' War.) However, it is interesting to note that Meinecke, while considering the issue of Belgium to be the serious one, still felt that it might be resolved by drawing her into some sort of expanded *Zollverein.*[25] In a May 6, 1915, letter to Walter Goetz, Meinecke indicated that Belgium could not be simply restored; otherwise a power imbalance against German interests would be created.[26] Furthermore, Meinecke began to evidence substantive interest in "strengthening the German character of Posen and West Prussia," while indicating that it would be a good thing if Courland could be placed at the disposal of German farmers.[27] In a later letter to Dove, this one dated July 31, 1915, Meinecke expanded his territorial concerns to include: a Maas line frontier in the West, a port on the Belgian coast, Courland, and pieces of Lithuania. Such territorial gains were not

---

23. Ludwig Dehio, *Germany and World Politics in the Twentieth Century,* Trans. Dieter Pevsner (New York, 1959), p. 58.
24. Meinecke, *Politische Schriften und Reden,* p. 85.
25. Meinecke, *Ausgewählter Briefwechsel,* pp 50–51.
26. *Ibid.,* pp. 58–59.
27. *Ibid.,* p. 61.

to be viewed as originating from desires for conquest, but rather were dictated by "bitter political necessity."[28] By 1917, as Meinecke noted in his *Erinnerungen,* most of these demands had wilted in the face of continued stalemate and the palpable threat posted by American intervention. However, it is obvious that, while Meinecke was adamantly opposed to the bastardized Machiavellism evidenced by the *Vaterlandspartei,* the actual substance of what he considered to be a Hubertusburg Peace tended to fluctuate in relationship to the military situation.

Out of his deep feeling for *Staatsnotwendigkeit,* Meinecke attempted to circumscribe German war aims in terms of the plausible. He worked toward this end to the same degree that he fought for a *Volksstaat* capable of attaining these goals. There was, of course, nothing unique or underhanded in such an approach. Nor was such a jerry-built synthesis of military necessity and political reform confined to the power-political schemes of Meinecke or even unique to Germany. National conscription and the gradual breaking down of class lines in Great Britain marked that nation's entry into the age of mass politics and mass armies. Yet, when seen in the context of German political history, Meinecke's tendency to justify political reform in terms of victory raised some questions regarding his appreciation of Germany's political needs. Germany had no parliamentary tradition. It had no established framework or even guidelines to provide for the implementation of republicanism, much less democratization. Meinecke disavowed the extremist war aims of the Pan-Germans, to be sure. However, victory, or at least the enhancing of Germany's power position, was the real purpose for political reform. The *Volksstaat* was merely the means for the full development of the *Machtstaat* of *Cosmopolitanism and the National State.* By binding political reform to reason of state, Meinecke was falling back upon a darker element in the troubled history of German liberalism. Constitutional monarchy, republicanism, democratization— each of these terms was merely the means to an end. If the particular means proved unsatisfactory, it could be altered or abandoned altogether.

The role that Meinecke assigned to proposed electoral reforms, particularly to reform of the *Dreiklassenwahlrecht* in Prussia, can be clearly seen in the descriptions, in *Erinnerungen,* of his occasional meetings with Bethmann-Hollweg. To the latter's statement that he felt it would be risky to promulgate electoral reform in a wartime situation, Meinecke replied that it would be infinitely more dangerous *not* to do so. Both Meinecke and Bethmann-Hollweg saw electoral reform as a means of strengthening the state by drawing the masses to it; and Meinecke admitted that, in 1917, he thought it best that a *plural* voting arrange-

28. *Ibid.,* p. 65.

ment be introduced into Prussia, in order that an aristocratic brake (*Hemmschuh*) be placed upon sudden overdemocratization.[29] Such an attitude on Meinecke's part is certainly understandable. However, it clearly indicates that one who calls for internal political reform in the name of externally determined *Staatsnotwendigkeit* need have only the most fragile of commitments to substantive reform measures.

Meinecke's demand for reform in the name of the state was in part predicated upon a rather questionable assumption: that the increase of strength enjoyed by the Social Democratic party represented a palpable threat to national interests. In this regard, it would appear that Meinecke was taking the Erfurt Program of 1891, where the Social Democrats vowed adherence to Marxist principles, more seriously than did many of the Social Democrats themselves. Certainly he took it more seriously than did Max Weber, who recognized that the Social Democratic party was becoming a "party machine" . . . like "the bureaucratically organized mass party" of America.[30] Weber's point was that the Social Democratic party was eschewing agitational and ideological goals for power on behalf of its increasing numbers of bureaucratic functionaries. Weber was well aware that the party was involved in gradually substituting ancillary and organizational goals for ideology during the years preceding World War I, and hence was well on its way to becoming a "party of order." Meinecke did not view the party in this fashion. While he did not consider the Social Democrats to be dangerous revolutionaries, he did regard them as an antistate, or at least antinational, phenomenon. After all, the Social Democratic party was supposed to be a class party.

Meinecke was, of course, correct in assuming that the continued domination of the old Prussian system posed a problem insofar as drawing the masses to the state was concerned. In his postwar writings he would maintain that the collapse of November 1918 was to some degree attributable to the lack of involvement in or commitment to the state on the part of the German masses. Perhaps there was some truth in this; perhaps not. What is important to note here is Meinecke's concept of the *role* of nationalism.

For Meinecke, at least during the pre-World War I years, nationalism was seen as a *state* phenomenon, or state-created phenomenon. In that

29. Meinecke, *Erinnerungen*, Vol. II, pp. 225–226.
30. Wolfgang J. Mommsen, *Max Weber und die deutsche Politik: 1890–1920* (Tübingen, 1959). On the subject of the gradual bureaucratization of the SPD, see also Richard N. Hunt's *German Social Democracy: 1918–1933* (New Haven, Conn., 1964), pp. 56–62, 241–256; also, Robert Michels's *Zur Soziologie des Parteiwesens in der modernen Demokratie* (Leipzig, 1910), of which Hunt makes use.

capacity, it was to be utilized by and for the state as the latter sought to attain well-defined and presumably rationally determined goals. As did Naumann, Meinecke viewed nationalism as something that could massively augment the power of the state. Meinecke recognized the dangers involved in unleashing power strivings within nationalism itself, and often tended to view the political emancipation of the German masses in terms of a gradual devolution of power from the state hierarchical structure. What Meinecke did was to extend the concept of the nation-building power of the state (as this had been presented in *Cosmopolitanism and the National State*) onto the field of practical politics. Meinecke viewed such phenomena of mass irrationality as racism and concepts of innate German superiority as being tangential or even harmful to the basic process of constructing a viable *Volksstaat*.

Meinecke felt that the lack of support for the Prussian state, as evidenced by the increase in the power of the Social Democrats and later by military collapse, was the result of certain oversights and mistakes in judgment made during Bismarckian and Wilhelmenian days. There were serious errors and oversights, yet they could be rectified in time.

As mentioned briefly above, Meinecke saw the bourgeoisie as filling a great role in enlisting mass support for the state. We have seen Meinecke's demand that all elements of society be infused with that "specific German sense of citizenship," which involved a combination of individualism and responsibility for the whole. Historically, such a sense of citizenship had been espoused by the political ideologists of Germany's middle class. The very word for citizen, *Bürger,* also means member of the middle class. For Meinecke, a self-confessed "old *Biedermeier,*" this identification had more than an etymological significance. As we have seen, he maintained (and would continue to maintain) that the representative liberals of Germany's middle class had the vital function of binding the masses to the state, no doubt, by infusing them with the "specific German sense of citizenship."

Meinecke's implied faith in the political abilities and sagacity of the German middle class raises the issue of just what had been the role of the bourgeoisie in pre-World War I Germany. In this regard, Max Weber castigated the German bourgeoisie for its failure to assume a sociopolitical role commensurate with its rising economic strength. According to Weber, this class had failed to develop that principle of accomplishment in the professions which was of "a specifically bourgeois character . . . ."[31] Rather, it had tended to exalt ideals of a "pseudo-aristocratic character" in order to better emulate the old, decaying Prussian nobility.[32] Throughout his writings, Weber accused both the bour-

31. *Ibid.,* p. 107.
32. *Ibid.*

geoisie and the workers of lacking "the great national instinct for power," and he blamed the "traditionally negative" attitude of liberalism toward power for this development.[33] Considering the rather unhappy history of German bourgeois political achievement since 1848, it would appear that the burden of proof regarding its political capacities rested on Meinecke. However, on this question he was almost studiously vague, even in his 1918 essay "German Citizenship in the War" ("Das deutsche Bürgertum im Kriege").

Throughout the prewar years and even during the war itself, Meinecke was able to remain fairly optimistic regarding the role of the bourgeoisie —or even its lack of a role. Apparently referring to the prewar gains of the Social Democrats and to the leveling effects which he saw as resulting from World War I, Meinecke remarked, "The relative decline in the value of the bourgeoisie is thus, in the first place, a sign of absolute growth in the national collective struggle." [34] Here, Meinecke obviously was attempting to assuage bourgeois-liberal fears by pointing out that the values of the bourgeoisie were beginning to infuse all of German society, and hence the bourgeois class itself would be of relatively less importance. (In postwar works, however, Meinecke would point out weaknesses and deficiencies he saw in the German bourgeoisie.) The problem involved here, of course, is that Meinecke himself was probably never certain as to the abilities of his own class to fulfill the role he assigned to it: strengthening the state. Its political role was certain. However, its spirit (*Geist*) was something of which Meinecke was never sure.

One can easily appreciate why Meinecke, as did Naumann, thought it preferable if the great mass of the German *Volk* received its cultural infusions from the bourgeoisie. Its very role as a "middle" class seemed almost to providentially ordain it as the class selected to bind the *Volk* together. Furthermore, Meinecke himself was of this class, and he was no doubt aware of its *Kultur*-bearing propensities. Nevertheless, particularly in later writings, Meinecke was never really certain as to the middle class's commitment to the strengthening of the state. Perhaps, Meinecke was not in error when he maintained that bourgeois social and political values should and would provide the matrix within which the broadened state-nationalism could thrive. Meinecke's basic problem was his own inability to determine whether or not his class was ready to address itself to its task in a mature fashion. Of particular significance for the future was Meinecke's feeling that nationalism could be a reasonable *state*-nationalism. In other words, he did not feel that irrational elements—such as racist teachings and chimerical war aims—had to be

33. *Ibid.*, p. 47.
34. Meinecke, *Politische Schriften und Reden*, p. 248.

part of this nationalism. Meinecke felt that nationalism should be utilized and expressed in a rational fashion. Raw and vulgar emotionalism had no role to play.

Meinecke's political attitudes during the prewar period and during World War I itself were based on the quasi-Rankean idea of the *Machtstaat,* in other words, upon that definition of the state which he presented in *Cosmopolitanism and the National State.* This can be seen in Meinecke's emphasis upon the nation-creating role of the German state and upon the rational employment of nationalism by the state in the name of *Staatsnotwendigkeit.* Moreover, the utilization of nationalism to strengthen the state was seen as being a necessary response to the demands of foreign policy. The demands were those imposed upon and created by the Rankean ego-state as it acted and reacted in a world of ego-states.

Meinecke was sufficiently aware of the problems of a mass age (and a mass war) to recognize the need for reform, and for this reason he drew close to the political ideals of Friedrich Naumann. However, he was enough of a *Biedermeier* to believe that power could be devolved, through the mediating link of an enlightened bourgeoisie, to the German masses, and that these masses (and, for that matter the bourgeoisie itself) could be trained never to overstep the bounds of real-political propriety in being nationalistic. The pre-1918 Meinecke, while not naïve, was in many ways extraordinarily optimistic. As the state idea was being concretized, he felt, the entire German *Volk* was being brought around to its support. Power and *Kultur,* the individual and the whole, were all neatly balanced. There was, admittedly, some doubt as to the bourgeoisie's capacities, but its *role* was certain; and this class, the bearer of German *Kultur,* could be brought around to recognizing it.

November 1918 brought a sudden and brutal end to the beautiful dream. Meinecke had had doubts and fears before. Now, old ones were augmented and new terrors came to the surface as Germany seemed to face a rapid future of enforced republicanism and bitter humiliation. Meinecke's reactions to the early post-World War I period constitute the concern of the next chapter.

4

Nach der Revolution

THE GERMAN EMPIRE had been put together in nine years, and had been purchased at the cost of perhaps fifty thousand German lives. In terms of the unemotional calculus of *Realpolitik,* the price had been reasonable. Now, in November 1918, the German people counted one million, eight hundred thousand dead. A generation had been sacrificed on a half dozen rainswept fields or left to hang on a curtain of wire from the Flanders Coast to the Vistula. Most bitter of all, the Empire had not even been preserved, but indeed seemed threatened with imminent destruction. The German people would respond in several different manners to the catastrophe, their respective responses being determined by the various combinations of intellect, raw emotion, and prejudice which had taken shape in Germany both because of and in spite of the grandeur of Empire.

Meinecke's own response to the 1914–1918 slaughter and, most important of all, to defeat, was calm, yet bitter, and it would color his intellectual efforts from this time on.

On September 27, 1918, when defeat was all but a foregone conclusion, Meinecke put down in his diary his fears for Germany's future. Most assuredly a German state could not derive its sustenance from the pap offered from the Left. "No state could rule for long on the basis provided by the protagonists of the left, with their Jewish, sentimental-soft ideas . . . ." A large measure of iron was needed.[1] A diary entry for October 13, 1918, reflects, with even greater clarity, the bitterness of Meinecke. The German public was too exhausted and demoralized to resist to the end. It had no stomach for a final, heroic effort. "The hero had been abandoned, and there remains only the shop-keeper!"[2] What

1. Friedrich Meinecke, *Erinnerungen,* Vol. II, *Strassburg, Freiburg, Berlin, 1901–1919* (Stuttgart, 1949), p. 266.
2. *Ibid.,* p. 271.

was to be done? In a rather poignant letter (of October 5, 1918) to his wife, Meinecke put down his thoughts about the apparently dismal future:

> ... to preserve the *Reich* and national unity, there is nothing left for us to do than to become democrats. And if we are successful in rebuilding ourselves democratically, under continued maintenance of state authority and without revolutionary distress, we will be satisfied. But now we must jettison a colossal ballast of conservative thinking, and we must have the courage to place ourselves and our efforts under severe judgment. Conservative Prussia is irretrievable! And the Majority Socialists, who under no condition want to see Bolshevism spring up among us, must now assist in keeping the masses orderly . . . .[3]

In the diary entries and in this letter, we can readily perceive Meinecke's dual reaction to the terrible events of 1918. Inwardly, he was embittered to an almost irrational degree. Yet, he seemed to be aware of the need to make those sacrifices necessary for adjustment to the unheroic period that seemed to lie ahead.

In volume two of his memoirs (*Erinnerungen*), Meinecke remarked that the period of World War I marked the end of a halcyon age of autonomous personalities, of individuals who preserved their individuality and yet were capable of maintaining fruitful links with the superpersonal life-forces that endowed history with meaning.[4] After the bloodbath, humankind had found itself in the region of the Shade, splintered and degenerated to simple life functions. Meinecke paraphrased Talleyrand's statement on the French Revolution when he remarked plaintively that "only he who has lived before 1914 knows what living meant."[5] Although there would be periods of optimism in Meinecke's life after 1918, the heroic intellectual hedonism of prewar years would never return.

Meinecke's political thinking after World War I was not readily unified. Indeed, it presents the reader with two almost contradictory strands. On the one hand, Meinecke made a brave attempt to reexamine German political and military failures in terms of the rather rigid critique of *Cosmopolitanism and the National State*. In other words, he adhered at least in part to a real-political analysis, examining this first twentieth-century German catastrophe in terms of statecraft and the failures of statecraft. On the other hand, the years immediately following World War I were marked for Meinecke by a slow turning away from purely

---

3. Friedrich Meinecke, *Ausgewählter Briefwechsel*, ed. Ludwig Dehio (Stuttgart, 1962), pp. 94–95.
4. *Erinnerungen*, Vol. II, p. 133.
5. *Ibid.*, p. 134.

political analyses and solutions. Practically, Meinecke became a member of the German Democratic party and devoted himself to a reason-dictated, if not heart-felt, defense of the Weimar Republic against the extremists of the radical Right and the radical Left. However, we will also be able to observe a rather profound intrusion of the nonpractical: pronounced, at times bitter, attacks on parliamentarianism and a perhaps unconscious empathy for the emotionalism of the extreme Right that also constituted a significant portion of Meinecke's post-World War I *Weltanschauung*. In place of almost monolithic adherence to statism, Meinecke in part yielded to the quiet turbulence of political Romanticism, that demon which always had lurked behind the unemotional Machiavellism of Germany's state apologists.

At first, the practical side of Meinecke emerged. Outside circumstances had dictated that Germany had to submit to massive internal constitutional reforms in order to preserve itself. Meinecke's primary task, as he saw it, was to calm the fears of the Conservatives and monarchists who felt threatened by the October 1918 reforms of Max von Baden. However, in an article that appeared on October 27, 1918, he warned that the "Conservative class-state must not be dissolved by a class state which calls itself democratic." [6] Such an idea can be seen as an extension of his prewar thinking; each citizen had a role to play in the state. Revolution not only could be avoided, but was in fact unnecessary. However, as we shall see, such a program would have a different meaning in the context of the Weimar Republic.

For the present, however, Meinecke adhered basically to his pre-defeat program of mollifying popular demands and providing tangible incentives for supporting the state. It was true, he mused aloud, that the old, noble state and the developing *Volksstaat* had been bound together, at least at the beginning of the war,[7] in response to the exigencies of military necessity. However, he realized that such sentimentalism was beside the point, at least for the moment. In "The Demand of the Hour" ("Die Forderung der Stunde") of December 13, 1918, he advised Liberals and Conservatives of the necessity of working with the Majority Socialists and the right-wing Independent Socialists in creating the new constitution. It would be, Meinecke maintained, impossible for a viable constitution to be created without the involvement of at least the Social Democrats.[8] Also, in an interesting and significant alteration in viewpoint, Meinecke pointed out that the values of bourgeois culture

6. Friedrich Meinecke, *Politische Schriften und Reden,* ed. Georg Kotowski (Darmstadt, 1958), p. 267.
7. *Ibid.,* p. 272.
8. *Ibid.,* pp. 277–278.

"could also be brought into accord with the goals of the Majority Socialists." [9] For Meinecke, it would appear that there was no longer any question of counting on the gentle infusion of bourgeois values into the German body politic. Rather, a reconciliation of such values with the more pressing needs of the revolution had to be affected.

Thus, during the days immediately following the November Revolution, Meinecke made several concessions to the demands of the moment. He recognized the necessity of working with the Majority Socialists and even with the right-wing Independent Socialists if an effective and meaningful constitution was to be promulgated. Moreover, he thought that the bourgeoisie had to acclimate itself—culturally as well as politically—to the establishment of a heterogeneous state that would reflect the interests of a plural society. When such concessions are viewed against the turbulent background of riot and revolt which marked Germany between November 1918 and the January 1919 elections, Meinecke's apparently calm judgment must appear all the more remarkable.

Another, and perhaps more concrete, manifestation of Meinecke's concern with day-to-day political affairs was his eventual joining of the German Democratic party, which had been formed in November 1918, less than a week after the Armistice. Meinecke's joining of the party, as well as the party itself, poses some rather interesting problems. It is true, as Koppel Pinson points out, that there was probably never before such a star-studded German political party. The variety of intellectual talent at its disposal was truly awesome. Friedrich Naumann, Walther Rathenau, Hugo Preuss, Hjalmar Schacht, Alfred Weber, Max Weber, and, of course, Friedrich Meinecke were all associated with it.[10] However, after 1922, the role of the party in the Republic became ever more nominal. After polling a highly respectable 5,641,800 votes in the January 19, 1919 election, the German Democratic party entered a period of almost uninterrupted decline which culminated in its fusion with the volkish *Jungdeutsche Orden* in 1930 to form the *Staatspartei*.[11] To make matters worse, the party's conception of what its role should have been is rather difficult to determine. As we shall see, its program was open to rather differing interpretations.

In his introduction to Meinecke's *Politische Schriften und Reden*, Georg Kotowski remarks that Meinecke had much to do with the ideological content of the German Democratic party. If he did, the pro-

9. *Ibid.*, p. 278.
10. Koppel Pinson, *Modern Germany: Its History and Civilization* (New York, 1954), p. 412.
11. *Ibid.*, p. 395.

gram of the party would not be one of which he could be proud. However, a survey of the 1918–1919 issues of the *Berliner Tageblatt,* issues covering the formative years of the German Democratic party, fails to reveal the precise role Meinecke played in the party's formation. Two of his colleagues, Friedrich Naumann and Hugo Preuss, are listed as being on the Provisional Committee, which was set up on November 29, 1918, thirteen days after the party itself was organized.[12] But Meinecke's name is not to be found, not even on the lists of distinguished supporters of the party which were published in the *Berliner Tageblatt* throughout November and December and up to the general elections of January 19, 1919.[13] Meinecke did submit most of his articles to Democratic newspapers and news agencies, for example the *Kölnische Zeitung* and the *Demokratischen Zeitungsdienst* (although, interestingly enough, only a few to the *Berliner Tageblatt* edited by Theodor Wolff). However, his actual role *in the formation* of the German Democratic party is not clear.

On the other hand, the ideological concerns of the party were clearly those shared by Meinecke. The authors of its "Call for the Establishment of a Democratic Party," which appeared on November 16, 1918, stated:

We wish the union of all those elements, men and women who are not today submerged in indolence, but who recognize the newly emerging facts and want to assure their opportunity for cooperation. What must come out of such a union is a great Democratic Party for the unified Reich.[14]

The "Call" (*Anruf*) went on to assure the good burghers of Germany that no radical reforms were needed. They certainly were not wanted because "the workers, as well as the bourgeoisie and farmers, can elevate themselves again only if the German economic policy is protected from Bolshevist or bureaucratic experimentation."[15] The party was coming out in favor of democracy and order. Such, as we have seen, were Meinecke's concerns. At times, it appeared that the party would

---

12. *Berliner Tageblatt,* November 29, 1918. Later, in his correspondences the party is mentioned in a rather interesting fashion. In a letter to G. von Below dated November 13, 1922, Meinecke described his visit to Riga to attend dedication ceremonies at the *Herderinstitut.* He praises those Baltic Germans he met as a ". . . highly . . . cultured aristocracy . . . ." He says that this is important to him" . . . for I also think aristocratically, as you know, in spite of my belonging to the German Democratic Party" (Friedrich Meinecke, *Ausgewählter Briefwechsel,* p. 11).

13. *Berliner Tageblatt,* November 11, 1918, to February 1, 1919.

14. Felix Saloman, *Die deutsche Parteiprogramme,* Heft 3 (Leipzig, 1926), p. 16.

15. *Ibid.,* p. 18.

be willing to emphasize order over democracy. As the Weimar period progressed, so would Meinecke.

Theodor Wolff pointed out that the actual goals of the Democratic party were so diffuse that some large industrialists and such geniuses of finance as Hjalmar Schacht seemed to experience no pangs of conscience at joining it. Indeed, Wolff maintained that there existed the overriding danger that the party would prove attractive "to all elements of German society." [16] Such might have been true. At first however, the party—one of the three that committed themselves to the Republic—seemed more concerned about left-wing disorders; and, in its "Election Call" (*Wahlaufruf*) of December 5, 1918, it came out against the disorders of the Spartacists and the disturbances created by "political strikes and senseless wage demands." [17] The *Wahlaufruf* went on to condemn the "meaningless internal splintering" of the *Reich*. If the Polish threat to the eastern territories was to be met, such splintering had to be ended. The party did go on to demand equality of all citizens before the law, regardless of class or sex, freedom of religion, and the concurrent separation of church and state. In the field of economics, the party was somewhat less clear. On this point, it declared itself against "the bureaucratization of economic life." [18]

Strangely enough, the party seemed to be concerned with a bit of radicalization of its own, the revival of an artisan class! Here, the Democrats indicated that the Social Democrats seemed to be somewhat insensitive to the plight of the craftsman and small trader.[19] The German Democratic party obviously was not, and it went so far as to promise adequate provisions for *apprenticeships* to the various crafts. Like Meinecke, the German Democratic party seemed to have a peculiar grudge against the industrial age. In his *After the Revolution* (*Nach der Revolution*), Meinecke expressed similar ideas.

In December 1919, the party produced a formal "program" for the first time. Understandably, it maintained that Germany had to work for revisions of the unjust treaties of Versailles and St. Germain. It also stated in a forthright fashion, "We shall never recognize the separation of segments of the German *Volk* from the Fatherland . . . ." [20] Other than this, the program really said little of palpable value that had not been mentioned before in earlier statements and decrees. It is true that, in a section entitled *Kultur,* the party did call for "strength of soul" on

16. Theodor Wolff, *Through Two Decades,* trans. E. W. Dickes (London, 1936), p. 142.
17. Saloman, *op. cit.,* p. 47.
18. *Ibid.,* p. 48.
19. *Ibid.,* pp. 47–48.
20. *Ibid.,* p. 86.

the part of the *Volk,* and it stated categorically that it believed in the ability of truth to overcome error.[21] Moreover, the party expressed interest in something with which Meinecke would become almost morbidly fascinated in the 1920s, the creation of a *"Kulturstaat."* [22]

To the Anglo-Saxon mind, it would seem as if the party program were written by a committee of frustrated metaphysicians rather than by one composed of politicians. Yet, in their own fashion, the members of the German Democratic party *were* being concrete. *Kultur* and the *Kulturstaat* had been part of the German political lexicon since the time of Kant and Fichte, and the roles of these two terms in German political philosophy always had been of great significance. However, the woes that beset Weimar Germany from the day of its inception were ones that defied the application of solutions drawn from the realm of Idealism.

As we have seen, the party was not completely submerged in generalities. When it was concerned with concrete goals, it came out for unity, freedom, and order. Briefly, it seemed to be adhering to the program espoused by Naumann, and implicitly, by Meinecke before the war. Also, the program had been tailored to meet the pressures imposed upon a weakened Germany from the outside. It is true that, in its *Wahlaufruf* of April 1920, the party did call for a "democratization of the economy" as the only way to end the class struggle. Unfortunately, at least in this *Wahlaufruf,* no specific program was described. The party also condemned the Kapp Putsch and called for an end to the disturbances in the Ruhr. It is significant to note that such fighting was condemned because it "support[s] the policies of our enemies, policies of annihilation." [23] The Democrats were no doubt upset by the violence. Nevertheless, in much the same fashion as did Meinecke, the party displayed the curious tendency to subordinate internal to external affairs. In a very real sense, the statist element of German historiography had found concrete embodiment in the only avowed republican bourgeois party in Germany.

At least one member of the German Democratic party seemed to be aware of its deficiencies. In a letter to Field Marshal von Bülow, dated November 25, 1918, Walther Rathenau pointed to the lack of specific action on the part of the bourgeois elements of the party. He maintained that this action was not forthcoming because these elements did not recognize the need "to socialize the state and economy." [24] In the autumn of 1919, Rathenau again expressed his disappointment in the

21. *Ibid.,* p. 88.
22. *Ibid.*
23. *Ibid.,* p. 51.
24. Walther Rathenau, *Politische Briefe* (Dresden, 1929), p. 216.

party. He pointed out that the Democrats had offered no concrete economic program, and he complained that they had "remained stuck in approximately the same position as had the old Progressive Party." [25] It is significant that this "old Progressive Party" had been the party of Friedrich Naumann. In a 1920 letter to Dr. Hugo Cassirer, Rathenau repeated the charge.

If Meinecke himself sensed these inadequacies in the party platform, his remarks on the subject were not recorded. While he was not altogether uncritical of the German Democratic party, he never questioned its spiritual underpinnings. Basic to these underpinnings was unity. Meinecke saw the German Democratic party as representing the best possible way to preserve the independence of the state, and as a means toward the unified *Volksstaat*. In other words, the party embodied the program to which Meinecke adhered in the seemingly halcyon prewar days. The German Democratic party was committed to parliamentarianism. So, at first, was Meinecke. Yet, when this parliamentarianism seemed to threaten the unity of the *Reich,* both the party and Meinecke displayed an almost frenetic desire to jettison it altogether. For many of the "republicans," as for the army, *Reich* stood above republic.

By January 1919, Meinecke's attitudes toward the Republic seem to have been fairly well established. In his significant essay, "Constitution and Government of the German Republic" ("Verfassung und Verwaltung der deutschen Republik"), he came to the defense of the then only formally existing republic by pointing out that "the republic is today the one form of government that divides us the least." [26] This attitude was perhaps implicitly shared, as Theodor Wolff suggests, by many of the adherents to the German Democratic party. In a famous statement, Meinecke commented upon his willingness to face the realities of 1919 Germany: "In regards to the past, I remain at heart a monarchist; in regards to the future, I am becoming a republican of reason [*Vernunftsrepublikaner.*]" [27] This forthright statement (and others) have established Meinecke's reputation as being one of the stronger defenders of the young Weimar Republic. Here we see the impassioned monarchist turning, admittedly with some reluctance, to the support of a form of government which had played no significant role in any of his earlier schemes for Germany's future. The imperial age was dead, and Meinecke recognized it. He would adjust to the new one —a Talleyrand minus cynicism.

25. *Ibid.,* p. 264 and pp. 277–278.
26. Meinecke, *Politische Schriften und Reden,* p. 282. Most revealing is Meinecke's stating, in the *Erinnerungen,* that what Germany severely needed was an "*Ersatzkaisertum.*" See pp. 258–259.
27. *Ibid.,* p. 281.

Yet, by divorcing heart from mind—and as effectively as any of the early Romantics he so roundly condemned in *Cosmopolitanism and the National State*—Meinecke revealed his own rather problematical position in regard to the Republic. To begin with, he did not, at this time, disavow his Rankean conception of the state. For him, it remained an organic unity, somehow above parties, somehow greater than the sum of its parts. In the very same essay in which he boldly declared himself a supporter of the republican form of government, Meinecke proclaimed, "Only the will of the collective *Volk* can save us, when all other lawful obligations and authorities are shaken." [28] This *will* was a concrete entity for Meinecke, as it was for many German political philosophers of his generation. It was at least as concrete as those *ad hoc* institutions that had been created to represent it. Further, "The power of the executive must have its own anchorage in the will of the *Volk*, independent from the changing parliamentary majorities." [29] Meinecke was not alone in maintaining this view. Depending on his mood, he would have been pleased or disturbed to know that many of the unreconstructed conservatives in the *Reichswehr* came to share it.[30]

It is of some significance that, in the very same essay in which he pledged support of the Republic, Meinecke had provided a reason to abandon its parliamentary framework, for he had not accepted the Weimar Republic out of republican principles, but because he thought that it could preserve the unity of the *Volk* and its concrete embodiment, the state. It is true, of course, that "overparliamentarization," that is, the system of proportional representation, has been considered as a salient weakness of the Weimar Republic.[31] Even if we accept this generalization at face value, however, we must also realize that the historically conditioned inability of the German people to work within a republican framework must be considered a primary cause for the failure of the Weimar Republic. At any rate, what overrepresentation there might have been was more than adequately compensated for by

28. *Ibid.*, p. 280.
29. *Ibid.*, p. 288.
30. See John W. Wheeler-Bennett, *The Nemesis of Power: The German Army in Politics, 1918–1945* (New York, 1967), p. 200. Kurt von Hammerstein, soon to be commander in chief of the army, made this statement in a Magdeburg newspaper on July 21, 1929: "The revolution has taught the German officer to discriminate between the *provisional regime* of the state and its *permanent identity,* and to serve the latter, which is symbolized by the *Reichspräsident,* elevated above ephemeral ministries and incoherent governmental bodies." The emphasis is von Hammerstein's.
31. Richard Hunt, in his work on *German Social Democracy: 1918–1933,* points out that the role of proportional representation in the collapse of the Republic has been grossly overestimated.

the emergency police powers contained in Article 48. Meinecke's own emphasis upon a superparliamentary will of the German *Volk* simply points out the ideological basis for this inability of the German people to accept republicanism at this time.

Meinecke's position concerning the role of "parliamentary majorities" in the new state was understandable, of course. The state could not base itself upon, or serve the interests of, only one party or a combination of parties. However, the means by which Meinecke sought to achieve integration of state and *Volk* raised some rather perplexing doubts as to the strength of his commitment to parliamentary democracy, for, as the Republic matured, he called increasingly for a strong executive divorced from parliamentary turmoil, the use of referendum and plebiscite, and, all in all, the virtual abandonment of parliamentary rule.

Meinecke's opinions on post-World War I German politics, as we have thus far considered them, were, taken together, a logical extension of those political ideas he had before the war. He called upon an integration of the German *Volk* into the state to strengthen this state. He, along with many of his comrades of the German Democratic party, seemed to favor order and unity over everything else. Although the title would not be applied until 1930, we can say that the German Democratic party was already a *Staatspartei* as early as 1918. In this regard, Meinecke's early negative attitude toward parliamentarianism becomes understandable if we bear in mind that unity of the state was of the utmost importance for him. The state represented the concrete embodiment of the people's will. Parliamentary disruptions could not be tolerated, at least not for long.

The aggregate of Meinecke's immediate thoughts concerning German collapse in World War I, as well as his considerations for the future, were tied together in his 1919 work *After the Revolution (Nach der Revolution)*. Here, his somber mood was augmented by an almost petulant reluctance to face the future in purely political terms. It is in this work that a curious Romanticism, born of defeat, can be observed. Thus, the book is of importance not because of any penetrating insights or sophisticated theoretical concerns that it contains, but rather for the insights that we can gain into the attitudes of the author. The German catastrophe of 1918 did not stem from the hideously embroidered pattern of spiritual collapse that characterized the rise and fall of the Third Reich. However, Meinecke's approach to it bears striking similarities to his approach toward Germany in World War II.

As in his more widely read *The German Catastrophe (Die deutsche Katastrophe)*, Meinecke attempted, in *After the Revolution,* to discern the causes for the German collapse not in the evolution of any element of German ideology, but in the course of German political development. He examined what he considered to be certain aberrations and malfunctionings in the German state. The one substantial difference between the two works is that, by 1946, Meinecke had grown weary of *Realpolitik* and hence did not emphasize it as much as he did in the 1919 book. In *After the Revolution,* Meinecke presaged much later historical thought on the German collapse by attributing a fair share of the responsibility for it to the failure of post-Bismarckian politics. His primary villains were Holstein and Wilhelm II. In considering them, he expounded a thesis that he would bring to mature fruition in his *History of the German-English Alliance Problem: 1890–1901* (1927), (*Geschichte des deutsch-englischen Bündnisproblems: 1890–1901*). The primary element of the thesis was that Wilhelm II was incapable of pursuing a course predicated upon a mature understanding of the rules and demands of *Realpolitik*. He could not pursue the prescribed Bismarckian course, that is, one that expertly guided Germany between Great Britain and Russia, yet he was spiritually unable to adjust himself to the new conditions, as a Bismarck might have been able to do. The logical corollaries of Wilhelm's real-political naïveté followed accordingly: the unwholesome influence of von Tirpitz and the Pan-German League, the overambitious goals of the wartime annexationists, and the failure to appreciate the value of a peace of reconciliation (often referred to as a "Hubertusburg Peace"; as mentioned before, the peace treaty that ended the Austro-Prussian portion of the Seven Years' War and essentially preserved the *status quo ante bellum*. All these influences had uprooted themselves from the wholesome soil of *Realpolitik*. Hence, they could have led only to disaster in a war in which Germany was virtually fighting the entire world. The nation was unprepared militarily, economically, and, above all, spiritually. Suffice it to say, Meinecke viewed the failure of post-Bismarckian policies as responsible for bringing about a situation that, in terms of *Realpolitik,* should have been unthinkable.[32] Whether or not the Bismarckian *Realpolitik* complex could have adjusted itself to the course of European affairs after 1890 must remain a moot point. However, in Meinecke's eyes, Bismarck's policies corresponded adequately to the external political situation of the period between 1870 and 1890. The policies of Holstein and Wilhelm II did *not* correspond to the post-1890 realities: the Franco-Russian alliance, Italy's gradual turning from the Triple Alliance, and the possibility for Germany to work more closely with Great Britain against Russia.

The most interesting aspects of *After the Revolution* concern

---

32. In an earlier essay, Meinecke pointed out the weaknesses of Bismarck's internal policies. Those weaknesses made it more difficult for Germany to live up to the possibilities created by successful implementation of his foreign goals.

Meinecke's considerations of German internal political developments. In looking at these, we must recall that for Meinecke internal and external policies had to be considered as being inextricably bound up together, and that, in terms of *Realpolitik,* the latter conditions, if it does not actually determine, the course of the former.

Meinecke set his task as follows: "We must attempt to divorce the . . . superfluous sources from the deeper-lying, more organic ones that extend further back . . . ."[33] These "deeper-lying" sources quite naturally led Meinecke to consider the evolution of the Prussian *Staatsidee* (at least insofar as he had previously treated it in his own terms). Meinecke made it immediately apparent that he intended to attack the "authoritarian stupidity and artificiality" of the Prussian state. However, he prefaced his discussion with this observation:

We can, however, draw a certain historical consolation from these observations. The noble, the pure Prussian system has not been destroyed in the catastrophe of 1918, but rather the degenerate [aspects] that had strayed from the path. We do not have the intention of holding our entire past to account and declaring the old Prussian *Staatsidee* to be an aberration because it had led to so fearful an end.[34]

Such a statement is certainly justifiable and, if we recall Meinecke's emotional attachment to things Prussian, understandable. Even in attacking the Prussian tradition, Meinecke felt for the stern glory it represented. Nevertheless, Meinecke did not hesitate to lay bare those "degenerate" aspects of it which, he felt, had led to disaster.

In attempting to delineate the course of events which had led to the tragedy of 1918, Meinecke at first turned to "the disruption of the course of reforms, through the non-fulfillment of the promises of 1815 . . . ." The return of reaction after the Napoleonic period had led to an "inner cleavage between the life of the state [*Staatsleben*] and the life of the people [*Volksleben*]."[35] Meinecke was of course here referring to the plans of Stein, Gneisenau, and von Boyen to provide for that much-needed synthesis between the state and its people. This was the synthesis that Meinecke had called for in his prewar writings, a synthesis that had been conspicuously lacking from the German political scene. For awhile, Meinecke shelved the more theoretical arguments against Stein's cosmopolitanism that had been voiced in *Cosmopolitanism and the National State.* In regard to von Boyen, he had essentially picked up where he had left off in his 1896 biography

33. Friedrich Meinecke, *Nach der Revolution* (München, 1919), p. 10.
34. *Ibid.,* p. 18.
35. *Ibid.,* p. 21.

of the great Field Marshal. The Prussian state had produced the possibility for reform only to have nipped it in the bud. A pivotal year in Prussian history, as far as Meinecke was concerned, was 1819, the year in which both von Boyen and Wilhelm von Humboldt were dismissed from their respective posts. State and *Volk* had been brutally separated, and the road to disaster had been laid.

Although Meinecke himself did not do it explicitly in this work, his reasons for the collapse of Germany in World War I can be broken down into three central or pivotal causes:

1) The dichotomy between *Volk* and *Staat* that had developed after 1819. Bismarck had attempted to bridge this through his social legislation; however, he had unfortunately preserved it through his failure to provide for the growing political desire of the masses.[36]
2) The growing demands of the masses, demands that stemmed from the accelerated urbanization and industrialization of the late nineteenth century, factors with which Wilhelm II, if not Bismarck, had to deal. Parenthetically, this problem of increasing urbanization was an important one in Meinecke's eyes. As we shall see, his solution to it was an extraordinarily interesting one.[37]
3) The failure of post-Bismarckian politicians and policy-makers to adhere to principles of *Realpolitik*.

As we can see, the first two points are rather tightly bound together, both logically and historically. Yet, here we confront the incredible paradox that had to result when a perceptive *Biedermeier* found himself immersed in an age of steel and mass destruction, for in his analysis of the causes behind Germany's collapse, Meinecke was both astonishingly right and terribly wrong. He was perceptive and, in his perceptiveness, terrifying. For in his consideration of these problems and in his solution to them, we can see—greatly aided, of course, by the cruel telescope of historical hindsight—for the first time in Meinecke's writings, spectral traces of Germany's radical Right. In Meinecke's troubled speculations, New Conservatism, the hot-blooded reaction of Germany's spiritually disinherited to the mass age, in part replaced an old Conservatism which had never had to confront it. This would appear in full measure as the 1920s passed.

In explaining one aspect of the German tragedy of 1918, Meinecke adhered with wonted vigor to his previous position: the fissure between *Volk* and *Staat* had been a fatal weakness. For Meinecke, the Prussian Junker, possessed of "strength, perseverance, industriousness, loyalty and the capacity for self-sacrifice upon the field of battle," was unfortunately culpable in this disaster.

36. *Ibid.*, pp. 18–22.   37. *Ibid.*, pp. 31–32.

He lacked the capacity to bring himself to make social sacrifices in the course of the life of the state, and he lacked the political foresight to recognize that aristocrats, in order to maintain themselves in modern life, must be able to practice the art of timely concessions.[38]

The Junkers had been originally culpable in failing to allow for the necessary synthesis of *Volk* and *Staat*. The bourgeoisie also had its own very special guilt. Its was the responsibility for the degeneration of *Realpolitik* into immature nationalistic cravings for power. "The ideal of national unity, power and greatness was first expressed by the German bourgeoisie, not by the Junkers." [39] This was well and good. However, it was the bourgeoisie that also led the way to the "narrowing and degeneration of national thought to nationalistic thought." [40] This accusation was an important one, inasmuch as it involved Meinecke's previously hallowed idea of *Realpolitik*. Admittedly, such a process had not been restricted to Germany. Furthermore, "German nationalism was not any more brutal or more materialistic than that of the enemy peoples." Nevertheless, Meinecke wisely pointed out, "it was more dangerous for us than for them, because we sat on the short end of the lever, while they [sat] on the long end." [41] Thus, more than any other nation, Germany needed leaders and statesmen well versed in *Realpolitik,* and hence able to guide her through the stress and strain brought on by her confrontation with other powers. The Junkers did not supply these needed individuals. The bourgeoisie did not materially help matters when it patronized the "little groups of Pan-Germans that . . . excited the suspicions and mistrust of the foreign powers." [42] Meinecke's admission of the bourgeoisie's lack of political wisdom was of immense significance. After all, it undercut the role he had previously assigned it and called into question its capability of being the bearer of the national *Kultur*.

The influence of such groups was mercifully small in prewar Germany. However, according to Meinecke, it grew alarmingly large during the war years. His own unhappy conflict with the *Vaterlandspartei* was no doubt foremost in his thoughts here. At any rate, the greatness and dignity of the August days of 1914 was dissipated as "those in the widest

38. *Ibid.,* p. 22.
39. *Ibid.,* p. 24.
40. What Meinecke has in mind here is probably the adherence of broad elements of the bourgeoisie to the dangerous concepts and goals that were expressed by such groups as the Pan-German League and the *Vaterlandspartei*. His earlier concern over the prominence of anti-Semitic thinking among the higher elements of society is not repeated.
41. Meinecke, *Nach der Revolution,* p. 24.
42. *Ibid.,* p. 25.

circles of the upper bourgeoisie lost the political assiduousness to discern what was possible and attainable for Germany in this way, and therefore worthy of desire and healthy." [43] On the surface of it, such a statement would appear to be rather casuistic. It was, to be sure, in the statist tradition.

Thus the political immaturity (or perhaps bankruptcy) of the middle class augmented the Junkers' unwillingness to adopt themselves to the more pedestrian realities of the twentieth century. The result could only have been disaster for Germany. Yet, for Meinecke, the ultimate source of collapse was the failure of the ruling bourgeois-Junker complex to recognize the need for a *Staat-Volk* synthesis, and its concurrent resistance to any efforts to affect its implementation. The masses ended up in the unfortunate position of being called upon to fight a war in which they could apparently gain nothing. Obviously, the masses could not support a politically myopic governing class, one whose lack of political acumen was revealed both in its denial of political freedom to them and in its failure to adhere to *Realpolitik*. Indeed, the war bore witness to palpable signs of real-political decay, for example, the exorbitant claims of the Pan-Germans and the introduction of unrestricted U-boat warfare. Meinecke quoted a statesman who had, in the unhappy summer of 1918, commiserated with him over the gravity of the situation:

Revolutions develop from errors in foreign policy. If the class that has been called upon to assume leadership of the nation does not understand its profession and does not know how to find the way to peace, it will lose authority with the masses, and the whole edifice will collapse.[44]

The situation was more desperate if "this military government does not derive its strength from the will of the whole *Volk*, but only from a part of the educated, propertied of leading elements." [45] Meinecke claimed that the ruling elements in Germany had failed to keep in touch with the mainstream of late nineteenth- and early twentieth-century developments. They seemed to act and react in blissful ignorance of such phenomena as increased urbanization, the growth of industrial complexes, and the rise in strength and influence of the Social Democratic party. However, if the ruling circles were ignorant of these developments, the more perceptive Meinecke was admittedly *sympathetic* with none of them, for while recognizing the need for social reform, he continuously expressed his distate for the "new" Germany. He saw in this new Germany a nation apparently lacking in any motivation toward

43. *Ibid.*, p. 25.
44. Meinecke, *Erinnerungen*, Vol. II, p. 251.
45. Meinecke, *Nach der Revolution*, p. 26.

higher purposes, a nation whose masses were unable to rise above mean materialism to fight to the death, a nation whose sailors would spurn a do-or-die venture against the British in November 1918. Meinecke felt that the crass society of egotistical capitalism had been responsible for inculcating this shocking lack of courage in the German populace. In an extraordinarily bitter examination of the problem, he revealed an almost romantic longing for past days, for a time in which almost thoughtless self-sacrifice in the name of home and Fatherland was taken for granted.

A remnant, a rump of the heroic-knightly ethic was yet prominent [enough] to preserve, until the end, the morale of an army doomed to ultimate collapse . . . . Would that this had been extant among the entire *Volk* during the bitter October and November days! But the prosaic egoism and materialism of the modern proletariat did not provide any more for such a spirit and we could count on its endurance only as long as it was able to see before it palpable possibilities for success.[46]

The realism Meinecke praised in the realm of foreign policy was condemned when it was displayed by the crude proletarians.

The army itself had been unfortunately raped of some of the old spirit. As the old officer corps became decimated in battle, younger lieutenants, whose rise in rank had been greatly facilitated by staggering casualties, were thrust into positions of command. The demeanor and capabilities of such men were forever being questioned by their own subordinates, and they did not receive the obedience to which they were entitled by rank.[47] Despite Meinecke's obvious appreciation of the military realities that existed after the failure of Ludendorff's grinding July offensive, he seemed to preserve a certain ingenuous wistfulness: If only the *Volk* had had more courage; if only the old officer corps had remained in charge; and—the unmentioned but omnipresent fantasy— if only Germany had won the war!

Of course, Meinecke continually pointed to the failure of the state in real-political terms. Its war goals had been unrealistic, and it had failed

46. *Ibid.*, p. 36. This is not meant to imply that Meinecke believed in the "*Dolchstosslegend.*" There is no evidence to indicate that he ever did. However, while Meinecke did reject the tendentious assumptions of the German right that Germany's defeat resulted from "treason" at home and revolutionary agitation at the front, *Nach der Revolution* would seem to indicate that, besides external military factors, Meinecke saw Germany's collapse as stemming from: (1) the inability or unwillingness of the government to adhere to a broad program of internal reform, and (2) the materialism of the German masses.

47. Meinecke, *Nach der Revolution*, p. 34.

to provide that organic fusion of *Volk* and *Staat* which could have established a framework resistant to collapse. The masses should have been brought into a more meaningful relationship with the state. Nevertheless, Meinecke was not too eager to accept the social and political ramifications of this thesis. Instead of confronting the harsh demands posed by the mass, industrial age, he took the course of least resistance and, like other Germans of his age, sought to transcend them. In this regard, he offered a most imaginative solution to the problem presented by the enervating effects of industrialization. The unhealthy and increasing dichotomy between countryside and city had to be ended. Minor industries should be set up in the countryside to ensure the periodic siphoning off of discontented members of the petite bourgeoisie and unhappy proletarians to a healthier rural environment. Conversely, this scheme would allow for the gradual synthesis of bucolic virility with the city-based *Kultur*. Perhaps Meinecke had in mind the revivification of the *Volk* through the conjuring-up of Cincinnatus. At any rate, that curious anti-industrial bias of the German Democratic party was also represented in Meinecke. In essence, Meinecke also called for a revival of the famous *Wandervogel* youth movements of the early 1900s:

> In the hearts of happy, wandering youth, the feeling for the homeland [*Heimat*] began to grow again. And the most German in our art and poetry was truly none other than the recapitulation of our landscape in the eyes of the artist—that . . . synthesis of idyllic *Herzlichkeit* with ascending, overpowering feeling for the infinite. . . . So, many of us today retain, even in our narrowness, a longing for the innermost recesses of our feeling, after the most German Germany in nature and spirit. . . . The danger that we might sink into dreamy contemplativeness and political indifference does not in fact exist, as the construction of the economy and of democracy will preoccupy us enough [to prevent it].[48]

In this rather remarkable solution to the problems faced by industrialization, cynical proletarians, and mony-grubbing petite bourgeoisie, we see Meinecke the romantic, a strange complement to Meinecke the student of statecraft. After World War II, the Goethe Study Group would replace the less cosmopolitan *Wandervogel*. In *After the Revolution,* there was a rather strange, if understandable, juxtapositioning of longing for the archaic Prussian ideal, demands for a democratization of the state, and a quasi-romantic emphasis upon youthful transcendence of the harsh realities of modern industrial society. We can see a head-on collision between the old statist thought, so prominent in Meinecke's pre-

---

48. *Ibid.,* pp. 69–70.

defeat political thinking, and newer, more superpolitical solutions. The latter did not have to be, and probably were not, antistate in overtone. Yet, they were certainly not in keeping with the coldly brilliant strictures of *Cosmopolitanism and the National State*. Thus, for the first time in our considerations of him, we see Meinecke the romantic. An obscure but meaningful break had been made in the Rankean wall of *Realpolitik*. As yet, this break neither complemented nor contradicted his concern for immediate and concrete answers to the overriding questions of democratization and reconstruction. Nonetheless a definite reaction to the previously hallowed statist doctrines was now clearly discernible.

As we have seen, Meinecke's reaction against the new Germany was also evidenced in a vague sort of antibourgeois feeling. This was coupled with his apparently renewed respect of the unselfish creed of the Prussian Junker, despite Meinecke's realization that the class was not only doomed economically, but actually had committed suicide. Out of the bitterness of defeat, he had romanticized at least the theoretical Prussian ethic and had elevated it to a position somewhat above the crass materialism and vapid policies of the post-World War I German situation.

In viewing Germany's international position after World War I, Meinecke minced no words and offered little comfort. Germany had been weakened; France had been wrecked; and Russia, at least for the moment, was out of the picture. Understandably, Meinecke saw Europe dominated by the United States and Great Britain, crushed beneath the weight of Anglo-Saxon economic and military preponderance. At least for the foreseeable future, Europe had been reduced to political and economic vassalage. This situation was unavoidable. Even if Great Britain and the United States were to split, Europe would have to suffer the gruesome bondage of a true Carthaginian peace. One can readily empathize with Meinecke's sense of desperation over the plight of Europe in general, and of Germany in particular.

In analyzing the situation in greater detail, Meinecke drew a historical parallel with the Roman domination over the Hellenic world. It was possible for temporary alliances to be formed. Philip V and the Romans had combined against the Seleucids in the late third century B.C. Macedonia and Carthage had allied against Rome. But, as these respective arrangements were abrogated at Pydna, and earlier at Zama, so must any sort of working arrangement with the victorious Anglo-Saxon powers prove transient. All of Western Europe would be united in a common despair.[49]

49. *Ibid.*, p. 80.

For the present, Meinecke saw a Germany stumbling in the darkness of a total political and economic eclipse. All she could do under the circumstances was to strive to maintain her spiritual integrity, her dignity as a distinct national entity. If Germany could present a brave and united front to the victorious powers, she might yet be allowed a certain degree of freedom. Certainly, she needed such freedom in order to continue along the path of self-development and to thus solve her problems in her own fashion. After all, Germany had her own unique spiritual heritage, and any attempted implantation of inorganic and therefore false (at least in the German context) governmental institutions could have led to the most tragic of circumstances. The same obviously would hold true if Germany was forced to endure the introduction of Anglo-Saxon political mores and philosophies. If Germany was to survive as a nation-state, she had first of all to retain the spiritual vitality necessary to demonstrate both to herself and to the Anglo-Saxon powers that she yet bore the spark of life within her.[50] Here again we can observe the intrusion of the romantic into Meinecke's thinking. Indeed, in maintaining that political institutions were organically bound to the national framework within which they developed, Meinecke sounded astonishingly similar to the Romantics he so roundly condemned in *Cosmopolitanism and the National State*. Meinecke had certainly indicated in his earlier writings that he considered the state to be organic in an operational sense. Now, at least for the moment, he felt it to be organic in an almost teleological sense. In the despair of defeat, the great historian was falling back upon the demonic. However, it is only fair to point out that so *clear* a romantic break in the statist wall was of a comparatively brief duration.

In considering the immediate external political situation in 1919, Meinecke displayed the same sagacious concern with statecraft as of old. Rather perceptively, he considered the possibility of a German-Italian rapprochement:

> We can think, to our great consolation, of the hoary and virtually perpetual clash between the Mediterranean interests of France and Italy and of the completely new clash of interests that [can develop] between them through the founding of the Yugoslav state . . . and that since the removal of Austria-Hungary, the area of friction between Germany and Italy has been greatly reduced.[51]

Meinecke then went on to point out that France, as well as Italy, was a second-rate power, and because this was true,

50. *Ibid.*, pp. 100–101.   51. *Ibid.*, p. 79.

Only a world-wide coalition of all the great second-rate powers—France, Italy and Japan [!]—and the ability of the other states of Europe to act will be able to fend off the pressure of Anglo-Saxon world domination.[52]

He also made the rather shrewd and far-reaching observation that Germany possibly could be able to come to some sort of rapprochement with England. Here, he foresaw the possibility that the latter might be able to prevent the development of the French hegemony on the Continent. Further, there was the joyful possibility that Great Britain and America might well fall out over the question of who should predominate in the Pacific. Meinecke envisioned the possibility of Great Britain's attempting to utilize Japan and America to balance each other out while she secured her own situation in that area. Perfidious Albion might very well work for Germany's good without knowing it.

However, Meinecke was adamant in maintaining that neither alliances nor the world power structure as a whole could save Germany. The Germans themselves had to do it.

Only a spiritual and intellectual renewal, nourished by a strong will, can help us to win back, sooner or later, our freedom in the ranks of the free peoples of the world; [only this] can preserve us as a nation.[53]

Thus, in the final analysis, Meinecke placed the burden for Germany's recovery upon the German nation, *in toto*. This time, however, no single class was designated as being the primary instigator of national renewal. Indeed, the appeal was directed toward the "nonpolitical" side of German life. Meinecke was calling upon the spiritual and intellectual faculties of the German people, faculties that could and had to exist untarnished by military defeat and economic disaster. It would seem that Meinecke was appealing here to a spiritualized Germany, a *Kulturnation;* in a word, to that variety of nation which had been extolled by the early cultural Romantics. In this regard, at least, Meinecke clearly broke with his Rankean legacy. His concern for a more spiritualized concept of the nation was a product of the disaster that four years of war had brought upon Germany. Meinecke the post-World War I cultural nationalist was the direct antecedent of Meinecke the post-World War II cosmopolitan.

Yet, it would be incorrect to maintain that *After the Revolution* manifested a complete break with Meinecke's spiritual legacy. The old concern for a politically conscious *Volksstaat* was yet quite strong. The work was in part a simple reiteration of earlier themes: all elements of

52. *Ibid.*, p. 80.   53. *Ibid.*, p. 104.

the population had to be brought into the state. The avowed purpose for such an integration remained very much the same as before: to allow Germany to assume her rightful role in the family of nations. Meinecke, at least in this instance, had effectively subordinated Germany's internal programs to the more significant task of, if not assuming a former place in the sun, at least moving part of the way out of the shade. Here, Meinecke's adherence to Rankean conceptions remained unbroken.

In *After the Revolution,* we are thus confronted with two different approaches to Germany's post-World War I problems. Two souls now strove mightily in Meinecke's breast. In part, he still adhered to the gospels of Prussian statism. Yet, a newer, well-nigh superpolitical approach had appeared. As yet, each of these unchaperoned strangers seemed to be oblivious to the presence of the other. A mechanical but brilliant statist critique contrasted sharply with the sudden appearance of a variety of cultural Romanticism, each as uniquely German a phenomenon as the other.

In considering Meinecke's reaction to World War I, we find that it was symptomatic of a *Weltanschauung* undergoing considerable stress. As we have seen, Meinecke's pre-World War I views on the respective roles of *Volk,* state, and internal reforms remained basically unchanged up to the time of the German collapse in November 1918. Meinecke had tended to view Germany's internal development in almost the same stolidly parochial fashion in which Guizot regarded pre-1848 France. The political and spiritual acculturation of the masses could and would be carried out through a gradual diffusion of bourgeois political and cultural values throughout the society. Meinecke had expressed, from time to time, genuine concern over the spiritual condition of this class. However, the sharper critiques of individuals such as Max Weber were not repeated by him, although he probably recognized some truth in them. Up to the defeat, Meinecke adhered with considerable tenacity to the seemingly almost simpleminded optimism of Wilhelmine days. The state would become a *Volksstaat.* The liberal bourgeoisie *would* have a significant role to play in this process. Power and the *Kultur* it was to protect *could* exist side-by-side. It was only after the November Revolution that Meinecke questioned his basic views and the underlying assumptions. But once he did so, the overthrow of prewar optimism took place with astounding speed.

We have seen that there was an almost perverse inconsistency in Meinecke's response to defeat. On the one hand, he blamed that "authoritarian stupidity" which had prevented mass participation in the state for leading Germany to disaster. After all, mass involvement, or perhaps even the illusion of involvement, was a *sine qua non* if the state was to be able to defend its own interests in an age of mass warfare. On the other hand, he denounced the new mass society as being cowardly and materialistic. While attacking the anachronistic political ideals of the Junker, Meinecke exalted his heroic qualities. Implicitly, he seemed to be drawing a distinction between his qualities and the more mercenary and unspiritual ones of the bourgeoisie and proletarians spawned by the industrial age. Meinecke was adamant about the necessity of bringing the masses into Germany's state structure. His sincerity on this issue is hardly open to doubt. Yet, he distrusted them, and one wonders if, in his heart of hearts, he might have felt that the state would suffer rather than gain from such a process.

Particularly in the newspaper articles, Meinecke clung to an organic conception of the state. Parliamentary government had to be introduced, and Meinecke recognized the necessity of doing so. Yet, even before the Weimar Constitutional Assembly met, he was raising questions and doubts concerning not only the efficacy but the validity of the introduction of parliamentary government into Germany. The executive had to be a strong one. A state could not be based on shifting parliamentary majorities. Somewhere, in back of the party blocs and vitriolic phrasemongering, there hovered the people's will. Meinecke had declared himself to be a *"Vernunftsrepublikaner."* He had become a republican out of real-political motives. Yet, *Realpolitik* had emerged tarnished and scarred from the trenches. Although "the republican is today the one form of government that divides us the least," heart was beginning to usurp the vast province of cold reason. "Only the will of the collective *Volk* can save us when all other lawful obligations and authorities are shattered." A substantive contradiction had intruded into the nascent republicanism of Meinecke, the same contradiction that would eventually turn his own German Democratic party toward political obscurantism and oblivion.

World War I had compelled Meinecke to divide sharply between heart and mind. His own genuine search for solutions led him, quite logically, to project this dichotomy onto the postwar German scene. The result of this was a curiously divided political personality. Organic state could live side by side with pluralistic state. Problems of the mass age could be at least partly solved by solutions drawn from the Romanticism of Germany's past.

What did it all mean? What was the significance of this for Meinecke's future political thinking? Meinecke had responded to defeat and revolution as a liberal constitutional monarchist would be expected to do. His prewar dreams had been shattered. Now, a combination of internal collapse and obnoxious Wilsonian piety was forcing an inorganic and undesired republicanism upon Germany. Mind had to yield to republicanism dictated by *Realpolitik*. Heart, however, did not have to do so, but could choose to live in the statist or romantic past. What Meinecke himself probably did not know was that solutions of the heart would become of ever greater importance as the Weimar Republic, born in chaos, matured into chaos. These solutions would be justified in terms of *Realpolitik,* to be sure. All this did was to underscore the spiritual confusion of a decent, nineteenth-century liberal adrift in a sea of twentieth-century troubles.

Meinecke, in the Weimar period, was on his way to the political never-never land of cosmopolitan Romanticism, a destination he attained after the second German catastrophe had taken place. In a way, he was marching blindly, but stolidly toward political death, toward the final rejection not only of power politics, but, in reality, of politics itself. As some varieties of fish die, they display, as if in pathetic defiance, all the colors of the rainbow. Meinecke, in the 1920s, displayed all the major political outlooks and prejudices of the decent, nonradical intellectual burgher. Before we consider his Weimar political views in detail, we must examine at length a phenomenon to which we have already referred: his rebellion against *Realpolitik* and his emphatic elevation of the *Kultur* portion of the state synthesis. To do so, we must look at Meinecke's conceptualization of power, a historiographical phenomenon of the 1920s which served both to rationalize his current political views and to justify his eventual withdrawal from politics.

5

The Clash between Power and Kultur

IF WE ARE TO TRUST HIS *Erinnerungen*, Meinecke had begun to question the Rankean tendency to sanctify power as early as 1917. Indeed, he seemed to feel that the roots of his monumental 1924 work, *Die Idee der Staatsräson*, went back to these musings.[1] His 1918 diary entries, which retain a certain bellicose flavor, would seem to contradict this. Nonetheless, as far as Meinecke was concerned, World War I destroyed a lot more than his naïve optimism in regard to German politics. The beautiful dream of a perfect balance of power, concretized in the state, and *Kultur* also died. The war itself had not killed it; rather stalemate and then Germany's defeat were the culprits. Nevertheless, it is a matter of record that the Weimar period saw a gradual turning away from power considerations on Meinecke's part. The almost jarring optimism of *Cosmopolitanism and the National State* was rejected in favor of Hamlet-like brooding over the impossibility of reconciling power with *Kultur*. Eventually, Meinecke discarded the *Macht* pole of state life in favor of *Kultur*.

For a long time, Meinecke's concept of *Kultur* was uncertain, as uncertain, perhaps, as the meaning of such a term would have to be. In 1928, however, he finally defined *Kultur* as "the manifestation and emergence of a spiritual element in the general causal nexus."[2] Further-

1. Friedrich Meinecke, *Erinnerungen*, Vol. II, *Strassburg, Freiburg Berlin, 1901–1919* (Stuttgart, 1949), p. 194. An excellent discussion of this problem is to be found in Georg G. Iggers, *The German Conception of History: The National Tradition of Historical Thought from Herder to the Present* (Middletown, Conn., 1968), pp. 207–215.
2. Friedrich Meinecke, "Kausalitäten und Werte in der Geschichte," *Historische Zeitschrift*, Band 134, Heft 1 (1928), p. 8. In such a definition (1928), Meinecke places a premium on the "individuality" of the free cultural breakthrough. Thus, individuality, either in terms of personal creativity or phenomenologically, was the substance of *Kultur*. Individuality, Free-

more, "*Kultur* emerges only when man takes up the struggle against nature with all his inner strength." This definition would prove to be of immense significance for Meinecke's future intellectual endeavors. *Kultur* was seen here as an almost superrational entity, drawing its essence from the wellsprings of the eternal. Implicit in such a definition of *Kultur* was the identification of it as being an embodiment of Spirit (*Geist*). Conversely, power (*Macht*), was seen as being closely bound to nature, to forces of external necessity.[3] What Meinecke had done was to sharply differentiate between *Kultur* and *Macht*. He had drawn a mystical, yet firm line between the intrinsic nature of the individual spiritual "breakthrough" and the elemental forces of causality that surrounded its emergence. Such a definition would have been unthinkable before the war. In the 1920s, however, after the corruption of power had been revealed in ignoble defeat, Meinecke established a sharp dichotomy between the two basic elements of state life.

In a way, Meinecke's recognition that the state could not be an ideal balance of *Kultur* and *Macht* was the most important change in his *Weltanschauung*. It represented the initial step on his troubled journey from statism to the cosmopolitanism of his post-World War II years. Meinecke, after World War I, had drawn closer to the brittle aestheticism of Jacob Burckhardt who, many years before, had recognized that power corrupted not only the administrative organs of the state, but also its ability to function as a preserver of the cultural heritage of past centuries. Walther Hofer and Richard Sterling considered this change in Meinecke's thinking to be crucial, but they did not examine the consequences of it at length.[4] We shall now examine Meinecke's polarization of *Macht* and *Kultur* in some detail, and follow this polarization to its logical conclusion.

As we have seen earlier, Meinecke, during the rather extensive statist period of his life, felt that power was the *sine qua non* of the development of the state, and thus of *Kultur*. Power was, after all, the very basis of state life. Without power, there could be no state. Since the existence of the state was necessary in order both to protect and to further the *Kultur* of a given people, power, as the underlying strength of the state, was possessed of a definite moral quality. Without specifically saying so, the prewar Meinecke adhered fairly closely to the Rankean

---

dom, and *Kultur* are thus possessed of the same spiritual substance, defining themselves in opposition to outside causal forces and crass power structures. This essay also appeared in *Staat und Persönlichkeit* (Berlin, 1933).

3. *Ibid.*, p. 24.
4. Walther Hofer, *Geschichtschreibung und Weltanschauung* (München, 1950); Richard Sterling, *Ethics in a World of Power: The Political Ideas of Friedrich Meinecke* (Princeton, N.J., 1958).

dictum that power was impregnated with a certain spiritual quality. Thus, before the German defeat in World War I, power and *Kultur* were virtually inseparable for Meinecke. Power was the support of the state, and this state provided the framework within which *Kultur* could develop to fruition. Eventually, of course, the development of *Kultur* would redeem those acts of pure Machiavellism which were necessary to assure its protection and growth. In a rather general fashion, the prewar Meinecke resembled the Jacob Burckhardt of *The Civilization of the Renaissance in Italy*, rather than the somewhat more somber Burckhardt in *Reflections on History (Weltgeschichtliche Betrachtungen)*. In the former work, Burckhardt felt that the ruthless clashing of Doge, Sforza, and Carrara was somehow redeemed through the cultural achievements of the Italian Renaissance. Indeed, there even occurred the philosophical transformation of the state itself into a work of art.[5] Meinecke never explicitly claimed that the state could be represented in the rather precious terminology of Burckhardt. Indeed, the latter's deprecation of power must have proved disquieting to him. Nevertheless, the prewar Meinecke also viewed the state as a vibrant synthesis of *Macht* and *Kultur*.[6]

5. Jacob Burckhardt, *The Civilization of the Renaissance in Italy*, trans. S. G. C. Middlemore (New York, 1958), Vol. I, Part I.

6. Burckhardt defined *Kultur* as ". . . the sum total of those mental developments which take place spontaneously and lay no claim to universal or compulsive authority . . . that millionfold process by which the spontaneous, unthinking activity of a race is transformed into considered action, or indeed, at its last and highest state, in science and especially philosophy, into pure thought. Its total external form, however, as distinguished from the State and religion, is society in its broadest sense" (Jacob Burckhardt, *Force and Freedom: Reflections on History*, ed. James Hastings Nichols [Boston, 1943], p. 140).

Thus, Burckhardt's view of *Kultur* was broad insofar as it consisted of the undifferentiated complex of spontaneous human activities as those activities were externalized in society. However, it was also rather narrow in that, for Burckhardt, the highest level of *Kultur* subsisted in pure thought. Assumed here, was a dialectic between mental activity and its objects; the highest possible level, of course, being mental activity for the sake of mental activity, i.e., pure thought. Of course, Burckhardt did not deny that the state had an important function to serve in the evolution of *Kultur*. In fact, the idea of the state was, for him, one of the most significant aspects of the Italian Renaissance (*ibid.*, p. 15). Moreover, the great states in history existed, not only "for the achievement of great external aims," but also for "the maintenance and protection of certain cultures which would flounder without it" (*ibid.*, p. 114). However, for Burckhardt, the juxtaposition of state power and cultural achievement was an uncomfortable one. Power *qua* power was evil; and the lifeblood and purpose of the state was power (*ibid.*, p. 115). Political life, as such, had little of a positive role to play in Burckhardt's view of *Kultur*. Spontaneity in mental activity directed toward

Until the 1920s, however, Meinecke's opinion of the state was certainly higher than Burckhardt's had been. The message of *Cosmopolitanism and the Nation State* was that the state had to be recognized as an organic, self-justifying entity. The historical situation of Germany lent Meinecke considerable empirical justification for such a view. Rankean theoretical confidence had been matched, if not exceeded, by the glorious achievements of Bismarck. Going beyond his mentor Ranke, Meinecke had even been able to dispense with much of the former's teleology. However he had alhered strenuously to the Rankean solution to that bugbear of historiography, the relationship of particular to general: the individual in history—whether this be a person, institution, or state—justified itself through its immediate and concrete relationship to general historical forces and trends. This concept provided Meinecke with a useful device in relating the creative roles of such figures as von Boyen, Stein, and Bismarck to the playing out of the general forces of which they were representative. Power and *Kultur*, and particular and general were all neatly synthesized for Meinecke before the German defeat shattered these convenient devices.

Before 1918, Meinecke did not bother to consider power as an entity. Germany seemed to be utilizing it fairly well, so there was little need to do so. However, after World War I, Meinecke became almost morbidly drawn to considering the nature of power. As Walther Hofer pointed out, prewar optimism over a final and historically satisfying synthesis of power and *Kultur* began to yield to agonizing doubts as to its possibility.[7] *Machtpolitik* had led to disaster. Even more disastrous, in Meinecke's eyes, was the pronounced lack of *Realpolitik* that had been displayed by even the better elements of German society during the war, a lack that had led, in fact, to defeat. In volume two of his memoirs, Meinecke noted that: "I experienced a fearful degeneration in the power-political striving [*Streben*] in those elements of the German people who, up to then, had been the main bearers of the national *Kultur*."[8] In his memoirs, Meinecke evinced a great deal of bitterness about the real-political maturity of the German people. Perhaps with the Treaty of Brest-Litovsk in mind, he asked rhetorically whether or not Germany would have offered an easier peace if she, and not the Allies, had won the war. Probably to quash some inner uneasiness, Meinecke said that

fulfilling human needs precluded power from the sphere of *Kultur,* even though its existence in the form of the state might have been a necessary prerequisite for such activities. In a very real sense, despite Meinecke's strong attraction to Goethe—one that we will soon consider in examining *Die Entstehung des Historismus*—his own definition of *Kultur,* at least after World War I, bore marked resemblances to Burckhardt's.

7. Walther Hofer, *Geschichte zwischen Philosophie und Politik* (Basel, 1956), p. 73.

8. Meinecke, *Erinnerungen,* Vol. II, p. 193.

he did not feel it necessary to accept Jacob Burckhardt's extreme views concerning power. However, he mentioned that the experience of the disaster of World War I had given him an appreciation of the "daemonic nature of power," something that he had sorely lacked during the brighter prewar years.[9] The 1920s period was a time of palpable change in Meinecke's attitudes toward the roles of power, the state, and *Kultur*. In reality, Meinecke developed an attitude *toward* power. Previously, the terms power and state had seemed almost to vanish into each other.

It is of immense significance that Meinecke did not really define *Kultur* until the 1920s. Perhaps he had not found it necessary to do so previously. Now, however, the prewar *Macht/Kultur* synthesis lay broken in the dust of military disaster. It was time that the elements that composed the state be examined. The Weimar period thus saw the appearance of several prodigious works in which Meinecke addressed himself to the task of determining the precise relationship of the various elements that previously had existed in that impressive synthesis called the state. These works were *Machiavellism (Die Idee der Staatsräson*, 1924), and *The Origin of Historicism (Die Entstehung des Historismus*, 1936). A somewhat lesser known work, *History of the German-English Alliance Problem: 1890–1901 (Geschichte des deutsch-englischen Bündnisproblems: 1890–1901*, 1927), was devoted to problems of statecraft during the period, and is important, for our purposes, for the light it casts on Meinecke's concept of creative *raison d'état*.

In his own rather prodigious *Ethics in a World of Power: The Political Ideas of Friedrich Meinecke*, Richard Sterling points out that Machiavellism was indicative of a significant break with Meinecke's earlier views on power and politics. Now, for the first time, Meinecke unequivocally recognized that "individual freedom and the welfare of the human community constituted the ultimate measure of the state's worth and they were precisely the values which the state again and again sacrifices in the name of its survival." [10] This statement is certainly borne out by Meinecke's considerations in the book, for, in *Machiavellism*, he was seriously concerned with the problems that arose from the confrontation between power and cultural values. He had committed himself to a study of *power as power*, and not merely of power as the underpinning of the evolutions of states. In fact, Meinecke was now concerned with the problem that arises when evil is turned into a means for obtaining good.[11]

Basic to these new considerations of Meinecke was a rejection of

9. *Ibid.,* p. 194.
10. Sterling, *op. cit.,* p. 233.
11. Friedrich Meinecke, *Die Idee der Staatsräson* (trans. by Douglass Scott as *Machiavellism;* London, 1957).

the Machiavellian conception of *virtù*. Machiavelli had seen *virtù* as being possessed of intrinsic justification for the unqualified use of power in the pursuance of political goals. Meinecke's attack upon this salient aspect of Machiavellism signified the end of the former's acceptance of the casuistic relationship of power to morality. Such an acceptance had to have constituted the linchpin of Meinecke's previously unqualified statism.

Times had changed. Or, it would be perhaps more accurate to say that the times had changed Meinecke, for certainly, there had been a shift in emphasis in Meinecke's historical and moral approach to the state. In *Cosmopolitanism and the National State*, he had considered the evolution of German thought as it had concerned the state. He had been particularly concerned with this evolution as it had been coincidental with the concrete development of the state. Now, in 1924, Meinecke was attacking the basic supposition that had to be virtually accepted a priori if the whole statist framework was not to tumble into the black abyss of amorality. We have dealt with this supposition before—the assumed ability of power and culture to exist in a wholesome fashion, side by side, within the same framework. Yet, in questioning the ability of power and culture to coexist, Meinecke did not at first reject *raison d'état*. Indeed, in his introduction to *Machiavellism*, he was adamant in maintaining that *raison d'état* did not have to be coterminous with naked power. In fact, Meinecke thought it to be located in the "twilight zone between impulse and reason . . . ," and that it could be indeed possessed of positive attributes if and when power "is no longer sought for its own sake alone [but] . . . is striven for solely as a means of attaining the common weal . . . ."[12] *Raison d'état* means *reason* of state. There was obviously nothing intrinsically atavistic about it, even if its material, power, happened to be. Meinecke's work was in fact devoted to a study of the rise of *raison d'état;* however, and most important for Meinecke, it was also the story of the hideous degeneration of this concept as a result of modern power drives.

In *Machiavellism* Meinecke traced the development of Machiavellism from the period of the Medicis up to and including World War I. This war represented, of course, the most fearsome product of the vulgar extrapolation of the ill-fated doctrine. In the work, Meinecke was concerned essentially with the spread of the power ideal throuhgout Europe and with its eventual diffusion, in a vertical fashion, through virtually all levels of society. Thus, in *Machiavellism*, the question of the state *itself* had become an almost peripheral one in terms of the broader question of power. Meinecke maintained that the roots of *raison d'état* could be traced back to the often casuistic concept of the "public good."

12. *Ibid.*, pp. 6–7.

This factor, which was both an antecedent and a logical corollary of Machiavellism, had been used by the rulers of states to undercut the concept of the immutability of law. This latter belief had been historically embodied in theories of "universal" natural law.[13] Obviously, if a state was going to relegate authority to itself, arguments based upon universal principles either had to be met and defeated, or at least ignored. The concept of the "public good" represented a convenient, if occasionally troublesome, counterargument. In discussing the evolution both of this concept and of the more significant doctrine it was to serve, Meinecke's methodology was somewhat similar to that he displayed in *Cosmopolitanism and the National State*. In other words he did relate the development of *raison d'état* and supportive ideas to the emergence of the power state. However, Meinecke had a further concern. He also attempted to show how such a development was *in itself* instrumental in clearing a wide philosophical field for the *expansion* both of state interests and state power.

According to Meinecke, the most far-reaching and potentially dangerous application of Machiavellism occurred in Germany. Here, *raison d'état* arrived as something new, an idea that was almost foreign to the rather slovenly political thinking of Germany's rulers. However, the German princes of the sixteenth and seventeenth centuries found it to be a useful tool in their wars with the nobility and the Empire. As such, it was exposed to

a specifically German radicalism which, precisely because it has its roots in ethical questions, is fond of carrying principles to extremes and of ruthlessly emphasizing their most terrible consequences.[14]

Raison d'état had been placed in the hands of a people who were alternately—and occasionally all at once—idealistic and cynical. Thus, it was only fitting that Frederick the Great displayed both an acute awareness of the totalitarian consequences that could result from the dichotomy between older ethical patterns and the casuistry of *raison d'état* and an equally acute awareness of the advantages to be gained by its employment. Significantly enough, it was in the eighteenth century, in the period of "mature absolutism," that Meinecke saw rational use of the doctrine as achieving its height. War, except perhaps for the forlorn grenadier, was not an emotional affair at all. Indeed, it was employed in an almost mechanical fashion to attain specific and palpable goals. Allies and enemies could be exchanged with wholesome alacrity, and a Prince Kaunitz could prosper amid the powder smoke.

13. *Ibid.*, p. 127. 14. *Ibid.*, p. 135.

As a historian of ideas, however, Meinecke was also interested in the application of *raison d'état* to historiography. Thus, it was in the philosophy of Hegel that Meinecke saw the triumph of Machiavellism in the world of ideas. Hegel's World Spirit might have been ultimately benevolent after its own Lutheran fashion, but, in everyday life it displayed a certain ferocity. Through "cunning of reason" (*List der Vernunft*) it illuded the passions and activities of men for its own transcendental purposes. Bitterly, Meinecke attacked Hegel's conception of the cunning and subtlety of Divine Reason. That demonic element in *raison d'état* had been recognized by Frederick the Great, Campanella, and even by Machiavelli himself. Now through Hegelian monism, it had been enshrined upon the altar of the eternal as the temporal embodiment of Universal Reason seeking self-fulfillment. In regarding this rather unfortunate turn of events, Meinecke acidly commented, "What happened now was almost like the legitimization of a bastard." [15]

For somewhat different reasons, Meinecke had already subjected Hegelian monism to a far-reaching criticism in *Cosmopolitanism and the National State*. The depth of his almost desperate concern with the moral issues raised by *raison d'état* was revealed in his new approach to Ranke. Previously the "hero" of Meinecke's 1907 work,[16] Ranke was now subjected to a severe critique. To be sure, Meinecke did not do a complete *volte-face* in regard to the great German historian. Indeed, he devoted a fair amount of space to discussing the latter's attempts to purify the otherwise rather shadowy concept of *raison d'état*. Ranke had insisted, after all, that states had to preserve a fundamental awareness of higher goals: "Religious truth . . . must . . . keep the state continually reminded of the origin and aim of earthly life, of the rights of neighboring states and the kinship between all nations." [17] However, a lot of blood had flowed under the bridge since the more tranquil nineteenth century, and Meinecke felt that the redeeming transcendentalism of Ranke's historiography was a moot point anyway. Ranke had been rather naïve after all, and "the veiled dualism which he used to help himself out and [to] cloak the nocturnal aspect of life, must be stripped of its veil." [18]

In the twentieth century, the irrational masses had become the inheritors of the awesome legacy of *raison d'état*. The days when Bismarck had been able to synthesize the old *raison d'état* of cabinets and mature diplomacy with the demands of popular forces was past. Now,

15. *Ibid.*, p. 350.
16. Friedrich Meinecke, *Weltbürgertum und Nationalstaat* (München, 1908), p. 285.
17. Meinecke, *Die Idee der Staatsräson*, p. 389.
18. *Ibid.*, p. 428.

the very question of "reason of state" had become fraught with perils unknown to the staid Junker. The atavistic power drive of mass nationalism, unfortunately rationalized by the German historical tradition, had been converted into terms of cold steel through the limitless resources of modern capitalism and mass militarism. In the twentieth century the question of war and national policy had been converted into "a question of being a great power or not being one." [19] The issues involved in modern state life were far more replete with significance and meaning than those that had concerned earlier states. The modern mass state literally laid its life, and the lives of other states, on the line almost every day. Hence, it was imperative for Meinecke that this "veiled dualism" of Ranke be revealed for the flimsy rationalization it was. Furthermore, sustained efforts had to be made to elevate *raison d'état* from the slough of "mere power deliberations." If at all possible, this now-tarnished doctrine had to be applied to the discovery and implementation of spiritual and moral values. In this approach, the beginnings of Meinecke's mature, post-World War II cosmopolitanism were already apparent.

Richard Sterling points to the above concerns as setting the stage for Meinecke's later rejection of "the *raison d'état* of National Socialist Germany." [20] Certainly, both Meinecke's new view of the term and his rejection of its application by Nazi Germany cannot be denied. However, in terms both of his methodology and of his ability to grasp the issues that concerned twentieth-century Germany, Meinecke's study of the development and degeneration of *raison d'état* raised more problems than it allayed.

Meinecke's approach in *Machiavellism*, as brilliantly as it is drawn out and ellucidated, points to the development of an exaggerated abstractness in his thinking. In earlier writings, Meinecke had been at least concerned with the vulgar, day-to-day aspects of power politics. It is true that his Rankean approach had tended to insulate him from such phenomena as the implications of the rise of mass nationalism. The Rankean emphasis upon the state's utilization of the "national idea" rather than upon nationalism itself led him in this direction. Nonetheless, Meinecke's own adherence to Historicism gave him a sophisticated appreciation of the time-bound (*zeitgebunden*) nature of historical phenomena. However, in the 1920s, Meinecke partly rejected his previous devotion both to Rankean statism and to the Rankean methodology. Instead, he began to evidence a concern with what Walther Hofer calls *Lebensgeschichte*. This was the tendency to try and grasp "Life" in all its complexities and obscurities, a tendency to consider history in

19. *Ibid.*, p. 418.   20. Sterling, *op. cit.*, p. 267.

terms of what Meinecke felt to be the almost impenetrable synthesis of rational and irrational life forces. Such an approach had a positive side to it, of course, for obviously it necessitated the merciful rejection of the stale and almost simplistic Rankean statist catechism. However, for Meinecke, the new approach also involved an estrangement of power from the concrete cultural circumstances that surrounded and conditioned its historical development. This process was most clearly revealed in *Machiavellism*.

Obviously power as power, that is, in terms of its dictionary definition, does not change. However, while the historical form of power remains constant, changing cultural circumstances involve changes in its content. The power drives and interests of a mass state involve substantially different motives and goals than did the power drives created and shaped by pristine absolutism. Meinecke was in part aware of this. However, his treatment of power and *raison d'état* in *Machiavellism* revealed a rather curious aspect in Meinecke's methodology: while *raison d'état* was the product of human minds, men and nations could, through *raison d'état*, only *relate* themselves to power. Such relationships were objectified by Meinecke in his considerations of Machiavelli, Campanella, Richelieu, and Frederick the Great. Yet, these individuals were relating themselves more to the form, power, than to power as it is influenced by the cultural circumstances in which its users are embedded.

Throughout his works, Meinecke rejected Hegelian monism almost out of hand. Yet, in *Machiavellism*, he displayed a very prominent Hegelian tendency. First of all, he virtually spiritualized power itself. He did not spiritualize it in a positive sense, but rather tended to see it as a partly rational, partly demonic life-force. He then tended to fuse intellectual apprehension of this spiritual force with its evolutionary development. In this regard, he pointed to all the misused applications and rationalizations of power, seeing them as milestones on the road to its ultimate demonification in the modern mass state. Meinecke attacked the Hegelian cunning of reason while at the same time viewing power as being immutable, if not virtually timeless. In *Machiavellism*, Meinecke never explicitly stated such a position. However, both his revised methodology and his revised *Weltanschauung* were leading toward the post-World War II conclusion that power represented a curiously rational form of nihilism. Meinecke had attacked Hegel for individualizing and absolutizing everything that served to promote the progressive realization of the Divine Reason. Yet, in *Machiavellism*, Meinecke had *conceptualized* power, and this was tantamount to absolutizing it. Meinecke maintained that "the doctrine of the cunning of reason was founded on the abyss of historical life."[21] However, he tended to emphasize the cunning of *power* as it passed through the at times all too flimsy filter of *raison d'état*. In *Machiavellism,* Meinecke clearly revealed a state of spiritual, or at least intellectual, confusion. First of all, he did adhere, at least in part, to his Rankean heritage. This was demonstrated in his fusion of the individual with the general, for example, Richelieu with the general level of sophistication of *raison d'état* characteristic of his time. However, his view of *power itself* was almost Hegelian. Yet, Meinecke continued to deprecate Hegel and to hold him largely responsible for some of the obvious perversions that had developed within the corpus of German historiography.

This spiritual turmoil did indicate, of course, that Meinecke no longer maintained his facile acceptance of the *Machtstaat*. In one sense, his abandoning of it was both admirable and necessary, for certainly the essential assumption upon which Meinecke's particular variety of statism rested—the symbiotic relationship between power and *Kultur*—seemed to beg the question all along. Now, by at least pointing out the "demonic nature" of power—the entity that, of course, was the taproot of the state's existence—Meinecke was apparently well on his way toward cosmopolitanism. In fact, both H. Stuart Hughes and Richard Sterling see a certain redemptive quality in Meinecke's first step on the road back toward Goethe.[22] It cannot be denied that the calling into question of the *Machtstaat/Kulturstaat* synthesis was a very palpable milestone on this road.

However, in considering this course of Meinecke's historical development, we must bear in mind Benedetto Croce's rather perceptive criticism of it. Croce in his own rigorous adherence to certain Hegelian principles, quite naturally eschewed any variety of dualism. At the same time, his Hegelian ancestry forbade him to admit the irrational in any form into history, except of course to the degree that it could be somehow correlated to "cosmic progress."[23] This sort of an approach naturally raised problems for Croce's own variety of historiography. However, this does not disqualify him as a critic of Meinecke. As might be expected, Croce was rather put off by Meinecke's willingness to admit irrationality into history, something Meinecke had done in several ways: (1) Meinecke's definition of *Kultur* emphasized its extremely

---

21. Meinecke, *Die Idee der Staatsräson*, p. 410.
22. H. Stuart Hughes, *Consciousness and Society* (New York, 1961), p. 245.
23. Benedetto Croce, *History as the Story of Liberty*, trans. Sylvia Sprigge (New York, 1941), p. 161; Benedetto Croce, *Philosophy of the Practical*, trans. Douglas Ainslie (London, 1913), p. 252.

spiritualized individuality. (Here, Walther Hofer's claim that Meinecke was really emphasizing "soul" (*Seele*) over Spirit or intellect [*Geist*] is both perceptive and probably valid.) [24] (2) Meinecke was willing to see general forces, such as power, as being *also* at least in part irrational and hence relatively immune to historical investigation. For Croce, this sort of almost vulgar mysticism defeated the purpose of the Historicism to which he and Meinecke were ostensibly devoted. According to Croce, Historicism ideally accepted the " 'irrational' and understands it within the framework of its own activity and thereby reveals it in a rational light and defines its peculiar forms hitherto misunderstood or only partially understood." [25] Croce agreed that such phenomena as the "abstract rationalism" of the eighteenth century were rather brittle, if not artificial, efforts to apply reason to life. Nevertheless, in exposing and understanding the admitted shortcomings of these approaches, Historicism revealed itself as being "more proudly rationalistic" than these previous *Weltanschauungen*. However, thought Croce, to be able to reject the admittedly artificial modes of eighteenth-century thought, only to fall prey to so-called irrational elements in history was both self-defeating and one-sided.

We have noted already Meinecke's tendency toward spiritualism in his definition of *Kultur*. However, in considering Meinecke's approach to power, Croce's remarks become even more relevant. Meinecke did not only fail to recognize that power must and can be understood only in its specific and time-conditioned forms. Besides rejecting this cardinal principle of Historicism, he also fell prey to what he felt to be the overwhelming perverse nature of power. Meinecke had made a noble effort to reject the statism of Wilhelmine days, particularly as he recognized that its misapplication in World War I had brought Germany to disaster. After the war, he went through great intellectual convolutions in a desperate attempt to theoretically preserve *Kultur* from the lust of *Macht*. However, in attempting to do so, he trapped himself into accepting the latter's demonic nature and its seemingly unconditional development. It is of immense significance for his future work and political attitudes that Meinecke failed to perceive this aberration in his historical thinking. He apparently did not realize that he had not revised his statism in the light of new discoveries concerning nature of *raison d'état* or of power. Essentially, these entities remained what they were before, only divorced from the redeeming touch of spirituality.

More important than Meinecke's failure to realize he had not revised his statism, however, was his apparent unwillingness or inability

---

24. Walther Hofer, *Geschichtschreibung und Weltanschauung* (München, 1950), pp. 478–482.
25. Croce, *History as the Story of Liberty*, p. 66.

to discern the cultural developments and transformations that led to fundamental changes within man's apprehension and employment of *raison d'état* and in his attitude toward power. It is certainly true that Meinecke had attempted to analyze *raison d'état* in terms of the increasingly dangerous ramifications that stemmed from its misuse. As mentioned above, Meinecke saw this as resulting from the awesome growth of mass militarism coupled with the development of mass nationalism and capitalism. Yet, in terms of its ideological content and its goals, power itself remained immutable. Power had been conceptualized and thus divorced from the political and cultural changes that had allowed for its increasingly more penetrating application to the affairs of men.

Attention has been already given to Meinecke's concern with the peculiar evolution of Machiavellism in Germany. However, it is important to note that the *spiritual* sources of this evolution were not discussed. Meinecke had indicated, apparently, that attitudes toward power—attitudes that were conceptualized as various forms of *raison d'état*—were subject to various national conditioning factors. However, his desire to maintain the dichotomy between power and spirit prohibited him from ever really exploring these factors within the context of Germany's spiritual development. Most certainly, Meinecke's esoteric definition of *Kultur* had much to do with this. In a *historical* context, *Kultur* obviously represented the spiritual heritage and life of the nation. However, it was, by the same token, a *superhistorical* phenomenon. It had a timeless aspect to it, one that allowed it to transcend the biological and mechanical chains of causality which bound man to pitiless nature. The problems raised by the definition will be considered in greater detail somewhat later. For the present, we can note that Meinecke's tendency to approach *Kultur* from the points of view of historian and idealist made it extremely difficult for him to consider attitudes toward power as developing *within* particular patterns of "spiritual" evolution.

Why had Meinecke, the historian, accepted a definition of *Kultur* which emphasized a virtually nontemporal, and thus nonhistorical, side? The answer to this question is most probably provided in his relatively minor work of 1919, *After the Revolution*. Here, Meinecke had advised his countrymen to seek out those eternal verities with which a benign Providence had graciously endowed Germany. He called for a turning toward spiritual concerns. If the Germans were able to do this, the agonies of physical defeat on the battlefields of Europe could be endured. It is obvious that, although Meinecke always could have qualified as a *Kulturmensch*, he did not emphasize the timeless glories of *Kultur* until the very mundane truisms of political history brought

Germany down to defeat. Meinecke's turning toward *Kultur* at least partially represented a turning away from the harsh facts of day-to-day historical life. Timelessness provided a convenient refuge for those injured by political and military events.

Meinecke adhered to a timeless conception of *power* to the same degree as he glorified the eternal verities embodied in *Kultur*. He did devote considerable space in *Machiavellism* to discussing the terrible development of that "mass Machiavellism" which he said characterized the twentieth century. However, it was the *continually* demonic nature of power which he saw as being catalyzed to new levels of horrible application through the triple development of militarism, nationalism, and capitalism.[26] The new motivations and demands that led to mass wars were not discussed. Rather, Meinecke seems to have assumed that the real danger lay in the extrapolation ad infinitum of national pride through the introduction of the masses into politics.

In conceptualizing power, in divorcing it from immediate and concrete relationships to the spiritual changes within the states themselves, Meinecke had virtually elevated it into an intellectual entity. *Raison d'état* had been transformed into a sort of diabolical *raison de puissance*. Power had become the timeless counterpart of *Kultur*. Meinecke had laid the foundations for his post-World War II quasi-cosmopolitan fantasies.

Meinecke ran himself into a corner in another, and perhaps more revealing fashion. Throughout *Machiavellism*, he pointed continually to the degeneration of *raison d'état* through mass involvement in politics. In a sense, Meinecke felt that the faceless, dully emotional man in the street had put the torch to the edifice so laboriously built over the centuries. He had hoped, however, for a "purified" *raison d'état*. Meinecke felt that this could at least in part be achieved through deemphasizing the vulgar political life of the Weimar Republic. In this context, he called for a strong plebiscite-based presidency to counterbalance the parliamentarianism of the Weimar Republic. Meinecke already had considered the more mundane political reasons for this constitutional arrangement in earlier works.[27] In *Machiavellism*, he added another one,

26. Meinecke, *Die Idee der Staatsräson*, p. 418.
27. Meinecke, *Nach der Revolution* (München, 1919). Also see *Politische Schriften und Reden*. This, despite Meinecke's maintaining (during the course of his discussion of Duke Henri de Rohan) that the "proper remedy" for dealing with the "quasi-State" nature of political parties "lies in the parliamentary State, where the separate parties and party-leaders themselves take over responsibility for the whole of the State" (page 190). In his *Erinnerungen, 1905–1933*, Theodor Heuss claims to have recognized the dangers to parliamentary democracy inherent in a plebiscite-based political system. In pointing out Conrad Haussmann's demands for such a system,

a reason supposedly stemming from his fear of the degeneration of *raison d'état* into mass Machiavellism. Essentially, he felt that *raison d'état* would be degenerated even further through the introduction and overweening influence of party politics! *Raison d'état*, already tarnished by a quarter century of misuse, would become prey to the divisive interests of the political parties, entities concerned with manipulation of the German masses for their respective nefarious ends. How, then, could one avoid the destructive influences of mass Machiavellism upon state life? By going directly to the masses, Meinecke answered.[28] Here again, we see the organic state of the German historical and political traditions rising to the surface. Somehow, the German people as a totality, that is, as a unit to be tapped through plebiscite and referendum, was greater than the sum of its parts as these were represented in the parties and in various interest groups.

Involved in these various inconsistencies and contradictions in Meinecke's thinking was a certain withdrawal on his part from political life. In *Machiavellism* (as in *After the Revolution*, although not quite so clearly stated as in that work), we see a certain longing on Meinecke's part to rise above day-to-day horrors and/or boredom. This attitude of Meinecke's is also revealed in the almost thoughtless manner in which he theoretically disposed of that most vital unit in Rankean historiography, the state, for, as we have seen, Meinecke's prewar conception of the state saw it as an entity consisting of power and culture. In *Machiavellism*, Meinecke had started to dismantle this synthesis; therefore, the destruction of this synthesis really involved the destruction of the state, at least as an heuristic principle in historical investigation. Naturally, Meinecke did not really feel he had destroyed the state. He would continue to refer to it throughout the remainder of his career, and indeed, it is difficult to see how he, as a historian, could have avoided doing so. Yet, he had extracted one element from the life of the state, *Kultur*, and posed it against the other element, power. It is also true that, in his later writings, Meinecke would tend to more and more identify the state with power, or rather *as* power.

Another problem emerged from *Machiavellism*. In his excellent study of Meinecke, *Geschichte zwischen Philosophie und Politik*, Walther Hofer implicitly praised Meinecke's polarization of power and *Kultur*, maintaining that Meinecke polarized the two in order to liberate Ger-

---

Heuss maintained that, if Haussman had been able to see how this doctrine was eventually employed, "no one would have more profoundly regretted this institutional enticement to brutal demagoguery" (see *Erinnerungen, 1905–1933* [Tübingen, 1963], p. 247). For more of Heuss's comments on this subject, see *Erinnerungen*, pp. 248 and 251.

28. Meinecke, *Die Idee der Staatsräson*, p. 430.

man historiography from what the latter felt to be the tyranny of Hegelian monism.[29] This polarization also involved for Meinecke the at least partial rejection of Ranke, his previous hero in German historiography. Walther Hofer implied that this separation of power from *Kultur* was laudable, as did Richard Sterling. In a sense, perhaps it was. However, in polarizing power and *Kultur*, Meinecke seems to have begged a rather disturbing question. He had assumed that there was a generic dichotomy between the two terms. Now, perhaps Meinecke felt that his own esoteric definition of *Kultur* had allowed it to remain snugly ensconced in the ethereal. He wanted to have things two ways, as a historian and as an idealist, for it is obvious that he was in fact utilizing the term *Kultur* in a double sense: it was a spiritualized entity embodying eternal values, but it was also the spiritual heritage of the nation. This latter use of the term was particularly apparent in *After the Revolution*. It is true that, in his formal definition of the term, Meinecke seemed to have placed *Kultur* out of reach of vulgar forces of politics and power. However this was an extremely artificial definition of the term. It represented, to be sure, an attempt to secure *Kultur* against the unseemly ravages of *Macht*. However, Meinecke had turned *Kultur* into something so precious and obstruse that he himself had trouble living with his own definition. This we shall see later. For the present, we should note again that Meinecke, in positing this dichotomy between *Macht* and *Kultur*, seemed unwilling to investigate power, or at least *attitudes* toward power developing within particular cultural situations.

One is tempted to ask how Meinecke would consider somebody like Johann Gottlieb Fichte. Certainly, this individual was a *Kulturmensch* in the profoundest meaning of the term. Yet, even while he dwelt in the world of spirit, Fichte displayed a willingness to indulge in matters of power and *raison d'état*. How could one divorce *Kultur* from *Macht* within the philosophy of Fichte? Obviously, Fichte's works have to be taken as a piece. Political concerns were most profoundly influenced by both his *Wissenschaftslehre* and by his *Ethik*. Attitudes toward power and the state had developed within the broader contours of Fichte's analytical philosophy.

Obviously, Meinecke's abstract approach to power was at the root of many of his problems. To make power into a construct implied divorcing it from specific cultural situations or specific patterns of evolution. Meinecke's unconscious Hegelianism in regard to power would wreak havoc in his later historiographical considerations.

Of course, the problems that appeared in *Machiavellism* were also

---

29. Hofer, *Geschichte zwischen Philosophie und Politik*, p. 83.

represented in some of Meinecke's other writing of the Weimar period. We have already examined his definition of *Kultur*. This definition was given in a 1928 article in the *Historische Zeitschrift* which was entitled "Causalities and Values in History" ("Kausalitäten und Werte in der Geschichte"). This definition had been given earlier in order to put his consideration of power in some perspective. Now, we must return to this essay and consider some of its ramifications in greater detail.

It is in this essay that Meinecke first made the rather well-known statement that "history is nothing else but *Kulturgeschichte*."[30] In other words, he felt that the historian must focus upon the various "spiritual breakthroughs" in the network of causality. The historian should empathize with the "searching after values" which is embodied in the various manifestations of spirit (*Kultur*).

These various manifestations of *Kultur* were placed under the rubric "historical individuality." In other words, each manifestation of *Kultur* or spirit was seen as something intrinsic and spontaneous, which Meinecke termed the "historical individuality." Here Meinecke was placing renewed emphasis upon the historicist side of Ranke, who himself had pointed to the importance of the "historical individuality." Taken together, Meinecke and Ranke agreed, these individuals were the very material (*Stoff*) of history itself. Ranke, however, had maintained that the historical individual *gained* its individuality only to the degree that it embodied general forces. Apparently without noticing he was doing so, Meinecke set out to redeem German historiography by placing exclusive emphasis upon the individuality itself; for in his definition of *Kultur*, Meinecke had sharply differentiated—at least qualitatively—between the individual and those general forces through which it had to break. For the universality of Ranke, Meinecke quietly substituted the Eternal. Meinecke was attempting obviously to salvage something meaningful from his dissolution of the *Macht/Kultur* synthesis. If history itself could be seen, not as a tragic story of clashing power states, but as the composite of individual quests for value, the situation might yet be saved.

To this end, Meinecke dedicated himself to a renewed appreciation of the Rankean dictum that world history was "only a great individuality filled with countless [numbers] of great and small individuals."[31] However, here Meinecke differed sharply from Ranke in his own rather interesting definition of the historical individualities. These were "only such phenomena which have intrinsic to them various tendencies in the direction of the good, beautiful or true and [which] therefore have

30. Meinecke, "Kausalitäten und Werte in der Geschichte," p. 23.
31. *Ibid.*, p. 8.

become meaningful or possessed of value for us." [32] In a way, Meinecke had done what Benedetto Croce had sought to do earlier. He had "positivized" history by seeing it as the temporal unfolding of spirit. However, unlike Croce, Meinecke adhered to a Rankean conception of the historical individual, while Croce based his speculations on a refined version of Hegelian monism.[33] Meinecke also, however, broke with Ranke in qualitatively separating the *Kultur*-laden historical individual from general forces. Apparently, though, he felt quite satisfied with his new approach. Since he chose to view history as a composite of constituent historical individualities, he apparently felt that he had succeeded in transforming history itself into a *Kultur* nexus; he felt that he had turned history into an ingeniously synthesized composite of historical individualities. In another essay, this one on Droysen, Meinecke pressed his point a bit further. He praised Droysen for recognizing "that the highest and most decisive phenomena in history were [those] which were not subordinated to mundane causality, but have a metaphysical background." [34]

Meinecke never went so far as to claim that the historical individualities, his bearers of *Kultur,* were or could be divorced *temporally* from the biological and mechanical chains of causality. *Kultur* always had been to some degree contingent upon power and external circumstances to provide the right order necessary for its emergence. Here, Meinecke attempted to reinforce the seemingly isolated historical individualities by creating a "spiritual-moral" ("*geistigsittlichen*") pattern of causality. Rather, he called upon others to create it for him. If one could join the "bearers" of *Kultur* into an integrated and cohesive totality, the historian could be always certain of being able to redeem history through the transcendental force of *Kultur*. Obviously the attempt to create a "*geistig-sittlichen*" pattern of causality stemmed from the considerations in *Machiavellism*, where power as a manifestation of those general patterns of causality seemed to have all its own way. It is just as obvious, unfortunately, that the problems touched upon in considering *Machiavellism* had carried over into Meinecke's *Historische Zeitschrift* essays.

Again, it is worth repeating that Meinecke did point out that *Kultur* was often dependent on such vulgar forces of nature as power. Nevertheless, Meinecke was adamant in maintaining that somehow *Kultur*

---

32. *Ibid.,* p. 18.

33. On Croce's positivizing of History, see his *History as the Story of Liberty,* pp. 161–164.

34. Friedrich Meinecke, "Johann Gustav Droysen," *Historische Zeitschrift,* Band 141, Heft 2 (1930), pp. 278–279. This essay also appeared in *Staat und Persönlichkeit* (Berlin, 1933).

stood pretty much above these forces. In a word, *Kultur*, which contained the breath of the Eternal, never could be *reduced* to any pattern of mechanical and biological causality. What Meinecke in fact had done was to separate power from *Kultur*, and then to transform each of the two terms into an essentially antihistorical, or at least *ahistorical*, phenomenon. Power had been made into a sort of demonic force. Perhaps it was such. Nevertheless, as we have seen, Meinecke's treatment of the evolution of thinking on *raison d'état* lacked a substantive examination of cultural conditioning in regard to concepts of power. Power was treated as a sort of demiurge which existed at the basis of state life and which alternatively revealed coldly mechanistic or irrational sides. In "Causalities and Values in History," Meinecke simply compounded the problem. This historian was to focus upon the cultural individuality. Meinecke indicated that, because the emergence of this individuality was dependent upon external conditions, it was necessary for the historian to relate forces of external causality to the *Kulturindividualitäten*. Yet, *could* he in fact do so? Could there not arise the tendency to view nature-conditioned phenomena like power as being almost nihilistic, in other words, as being essentially opaque to historical investigation? As a matter of fact, Meinecke's post-World War II attitudes in regard to Nazism would suffer from this tendency. Meinecke's view of power, heavily conditioned by post-World War I musings and regrets, allowed for nihilism to pervade the historian's realm.

On the other hand, Meinecke's very conception of *Kulturgeschichte* was fraught with problems and contradictions, for obviously, *Kulturgeschichte* was very much a contradiction in terms. The essentially noncontingent "historical individualities" derived their substance from unfettered spirituality. In this regard, they could scarcely have been related to history, at least insofar as the discipline is normally understood, for the "historical individualities" were really superrational. They embodied Eternal and therefore nontemporal verities. Meinecke never denied that these entities were dependent upon external conditions, "tendencies," as he would refer to them later. However, the historian could not really be expected to understand them rationally. What was implied was a sort of intuitive/emotional grasping for the infinite that was to be discovered in each of the individualities.

Meinecke's calling for the discovery of a casual chain of "*geistigsittlichen*" individualities would have served only to divorce *Kultur* from history even further, even if we were to admit to the feasibility of linking together *essentially* unique entities into any sort of consistent pattern. It is true that Meinecke's mentor, Leopold von Ranke, had placed great emphasis upon the individual. But Meinecke had turned the Rankean historical individuality into a manifestation of the Eternal.

This curious being no longer embodied general forces, but rather timeless verities.

Meinecke was not the only historian to place heavy emphasis upon intuition: Dilthey, Collingwood, and even, to some extent, Croce also did so.[35] Nevertheless, there is an important quantitative difference in application here. Meinecke was not calling upon the historian to "re-experience" the past; he was not calling upon him to place reliance in an admittedly obscure "historical imagination." Most important of all, he did not recognize the wisdom in Croce's point that too great a reliance upon intuition and too little reliance upon reason would turn history into aesthetics.[36] Admittedly, the difference between other historians' use of intuition and Meinecke's use of it was a quantitative one. Yet, quantitative differences can be significant. Perhaps one would not be unjust in saying that Meinecke wanted to turn history into aesthetics. Perhaps his renewed interest in, and strengthened respect for, Goethe was indicative of this desire. At any rate, this much is certain: By the 1920s, Meinecke had begun to capitulate to what he considered to be the irrationalities and meanness of history. As if in anticipation of unhappy post-World War II questioning, he had begun to place *Kultur* in the snug and serene environment of the spiritual. *Kultur* was superrational spirit. *Macht*, power, was a nihilistic offshoot of vulgar biological and mechanical patterns of causality. What was the role of the historian? He could concern himself with the transient, the epiphenomenal. After World War I, Meinecke's writings give the distinct impression that their author was placing greater and greater importance upon a sort of netherworld in which mighty forces moved with the dignity of eternity, occasionally erupting into events of a beautiful or tragic nature.

Yet, Meinecke was still writing definitely "historical" works. In one of these, *History of the German-English Alliance Problem: 1890–1901* (1927), Meinecke placed a renewed emphasis upon creative statesmanship. This work seems to be Meinecke's final effort to extoll creativity in statescraft, for, in this book, Meinecke points to the creative use and understanding of *raison d'état* on the parts of several British and German statesmen during the period 1890–1901. Such individuals as Landsdowne, Chamberlain, and Ambassadors Metternich and Hatzfeldt of the German Foreign Office were praised as having a sophisticated understanding of the rather tricky doctrine of *raison d'état*. Others, such as Salisbury, Holstein, Bülow, and Wilhelm II, lacked it.

---

35. See Croce, *Philosophy of the Practical*, pp. 27–28.

36. Benedetto Croce, *Logic as the Science of the Pure Concept*, trans. Douglas Ainslie (London, 1917), pp. 283–288.

The thesis of Meinecke's book was that an alliance between Germany and Great Britain could and, in terms of *Realpolitik*, should have been implemented during the period in question. Failure to do so was the result of an overly suspicious attitude toward German colonial and naval policies by Salisbury and of Holstein's irrational suspicion of England's motives in seeking such an alliance. Meinecke was particularly critical of Holstein's monomania in regard to the "perfidious Albion" who utilized the nations of Europe to "draw her chestnuts out of the fire." According to Meinecke, Holstein seemed to have believed that England enjoyed and certainly benefited from continental disorder and lack of unity. Also, Meinecke quite logically castigated the hapless Wilhelm II and Bülow, who had been given the unusual opportunity of displaying his incompetence at two important posts: that of foreign minister (1897–1900), and that of chancellor (1900–1909). Both of these gentlemen tried to practice *Realpolitik* by keeping Germany always between England and Russia. However, neither of these individuals had any sense for the game, and this spelled disaster for Germany.

Essentially, Meinecke felt that Germany should have gone along with Great Britain. She should not have engaged in the futile naval race. Bismarck himself had advised against it; and, if Germany had not done so, she might have been able to preserve her colonies under the guns of the British fleet. Meinecke was extremely critical of the naïvely arrogant policy practiced by Holstein and Bülow of alienating Russia while at the same time expecting Great Britain to come to Germany on German terms. If Germany *had* to alienate Russia, she could have played much more sensitively than she did upon British fears of Russian expansion in China and, for that matter, of French expansion into Africa.[37]

The net result of the book was a rather well-written and ingenious account of the efforts of specific German and British statesmen to thwart fate and to form an alliance. This was diplomatic history par excellence, one that was written almost solely in terms of the diplomats themselves. There were only the most tangential of references to underlying social or even political trends in either of the great powers. Such events as the Treaty of Shimonoseki of 1894, the Fashoda Crisis of 1898, and the Boxer Rebellion of 1900 were all described pretty much in a vacuum. The book was almost exclusively concerned with the course of German-British diplomatic problems as these were manifested in the day-to-day activities (or lack of them) of a score or so diplomats and statesmen. As such, this is an interesting book, although

37. Friedrich Meinecke, *Geschichte des deutsch-englischen Bündnisproblems 1890–1901* (München, 1927), p. 92.

the recent publication of Holstein's papers does much to undecut Meinecke's portrayal of him as a vain and irrational civilian Colonel Blimp, completely possessed by his own prejudices.

Yet, the book has several damaging flaws. First of all, Meinecke failed to give adequate weight to the very unique position of Germany vis-à-vis Great Britain. A general world picture of 1890–1901 is also curiously lacking, and the crises and efforts at *detente* during this time were seen as being largely the results of the machinations of individual men. The old and in this instance very useful Rankean scheme of linking individual effort to general trend was lacking altogether. *Realpolitik* was being studied, and in the most limited possible fashion. Some diplomats had an understanding of it; others did not. Meinecke's approach was thus quite limited, and this resulted in occasionally questionable statements. Meinecke speculated as to the wholesome results that might have followed upon an anti-Russian alliance between Japan, Germany, and Great Britain around the turn of the century. If Russia had been defeated by all of these powers, rather than merely by Japan, the rather hollow Revolution of 1905 would have occurred "in the dimensions of the one it [Russia] experienced in 1917. We would have been thus liberated from the Eastern nightmare, for the foreseeable future." [38] For a *Realpolitiker,* this was a rather remarkable statement. It indicates that, in this instance at least, Meinecke gave little attention to the social and political developments within Russia itself. In a way, he was still adhering to a sort of debased Rankean approach, for, as in *After the Revolution,* Meinecke still believed that such things as revolution occur mainly as responses to foreign adventures and disasters. Yet, Meinecke appears to have given little consideration to the state of the balance of power within Europe, the consequences of which a war with Russia could only have delayed. For a former adherent to Rankean statism, this was quite an oversight on his part.

In *Machiavellism,* Meinecke had been concerned with the concept of *raison d'état* itself. Meinecke's diplomatic history of 1927 examined this concept in a personalized, almost idiocentric fashion. It is not unusual, of course, for one to read diplomatic histories largely concerned with the attitudes, actions, and prejudices of the individual diplomats themselves. What is unusual in this instance (particularly when one bears in mind Meinecke's intellectual pedigree) is the author's failure to link individual diplomatic actions to the overall pattern of general forces and conditions extant during the period under consideration.

History of the German-English Alliance Problem represented Meinecke's last serious foray into the field of statecraft. When we bear this

---

38. *Ibid.,* p. 225.

in mind, and when we consider the themes of *Machiavellism,* the tenor of the work should not surprise us. In *Machiavellism,* Meinecke had been concerned with the degeneration of *raison d'état* under the inhuman pressures of the mass state. One has the feeling that, in his 1927 book, Meinecke was trying to show what "positive" *raison d'état* could be like. Here *raison d'état* had been elevated to the position of being an art practiced by cool-headed men, who acted oblivious to mass pressures and vulgar mass politics. In *Machiavellism,* Meinecke had elevated power to a position that was over and above specific factors of historical conditioning. In *History of the German-English Alliance Problem,* the creative roles of individual statesmen were almost abstracted from historical context. Their activities were described in almost aesthetic terms as Jacob Burckhardt might have described the actions of a Sforza or a Medici. Meinecke's last, and in its own way, impressive work on statecraft was really a wistful backward glance at an era when heroic individuals sought to head off forces of mass destruction. A more refined, humane age had gone down with the German defeat. Understandably, Meinecke hesitated to take to the boats.

History of the German-English Alliance Problem was not merely unusual because of its seemingly restricted methodology. It was also unusual because this book, concerned with the most unemotional of subjects, diplomatic history, was perhaps one of the more nostalgic of Meinecke's intellectual excursions. It is doubtful if Meinecke had intended this. Yet, there can be but little doubt that Meinecke's 1927 book was a least in part intended as a salute to those cool, nineteenth-century practitioners of *raison d'état* who were just as much victims of mass Machiavellism as the ten million dead of World War I. Furthermore, it is of immense importance that Meinecke was writing this book during a period in which his own gaze was gradually turning away from the state and toward more remote, yet spiritually more satisfying, concerns. *History of the German-English Alliance Problem* cannot be fit neatly into the context of the *Kultur/Macht* dichotomy which was perplexing Meinecke at the time; however, it was symptomatic of it, and was perhaps Meinecke's last effort to have *raison d'état* in the name of creative individuality.

The ramifications of Meinecke's fixation with the demonic nature of power and of his elevation of individuality carried over into several works of the Nazi period. This is extremely interesting inasmuch as it reveals Meinecke's complete sincerity and his courage in his consistent adherence to his newly founded theses. It also presents us with one of the issues raised previously: the conceptualization of *Kultur.*

The issues raised in *Machiavellism* carried over into Meinecke's most significant methodological work, *The Origin of Historicism* (*Die Ent-*

stehung des Historismus 1936). This work, which was concerned with the evolution of Historicism, was also Meinecke's most thoroughgoing and elaborate defense of historical individuality. In considering it, Walther Hofer pointed out that Meinecke's adherence to the principle of individualism was aptly revealed in his rejection of the "development" (*Entwicklung*) theories of Vico. (It is of some significance, perhaps, that Vico was one of Croce's heroes.) Meinecke was adamant in rejecting Vico's cyclical theories because, as he saw it, theories this mechanistic precluded any meaningful assertion of individualism in the historical context.[39] Meinecke was being quite consistent with earlier positions here. In this regard, we must bear in mind his specific rejection of Hegel in *Cosmopolitanism and the National State* and more pointedly in *Machiavellism*. However, Hofer pointed out that *The Origin of Historicism* represented the apotheosis of Meinecke's historiographical concerns, for, in describing the development of Historicism, Meinecke had attained his highest intellectual level in his attempts to: (1) exalt the historical individual, and (2) to somehow *reconcile* the individual with the general forces.

The Origin of Historicism also can be viewed as Meinecke's most singular effort to exalt the superiority of a specifically *German* mode of thought, or at least concern: the reconciling of universal and particular. To be sure, in volume one of *The Origin of Historicism,* Meinecke focused upon a variety of European thinkers, each of whom seemed to be concerned with overthrowing rigid adherence to natural law in favor of a more individualized approach to man and to his history. Here, Meinecke focused upon Shaftesbury, Leibniz, Gibbon, Voltaire, and the English Pre-Romantics, among others. Nevertheless, Meinecke was adamant in maintaining that only in *Germany* had the problem of reconciling universality and individuality been elevated to a position of prominence. However, the primary concern of *The Origin of Historicism* was somehow reconciling *Kultur* with the vulgar external causal forces that both conditioned and frustrated it.

In this regard, Hofer pointed to Meinecke's efforts to provide for a new conceptual framework, a framework within which the polarities of individuality and generality could be somehow synthesized. Hofer was concerned here with Meinecke's extraordinarily sophisticated analysis of the role of *Idee*. Literally, *Idee* can be translated as "idea" or "notion." However, this cognate is rather deceptive (in this, it is similar to *Kultur*) because *Idee* can be laden with spiritual overtones. In fact, in *The Origin of Historicism,* it is. Here Meinecke stated that the *Idee* represented a sort of synthesis of a spontaneous spiritual outburst (the *Kultur*

---

39. Hofer, *Geschichtschreibung und Weltanschauung*, p. 488.

phenomenon) and a tendency in the amalgam of external causal forces. Thus, a cultural phenomenon could only emerge into the phenomenal world if this manifestation of spiritual spontaneity was *somehow* connected with an "inborn" or "innate tendency" (*"angeborner Tendenz"*) in the developmental processes. The possibility for the emergence of the *Kultur* phenomenon thus had been made dependent upon the synthesis of spontaneity and general forces embodied in the *Idee*.[40] Through this ingenious and seemingly logical device—the *Idee*—Meinecke had attempted to resolve the dichotomy between the *Kulturindividualitäten* and general forces (power, of course, being among them). He had attempted once more to fuse them together, in this instance by describing the emergence of the particular individual as being dependent upon its being an "inborn tendency" in the causal nexus. So, the cultural individual had been made dependent upon forces of external necessity. In a way, Meinecke simply had enlarged the perspective of *Cosmopolitanism and the National State,* where the power-based state provided the framework within which *Kultur* could mature.

Whether Meinecke had actually affected a reconciliation between *Kultur* and the more developmental natural processes must remain a moot point. Curiously enough, he may have theoretically exalted generality over particularity, inasmuch as one could see the "inborn tendency" as usurping the role of spiritual spontaneity. The cultural event would thus be as illuded by developmental processes as was, according to Croce, the historical individual by Hegelian Providence.[41] However, the actual fusion of spirituality with developmental process was a rather artificial one, and Carlo Antoni, a student of Croce, seemed to be aware of this artificiality:

Meinecke thought to mediate the dangers of individualism by refusing to conceive the individual as a monad and by linking its development to the processes of the external world. The resultant relationship is therefore conceived as an intermixture or interweaving, a reciprocal determination of two entities, remains, that is, in an extrinsic and, in the last analysis, purely mechanical relationship.[42]

Antoni was quite perceptive here, for even in so sophisticated and so painfully thought-out an analysis, Meinecke had not really fused individuality and developmental processes. *Kultur* and outside forces had been fused in *time*. However, there was no qualitative fusion of them,

40. Friedrich Meinecke, *Die Entstehung des Historismus,* Vol. I (München, 1936), p. 171.
41. See Croce's discussion of this in *History as the Story of Liberty,* pp. 163–164.
42. Carlo Antoni, *Dallo storicismo alla sociologia* (trans. by Hayden V. White as *From History to Sociology;* Detroit, 1959), p. 116.

and the cultural individual was still surrounded by the halo of spirituality. Meinecke never repudiated his elevation of individuality which we saw in the *Historische Zeitschrift* essay. The brilliant, but unsatisfying constructivism he displayed in *The Origin of Historicism* was more of an intellectual exercise than a serious effort to counterbalance the almost mystical attempts Meinecke was making to sanctify history and to exclude those forces that appalled him.

Seen in a broader context, then, *The Origin of Historicism* leaves Meinecke's readers with much the same problem that was considered in the context of *Machiavellism:* the artificial dichotomy between two rather artificial concepts of power and *Kultur*. Furthermore, Meinecke accentuated this dichotomy—although he certainly did not intend to do so—by placing great emphasis upon the differences between Goethe and Ranke.

In *The Origin of Historicism,* Meinecke displayed a sympathy toward Goethe which had been lacking in earlier writings. He found a certain spiritual contentment in Goethe's "synthesis of Enlightenment and Neo-Platonic elements" which transcended the antiseptic rationalist egoism of the eighteenth-century.[43] No doubt, Meinecke sensed a certain spiritual affinity between himself and Goethe. He realized that Goethe, to a marked degree, had concerned himself with some of the same problems which he, in an historical context, had faced in the 1920s. The problem of individuality had been an important one to Goethe. In his *Sturm und Drang* period, Goethe had been greatly preoccupied with "the . . . developing consciousness of unity and the totality of strengths of all souls: similarly, however, also [with] their individuality . . . and the source of all individuality . . . the immutable, creating nature . . . the universe."[44] Thus, even though Goethe seemed to have been considering "creating nature" in a somewhat different fashion than Meinecke, the problem of individual and general forces was an important one for him. Before carrying this discussion further, however, we would do well to consider some of Goethe's own conceptions of the individual and the *Kultur*.

Kultur, for Goethe, was a term that had both a narrower and a broader connotation than it did for Burckhardt, and even for Meinecke. *Kultur*, for the individual human spirit, was attained through the broadest possible *Bildung,* that is, the total intellectual and spiritual education of the individual. It also implied the ability of this individual to relate himself—as a *gebildeter Mensch*—to other individuals in society. *Bildung* thus implied a delicate balance of aesthetic appreciation and morality, one that was valid, however, only insofar as it functioned in

43. Meinecke, *Die Entstehung des Historismus*, Vol. II, p. 541.
44. *Ibid.*, p. 540.

society. This was the lesson that had to be learned by Goethe's archetype of *Bildung,* Wilhelm Meister.⁴⁵ The individual man, as he partook of *Bildung,* was the *subject* of *Kultur* for Goethe. The *object* of *Kultur* was Truth, in both its general and particular manifestations. As Goethe saw it, it was the duty of science to be concerned with the general, with Necessity, which was the *highest product* of Nature. Although the scientist was to be concerned with the manifestation of Necessity in the various unique forms of plant and animal life, his focus was on the general rather than on the particular. The artist was to concern himself with the creation and perception of the beautiful which, for Goethe, represented an aspect of God's Truth as this was captured and concretized through the cognative processes of man. In a word, the scientist was to arrive at an understanding of Nature, the general, by becoming aware of the developmental processes inherent in all organic life. The artist was to arrive at an understanding of the particular as this manifested God's Truth in beauty.⁴⁶ For the scientist, individuality served as a point of departure from which to arrive at an understanding of intuitively sensed generality. For the artist, individuality was both the goal of his efforts and a particular manifestation of the general.

Differing considerably from Meinecke in this regard, Goethe had maintained that art and nature both stemmed from the same all-encompassing source.⁴⁷ Obviously *Kultur,* for Goethe, consisted of an extraordinarily broad *Bildungsideal* in which the processes at work in the becoming of the human spirit were to be seen as representative of the general developmental processes at work in the universe. Description and creation, the respective realms of the scientist and aestheticism, were both part of it. Thus, from Goethe's point of view, *Kultur* meant two things: (1) the process and idea of *Bildung,* as applied to the individual, and (2) the highest realms of spiritual life, that is, scientific and aesthetic endeavors. In brief, *Kultur* was the composite of man's spiritual existence.

Social life, as depicted in *Wilhelm Meisters Wanderjahre* and *Faust,* represented the all-important matrix within which *Kultur* was objectified. However, it is true that, particularly after his Italian journey and the outbreak of the French revolution, political life tended to play less of a role in Goethe's conception of *Kultur.* War and *Staaträson* were

45. Johann Wolfgang von Goethe, *Wilhelm Meisters Lehrjahre* [Wilhelm Goldmann Verlag] (München, 1964), pp. 394–395 and 441–442.
46. Albert Bielchowsky, *Goethe, Sein Leben und seine Werke* (München, 1908), pp. 238–239 and 429–431.
47. *Ibid.,* pp. 430–431. Since the individual was as such an embodiment of the External, the subjects and objects of *Kultur* tended to have a timeless quality for Goethe. Goethe's antipathy toward history is well known.

anathema to him, and it was his unwillingness to recognize the role of the state and of the interactions of states in the evolution of *Kultur* that Meinecke singled out as indicating Goethe's lack of a historical sense. At least in this instance, Meinecke seemed to have overlooked the fact that he himself was tending in much the same direction.

Nevertheless, the syncretic side of Goethe's intellectual endeavors—the fusion of individuality with the course of development—was important to Ranke. Meinecke did make much of Goethe's concern with the fusion of Individuality and Necessity, and, in terms of the transcendental aesthetic experience, of past and present. However, he did not treat Goethe as a historian, for, as he himself states, Goethe was "a child of peace." Thus, according to Meinecke, "He built his *Kultur* essentially without the help of the state," never being able to appreciate the positive aspects of the state as an entity of power.[48] "Causality in history interested him only insofar . . . as it facilitated or strictured the general advance of human cultural values." [49] The fusion of the creative particular and the general *in a historical sense* would have to wait until Ranke who, much as he did in *Cosmopolitanism and the National State,* here represented for Meinecke the "highest achievement yet attained in the marriage of Idea and Reality." [50] Considering Meinecke's own increasing concern with the problems rising from statism, this is certainly an interesting statement. It would seem that, by this time, his attitude toward power and the state were, if anything, closer to those of the nonhistorical Goethe than to the historian Ranke.

It is significant, nonetheless, that unlike in *Cosmopolitanism and the National State,* there was evidenced great sympathy for the concept of cosmopolitanism in *The Origin of Historicism.* There was shown a profound respect for Goethe, and he was perhaps one of the most notable examples of this outlook. Also, Meinecke respected Goethe as the "ground-breaker" for the later synthesis that Ranke so effectively utilized in his own statist version of Historicism, for it was Goethe who transcended both the developmentalism of Vico and the raw individualism of the eighteenth-century Enlightenment thinkers by "showing how one and the same happening is completely individual and unrelated and yet blended into a general coherence." [51] Meinecke had drawn the cosmopolitan Goethe and the historian Ranke into a fairly close relationship here. Perhaps Meinecke felt that in so doing he was pointing toward that desired synthesis of general and particular. Perhaps raw, natural-bound power and *Kultur* could be yet reconciled. It must be

48. Meinecke, *Die Entstehung des Historismus,* Vol. II, p. 555.
49. *Ibid.,* p. 587.
50. *Ibid.,* p. 680.
51. *Ibid.,* p. 649.

THE CLASH BETWEEN POWER AND *KULTUR* 77

seen, however, that this was not true. Indeed, the cleavage between Goethe and Ranke and the respective viewpoints they represented was widened rather than bridged over by considering the two in tandem.[52]

Even if he did consciously utilize Goethe's synthesis of the general and the particular, Ranke merely was borrowing a methodological device rather than a *Weltanschauung*. For Goethe, this synthesis had been an aesthetic and a "natural" one, central both to his scientific endeavors and to his conception of *Kultur*. The involvement of historical processes in *Kultur* was certainly not parenthetical to it. However, for Goethe, historical considerations served more to *color* the synthesis rather than to give it significance in terms of temporal development. Goethe certainly provided Ranke with a frame of reference—the fusion of the particular and the general—that would prove to be salient to the latter's conceptions of the roles of individual, state, and general forces in history. However, as Meinecke knew very well, Goethe himself was not a historian. His very concern with *Kultur,* one that was divorced from supportive power considerations, precluded him from a sophisticated understanding of the primary actors in world history, the nation-states. As mentioned above, it is rather curious that Meinecke would fault him for this, inasmuch as he was tending to do the same thing himself.

Moreover, Ranke's "use" of Goethe's conception of fusing the particular to the general raises some profound problems, as does Ranke's conception of *Kultur* and its role in history. To begin with, his own application of Goethe's principle has to be seen on two levels. This serves to put Ranke's considerations of *Kultur* in a much different light than that cast upon the subject by Goethe and, although he was apparently loath to admit it, by Meinecke also.

First of all, Ranke maintained that each state embodied a spiritual reality of its own; it was a particular individualization of *Geist*.[53] In a word, each state had its own "idea" or tendency, and it was this idea that described the state's intrinsic relationship to God. A state, or institution of the state, was considered by Ranke to be a "particular" (*Besondere*), while the force of which it was an individualization was the "general" (*Allgemeine*). Thus, the course of the political life of the particular state in question, the *Besondere,* represented a striving toward the *Allgemeine* in terms of the fixed nature or *idea* of this state.[54] On this level, then, there appears a rough approximation of Goethe's emphasis on individualism, of his tendency to merge general

52. The chapter on Ranke was based on an address given by Meinecke on January 23, 1936, and was appended to the book.
53. Leopold von Ranke, *Das Politische Gespräch,* with an introduction by Friedrich Meinecke (München and Leipzig, 1924), p. 32.
54. *Ibid.*

and particular. For Ranke, however, the general did not *live* in the particular, and he could not have rejected teleology if he was to have avoided the type of monism to which Goethe held. For Ranke, God had to stand apart from the entities in which He manifested himself.

Ranke's own fusion of the particular and the general was operative, however, on yet another level, that of the state itself. Here, the unique or individual phenomenon was the particular variety of spiritual or "moral energy" that was at the basis of the state's existence and was elaborated upon and reinforced by the state's interactions with other states.[55] This "moral energy" constituted, of course, the taproot of the state's particular idea. *Kultur, for Ranke, did not constitute the base of the state's spiritual existence* but was, rather, simply a social manifestation of the particular variety of moral energy which was the source of the very life of the state.[56] "Moral energy" was not *Kultur*, but *power;* or rather, power *plus* the other components of the life of a particular people. It is difficult to see how Meinecke could have overlooked Ranke's view. Probably, he did not, but chose instead, to focus upon the spiritual content of Ranke's historical individual, ignoring Ranke's tendency to spiritualize power itself. At least he ignored this particular Rankean tendency in *The Origin of Historicism*, for in *Machiavellism* he displayed an acute sensitivity to this problem. The *general tendencies* at the level of the state itself were those activities that governed relationships between states: wars, diplomacy, armies, and so on. On the level of the individual state, then, Ranke fused the creative individual, that is, the state's own moral energy (with *Kultur* as a manifestation of it) with the crass external forces necessary for its development. It is obvious, however, that Ranke's use of Goethe's synthesis was relevant—and, as we have seen only partially so—only on this last level. Furthermore, Ranke's own extremely limited concept of the role of *Kultur* was something with which Meinecke was apparently not concerned. Certainly it would appear to call into question the emphasis that Meinecke placed upon Ranke as representing "the highest achievement yet attained in the marriage of Idea and Reality." Despite his efforts to reconcile external forces with the historical individual, Meinecke was cognizant of a rather great difference between Ranke and Goethe. This difference was, of course, the former's willingness to fuse *power* (in the form of the state) and *Kultur*.

Ranke did qualify power through his teleology and through his endowing it with a certain moral energy. His conception of history, however, was necessarily predicated upon an acceptance of the relevance

---

55. *Ibid.*, p. 37.
56. Leopold von Ranke, *Die grossen Mächte in Zeitbilder und Charakteristiken* (Berlin, 1834), p. 293.

of power, something which Goethe, despite his Weimar experience as an administrator, never fully understood. This difference was an extremely important one for Meinecke. For, as we have seen, Meinecke excluded Goethe from the ranks of historians because of the latter's unwillingness to provide for a meaningful integration of power considerations into his conceptual framework. While certainly understandable, it is significant that, in *The Origin of Historicism,* Ranke was never discussed as a *Kulturmensch.* Naturally, Goethe was the *Kulturmensch* par excellence. He was so because of his almost timeless conception of *Kultur* and his unwillingness to tarnish it with the meanness of day-to-day political life. Despite some differences between his idea of *Kultur* and Goethe's, Meinecke apparently felt that he was accepting Goethe's notion of it. His virtually timeless conception of *Kultur,* something that we have seen in the *Historische Zeitschrift* essay, represented Meinecke's initial effort in the direction of his post-World War II cosmopolitanism.

Meinecke's considerations of Ranke and Goethe raised several perplexing problems for him. Meinecke considered Ranke to be a historian because he was concerned with power states and recognized the importance of power in the development of a *Kultur.* Goethe was *not* a historian because he was unwilling to do this. In defining the concerns and role of the historian, then, Meinecke seemed to be reaching back to his pre-World War I statism. However, as we have seen, the 1920s saw Meinecke turn his interest toward the *Kulturindividualitäten* as being the very material of history. These entities, while dependent on external forces of one kind or another, were yet qualitatively different from them, and external forces were not supposed to be the objects of historical analysis. The historian, rather, was to concern himself with the manifestations of eternal *Kultur,* the historical individualities. Meinecke himself was tending more and more in this direction. Although he had certainly not intended to do so, he had really divorced history, as it consists of the egoistical interactions between states, from *Kultur,* thus violating the canons of his own Historicism. Naturally, he still considered himself to be a historian, but the Rankean underpinnings of his earlier approach had been knocked out by his recent focus upon an almost mystical idea of *Kultur.* Certainly, in terms of his own work and methodology, Meinecke was a historian. The very existence of *The Origins of Historicism* is adequate proof of this fact. However, in the innermost reaches of his rather confused psyche, Meinecke was turning toward timeless entities, toward that abstruse and historically unapproachable conception of *Kultur* which he, perhaps mistakenly, attributed to Goethe. Timeless demonic power was being carefully balanced by timeless, meaningful *Kultur.*

In a sense, Meinecke had fallen prey to a historiographical problem that had been extant since Kant's writings on history. As Bruce Mazlish so accurately points out in his *The Riddle of History,* Kant's emphasis upon morality as the teleological goal of the history of the human race foundered upon the difficulties imposed by his phenomenal-noumenal dichotomy.[57] History, both as a discipline and as a process, was by definition relegated to the phenomenal world, the world governed by rationality. To attain the goal of morality, history would have had, in effect, to transcend itself. Kant was never too precise as to how this dialectical jump would be accomplished. Thus, his historical writings give the impression of being intellectual exercises devoted to extolling the cunning of reason, rather than serious attempts to arrive at either an understanding or a justification of history. Meinecke fell into much the same problem. His concept of *Kultur* was not merely a superhistorical term; it was virtually *ahistorical*—a timeless, supercausal category, in reality, a moral category. Thus any effort that might have been made to link the various manifestations of *Kultur,* the historical individualities, into a causal pattern would most certainly have been doomed to failure.

History, for Kant, had been essentially the story of the rise and the diffusion of Civilization. It was a quantitative story, describing mainly technological and material, and not spiritual, improvements. The story would be redeemed, somehow, through the eventual acceptance by the human race of freely willed submission to universal law. Only at this point would man become moral, and it was this transcendental condition that Kant dignified with the word *Kultur.*[58] Kant had imposed a traditional dualism upon history, one that he concretized through the terms *Civilization* and *Kultur.* During the interwar period, Meinecke had turned "history" into approximately the same thing as it had become for Kant. Meinecke's conception of *Kultur,* at least definitionally, was somewhat different from that of Kant. However, the problem that had been posed by Kant's dualistic conception of history was essentially the same problem that ensnared Meinecke. After the war, Meinecke would make the same differentiation between *Civilization* and *Kultur* that Kant had made a century and a half before. However, the most important problem was this: *Kultur* could not have provided either meaning or justification for history as it could never have been related to the course of human events. Could one in fact say that the "historical individuals," at least as Meinecke conceived of them, were *historical?* Could they be seen as deriving, if not their essence, then at least their utility from history. The answer is, of course, that they could not.

57. Bruce Mazlish, *The Riddle of History* (New York, 1966), pp. 117 and 122.
58. *Ibid.,* p. 109.

Considering the problems with which he was concerned, it is rather remarkable, as Antoni points out, that Meinecke spent virtually no time in *The Origin of Historicism* considering the historiographical significance of Kant.[59] Yet, perhaps the position in which Meinecke found himself, that is, his conceptualization of *Kultur* and the relationship he established between *Kultur* and history, was so similar to that of Kant that Meinecke was unable to recognize it. Perhaps we can find a hint of this in Meinecke's curt rejections of Hegel and in his concurrent tendency toward a Hegelian conception of power.

Meinecke's efforts to reconcile the individual in history with the often pernicious elemental forces that surrounded it had failed. *The Origin of Historicism* is a work that reflects immense labor and synthesizing genius. Yet, as seen above, it also reflected the spiritual confusion tormenting Meinecke during the 1920s. In the impasse between the *Kultur* of Goethe and the necessary statism of Ranke's historiography, Meinecke had really destroyed the unity of history. History was no longer process, but a set of unhappy polarities tied together by the crudest constructivism. Meinecke's efforts to save history in the name of *Kultur* had led him, spiritually at least, out of the realm of Clio and into the haunted kingdom of the German Idealists. This process is of interest not merely because of its significance for Meinecke's historiography. Of far greater importance for our considerations is the fact that Meinecke's efforts to seek a unity of soul far above the ordinary interests of historians was reflected in his political writings of the 1920s. In this regard, we shall see that Meinecke's attempt to escape the travails of history was reflected in his fervent wish to avoid the political realities of republicanism.

For the present, we can state that Meinecke's sharp division between elemental forces of causality (power, of course, being among them) and *Kultur* aided him in his partial withdrawal from political reality during the 1920s. Yet, during this period, he continued to adhere to the power-based political ideas of Friedrich Naumann. Naumann, an individual who seemed to have a greater understanding of mass society than did Meinecke, continued to exercise a great fascination for him. Meinecke's faith in Naumann's statist-conditioned national socialism survived the substantive changes in the former's political and methodological approaches. Naumann represented a nostalgic embodiment of what might have been. Meinecke was aware, no doubt, that Naumann's proletarian/bourgeois idyll was based upon the needs of a power state. Naumann was certainly not a Goethean *Kulturmensch* suddenly brought to life in an age of smoke and steel. What Naumann represented for Meinecke was a vestige of statism, a sort of intellectual fig leaf on an

---

59. Carlo Antoni, *op. cit.*, p. 117.

otherwise obscene and embarrassing structure which Meinecke was attempting to reject. During the 1920s, Meinecke's thinking was becoming more and more divorced from pedestrian political concerns. However, he seemed to set aside a small portion of his mind for issues of state. This resulted in a very curious juxtapositioning of *Weltanschauungen* in some of his pre-World War II works.

Such a phenomenon can perhaps be illustrated best by considering his brief work *State and Personality* (*Staat und Persönlichkeit*), published in Berlin during the rather active year 1933. In the introductory essay of the work, "Natur und Kultur," Meinecke clung to a theme that had been prominent in his writings since the middle 1920s: the superiority both in historical and ethical terms of *Kultur*. "Out of all that we have said, one thing is clear: that unidiomatic history is nothing else but *Kulturgeschichte,* whereby *Kultur* signifies the emergence of . . . intrinsic spiritual values, historical individuals." [60] This was a logical carry-over from his concerns of the 1920s. Of course, Meinecke was again raising problems we have considered earlier in different context. Nonetheless, this statement was a simple, straightforward description of the position he had attained by the end of the 1920s.

However, *State and Personality* was significant for yet another reason. In this collection of essays, Meinecke included one that had been published in 1916. The title of this work was "Reich und Nation von 1871 bis 1914." Meinecke felt, apparently, that this essay was still substantially correct and meaningful in regard to the course of German political development. Perhaps, at least in 1916, it was. The subject of this essay was very much in keeping with the themes of national integration that were so prominent in his writings before and during World War I. It was, first of all, a gentle attack on some of the inadequacies of the Bismarckian system. It also contained a joyous paean dedicated to that unique synthesis of individualism and subordination to the whole which constituted German Freedom. Development of this synthesis would most certainly allow the full strength of German nationalism to be tapped. It was in this regard that he praised the fusion of democracy and Empire which he saw in Friedrich Naumann. It is interesting to note that he also praised Naumann for appreciating the supremacy of foreign policy demands over internal developments. Naumann understood that democratization should take place as a response to the more important dictates of external policy.[61] In this earlier essay, Meinecke obviously revealed his Rankean heritage.

In view of the time in which this essay was written, such attitudes were not particularly unusual. However, the inclusion of an essay colored

60. Meinecke, *Staat und Persönlichkeit* (Berlin, 1933), p. 53.
61. *Ibid.*, p. 185.

with the statism of Ranke with one that was concerned with preserving history in the name of *Kultur* points to the departmentalization that had afflicted Meinecke's historiography by this time. Political concerns and cultural concerns could exist side by side in his mind and in fact did so. This would be most laudable under ordinary circumstances; however, the 1920s saw Meinecke push *Kultur* and politics further and further away from each other. On the one hand, Meinecke could display a quite genuine interest in the concrete, if perhaps unrealistic, solutions Naumann provided for the problems that arose during the historical development of the mass state. On the other hand, Meinecke's view of history was well on its way to that unhappy point where its relationship to the one spiritually redeeming factor, *Kultur,* would become ever more uncertain. Strangely enough (or perhaps, not so strangely), these two concerns seldom crossed paths or influenced each other. When they did, however, the results were disastrous.

Meinecke's 1920 efforts to divorce power from culture bore strange fruit. First of all, it must be understood as a palpable sign of the deep inward reaction Meinecke experienced after the German defeat against the simplistic optimism concerning the state and *Realpolitik* which characterized his pre-World War I writings. Certainly, when this is borne in mind, it can be easily appreciated and understood. However, the 1920s were also a period in which all the elements of the state idea itself, the very unity of history for the pre-World War I Meinecke, became polarized. Although he would continue to write history and to concern himself with the state, these polarizations really destroyed the state as a viable element of historiographical analysis. From this angle, they can be seen as marking the first steps on the road to Meinecke's post-World War II avowed dedication to cosmopolitanism. Meinecke's retreat from statism *implied* a retreat from parochial national-centered historiography. For this reason, it is easy to see a certain ethical aura about it.

In a larger sense, however, Meinecke's division between power and *Kultur* led to extremely dangerous consequences for both his methodology and for his political viewpoints. First of all, as we have seen, it led to a certain mystification of power which elevated it into the realm of quasi-Hegelian Idealism. Meinecke had not concerned himself with the great changes in understanding and utilization of power which alterations in the national culture could bring to the term. He pointed with justifiable alarm to the immense quantitative changes wrought by the introduction of the masses into the state; however, he did not consider changes in both the content and meaning of *raison d'état* and of power. The new power drives and the new *raison d'état* of the mass society may have been more pitiless than earlier samples. Wars of annihilation were now being demanded, and Meinecke certainly did recognize these demands as products of the degeneration of *raison d'état* as a result of its exposure to a mass society. Yet, Meinecke failed to consider the needs and perversions of this new mass society, needs and perversions that would be externalized in the decay of the once-dignified *raison d'état*. Meinecke's willingness to utilize the impedimenta of totalitarian ideology, the plebiscite and referendum, in part to supplant parliamentarianism shows that he had virtually no idea of the increasing influence and elements of mass ideology.

Meinecke's divorcing of power and *Kultur* raised problems. It also, unfortunately, begged the question, for such an approach precluded the study of power as being the product of a specific cultural tradition. Meinecke's esoteric definition of *Kultur* perhaps represented an attempt to remove it from the arena of war and other forms of national pathology. However, as mentioned before, Meinecke also used *Kultur* in the sense of its being the spiritual heritage of a nation. It was spirit, but spirit in the form of philosophy, music, religious ideals, and so on. In assuming that ideals of power were divorced from this amalgam of spirituality, Meinecke was making a grave error, for, *particularly* in the German context, philosophy often had served not only to rationalize power but to define it in *spiritual terms*. By slavishly adhering to his own parochial application of *Kultur* to historical investigation (or perhaps, even divorcing it from historical investigation), Meinecke had fallen into the error for which he so rightfully criticized the eighteenth-century rationalists: the failure to study a historical phenomenon as the product of a given historical tradition. Parenthetically, both Goethe's and Burckhardt's conceptions of *Kultur,* with their strong concessions to social life, could have allowed perhaps for studies of this nature, despite their respective emphases upon the qualitative differences between power and *Kultur*.

In *Ethics in a World of Power,* Richard Sterling pointed to the unwillingness of Meinecke "to absolutize any of the values in his polarities" as the latter's stabilizing strength.[62] Such a statement begs the question. For, in the 1920s, Meinecke was well on his way to absolutizing *Kultur* and thus divorcing it from the pitiless scrutiny of the historical mind. He was also in the process of absolutizing power and, by committing it to the realm of the nihilistic, also removing it from the same scrutiny. Already, Meinecke had prepared the shrouds with which, after World War II, he was to cloak those aspects of Germany's spiritual tradition too painful to confront.

Mention has been made of Meinecke's efforts to obtain solace on the level of day-to-day political life to the same degree as he sought this on

---

62. Sterling, *op. cit.,* p. 245.

the level of the spiritual. This produced a most interesting phenomenon: Meinecke had overthrown statism in the name of the eternal verities manifested in *Kultur*. In the day-to-day life of the Weimar period, he also strove for peace, political peace, a peace through unity which could only be assured through the state. In Meinecke's political writings of the 1920s, we shall thus see a continuation of some of the pre-World War I themes, as well as the intrusion of more romantic concerns, of which his historiographical efforts of the period were symptomatic. Thus, it is to a consideration of these writings that we must now turn.

6

Friedrich Meinecke
and the Weimar Republic

IN HIS WORK *Geschichte zwischen Philosophie und Politik,* Walther Hofer made the remark that the Weimar Republic was "the high point of Meinecke's political involvement." [1] Certainly if the plethora of political essays he produced during this period are considered, the validity of this statement can well be appreciated. Moreover, for Hofer, it would appear that Meinecke's commitment to the Republic was genuine, one that stemmed "not from cheap . . . opportunism . . . but because he recognized it as an historical necessity." [2]

Yet, most commentators on Meinecke recognize that there were several problems and contradictions implicit in his support as a *Vernunftsrepublikaner* of the Weimar Republic. Even his perhaps most sympathetic critic, Richard Sterling, pointed out that Meinecke tolerated democratic republicanism "only as an historically necessary political form, not without certain virtues but wholly lacking in virtue if it did not make possible the realization of aristocratic individualism as well." [3] Sterling correctly points out that Meinecke at heart remained an aristocrat, often fearful that mass democracy would swamp the individual and sweep away time-honored cultural and political values.[4] One year after Sterling's *Ethics in a World of Power* was published, Waldemar Besson's curt, penetrating article "Friedrich Meinecke und die Weimarer Republik" appeared in the April 1959 edition of the *Vierteljahrshefte für Zeitgeschichte.* Here Besson evinced rather deep reservations

1. Walther Hofer, *Geschichte zwischen Philosophie und Politik* (Basel, 1956), p. 81.
2. *Ibid.,* p. 80.
3. Richard Sterling, *Ethics in a World of Power: The Political Ideas of Friedrich Meinecke* (Princeton, N.J., 1958), p. 174.
4. *Ibid.,* 173–176.

regarding Meinecke's commitment to the Republic in particular and to republicanism in general. Meinecke, Besson maintained, had always desired "as much of the old as possible, without examining precisely the other side: as much of the new as necessary." [5] Besson pointed out that this deep-seated reluctance to accept the risks of change, much less those of an apparent revolution, tended to vitiate Meinecke's republicanism, particularly inasmuch as Meinecke was never able to prevent himself from attributing the darkest of motives to those important phenomena of republicanism: pressure groups and political parties.[6]

In one respect, however, Hofer, Sterling, and Besson were in agreement: that Meinecke did become a *Vernunftsrepublikaner*, albeit strongly against his will. All accepted both the validity and the importance of Meinecke's claim to have become a republican of reason as opposed to a monarchist of the heart. More recently, Georg G. Iggers, in his article "The Decline of the Classical National Tradition of German Historiography," gave a somewhat more negative appraisal of Meinecke's commitment to the Weimar Republic, emphasizing that his, as well as others', extremely grudging acceptance of the Republic as "that form of government which divides us least" did not even necessitate a break "with traditional historical concepts." [7] In this context, Iggers meant the traditional emphasis of German historiography upon the state as the unit of historical analysis, the sharp differentiation between power and *Kultur*, and above all, the tendency to either ignore or deprecate the role of social forces in history.[8] Obviously, even if Meinecke did in fact endorse republicanism, there were problems involved of which even his admirers, such as Sterling and Besson, were aware. It is the purpose of this chapter to examine in detail Meinecke's attitudes toward republicanism and the significance of these attitudes, particularly, as we bear in mind that Meinecke was a representative of perhaps the most enlightened stratum of the German bourgeois intelligentsia of pre-Hitler Germany.

A rather cautious attitude toward republicanism evidenced itself in Meinecke's writings rather early. Almost from the very beginning of the Weimar period, there were several contradictory elements in Meinecke's efforts to justify that which he had once almost condemned. Such contradiction stemmed from that complex of statist and neoroman-

5. Waldemar Besson, "Friedrich Meinecke und die Weimarer Republik," *Vierteljahrshefte für Zeitgeschichte*, 7 Jahrgang, 1 Heft (April 1959), p. 124.
6. *Ibid.*
7. Georg G. Iggers, "The Decline of the Classical National Tradition of German Historiography," *History and Theory*, Vol. VI, no. 3 (1967), p. 386.
8. *Ibid.*, pp. 386–387.

tic ideals which was the bitter legacy of World War I. Throughout the Weimar period, this spiritual confusion was reflected in Meinecke's attempts to persuade an obviously recalcitrant German body politic of the desirability of republican constitutionalism; for, even in his efforts to defend republicanism, he made obvious attempts to circumvent it. Meinecke did so by theoretically grounding the rationalization for the existence of constitutionalism (as well as the means for overcoming difficulties raised by its implementation) in a superconstitutional concept of the *Volk*-community (*Volksgemeinschaft*). In part this concept was, of course, merely the legacy of statism as applied to the vicissitudes of republican life. However, as we have seen, newer, romantic concerns also were beginning to influence Meinecke at this time. These statist and romantic concerns were reflected in his apparent unwillingness to accept the ramifications of a pluralistic society. As time went on, he revealed an ever-growing distrust for the particularism of the political parties of the Weimar period. Such groups seemed to him to be unwilling to sacrifice their immediate interests for the overriding interest of state preservation. To some degree, then, Meinecke's efforts on half of constitutionalism and parliamentary government were vitiated almost as they were being made.

It goes without saying that political life, hypothetically and in practice, is replete with concessions to superconstitutional demands. Nevertheless, in view of Germany's rather feeble republican tradition—something of which Meinecke was well aware—it must appear strange that he, as a *Vernunftsrepublikaner,* felt little hesitation in imposing limitations upon parliamentary republicanism from the beginning.

We have considered previously his significant essay "Constitution and Government of the German Republic" which did contain some concessions to republican interests. Meinecke had recognized the validity of the majority will,[9] and he was concerned that the influence of Prussia not be too strong. Particularly if some sort of Austro-German unification took place, an influential Prussia would be disastrous.[10] However, we have seen also how Meinecke severely qualified his republicanism by emphasizing the need for a strong central government.[11] Furthermore, he had demanded that the executive not be dependent upon "parliamentary majorities," but have a strong "anchorage in the will of the Volk." [12] Here, Meinecke justified this point of view by maintaining that such a

9. Friedrich Meinecke, *Politische Schriften und Reden,* ed. Georg Kotowski (Darmstadt, 1958), p. 280.
10. *Ibid.,* p. 283.
11. *Ibid.,* pp. 282–283.
12. *Ibid.,* p. 288.

strong, central power would be necessary if the government were to be able to forestall any militaristic or otherwise authoritarian usurpations from the right.

It is certainly true that Meinecke's desire for a strong presidency rooted *im Volksleben* was shared by others, Max Weber being probably the most significant individual among them.[13] Furthermore, one must note, Meinecke was adamant in rejecting any sort of "Caesarism," whether it came from the Right or from the Left. However, his rather early demands for a strong presidency and his concurrent suspicion of political parties indicated that Meinecke had strong reservations regarding the political pluralism to which he was ostensibly devoted. Moreover, it is important to note that Weber at least defended his demand for a strong executive by pointing out that such an institution would be necessary to implement the processes of socialization which he felt should be carried out in Germany.[14] Meinecke, on the other hand, indicated his disapproval of Weber on this point. It would be a shame, he thought, if the bourgeoisie would turn against a strong central government because of *fears* of socialism and concurrently "seek protection in a weak central power and, in particular, in the parliamentary system."[15] Obviously, for Meinecke, a strong, centralized executive was not a precondition for social, or at least economic change, but was rather a precondition for the very existence of the state. That the statism being expelled from Meinecke's historiographical concerns remained ensconced in his considerations of mundane political life was plainly reflected in his opposition to what he felt to be rigid adherence to the parliamentary system.

In a somewhat later essay, "Remarks concerning the plan of the *Reich* Constitution" ("Bemerkungen zum Entwurf der Reich Verfassung"), which appeared on February 7, 1919, in *Deutsche Politik,* Meinecke continued to emphasize several of the themes with which he had been concerned in previous writings. He evidenced concern over the division between Prussia and the *Reich,* indicating that he thought his own Democratic party was too cautious in its position.[16] The Prussian hegemony had to be ended once and for all. Possibly, some of the frictions between Prussia and the *Reich* could be alleviated by merging various state offices of the two powers and by establishing contacts be-

13. See Max Weber, *Gesammelte Politische Schriften* (2d ed., ed. Johannes Winckelmann; Tübingen, 1958), particularly "Der Reichspräsident" (written in February 1919), p. 486.
14. *Ibid.*
15. Meinecke, *op. cit.,* p. 297.
16. *Ibid.,* pp. 300–301.

tween leading figures in the Prussian Ministry of State and the *Chef der Reichsämter*.[17] In proposing this solution, Meinecke was somewhat ahead of the thinking of his own party on the subject. The German Democratic party would not be intensively concerned with this problem until the last few years of the Weimar Republic.[18] In the same essay, Meinecke indicated another concern: the lack of discipline on the part of Germany's rather mercenary workers and soldiers. Meinecke thought that an appropriate solution for this problem could be found in a type of limited "dictator of trust" (*Vertrauensdiktatur*) freed from the pressures of parties and their ephemeral attitudes.[19] Meinecke thought that, if such a *Vertrauensdiktatur* was firmly rooted in the will of the *Volk*, Germany would have little to worry about. Also, he reemphasized his view that the weak point of the Republic would be its dependence upon parliamentary majorities and their continual vacillations.[20]

From considering these very early Weimar-period essays, it may be seen that Meinecke was not really concerned with republicanism qua republicanism. The issue that rested most heavily upon his mind was that of maintaining a unified and organic state, one that would somehow exist above and beyond the transient and mean issues of day-to-day politics. Again, it is well to point out that every state, no matter how strong its commitment to republicanism might be, frequently makes concessions to demands for centralization. However, such concessions are usually made against a background of sophisticated constitutional development. Meinecke's questioning of republicanism was symptomatic of the inability of Germany's intelligentsia to confront the challenge of pluralism.

This inability also was reflected in Meinecke's attitudes toward his own political party. In his "Easter Observations" ("Osterbetrachtungen") of March 26, 1921, Meinecke pointed out that the German Democratic party's (DDP's) importance did not stem so much from election statistics (a rather comforting observation in 1921) as from its very *existence* as a middle party.[21] In this happy position, the DDP might

17. *Ibid.*, p. 302.
18. See the discussion of the German Democratic party in Eric Matthias's and Rudolf Morsey's *Das Ende der Parteien 1933* (Düsseldorf, 1960). For the views of an individual of the German Democratic party, see Otto Gessler, *Reichswehrpolitik in der Weimarer Zeit* (Stuttgart, 1958), particularly pp. 497–499. In his introduction to the book, Theodor Heuss mentions Meinecke's participation in the *Bund für die Erneuerung des Reichs,* a group founded in 1928 by Hans Luther and concerned with the Prussian/Reich issue, among others (pp. 80–81).
19. Meinecke, *op. cit.*, pp. 306–307.
20. *Ibid.*
21. *Ibid.*, p. 316.

be able to infuse the right-of-center German People's party with its ideas. It could then perhaps allow for some sort of future unification between the Social Democratic party and the bourgeois middle parties.[22] Meinecke did not view the German Democratic party as representing a particular interest, even that of republicanism. Rather, it represented a party of national reconciliation, a means to the end of finally transcending the class struggle in Germany (many socialists no doubt would have been astounded to learn that one was taking place). In other words, the overriding interest or function of the Democrats was that of maintaining the unity of the state. This was a rather unpluralistic view of political parties and their roles. It is a view that Meinecke expressed fairly often during the Weimar period. In a June 11, 1922, article entitled "Signs of Political Progress in Germany" ("Zeichen des politischen Fortschritts in Deutschland"), Meinecke pointed out the valuable role being filled by the German Democratic party—in conjunction with the Center party— in bringing to an end the monarchical era and in attempting to build bridges between the working class and the bourgeoisie.[23] After Versailles he said, the extremist parties had gained electoral strength. Some of them had found anti-Semitism to be a convenient political weapon. However, the German Democratic party, despite its losses, should recognize that it was being punished merely for fulfilling various unenviable functions in the national interest.[24] Meinecke went on to state that the democrats of the Weimar period had not become democrats out of democratic predilections. Reason of state was why the erstwhile "liberals" of the prewar period became democrats after the war. There was no enthusiasm for democracy as such, and Meinecke comforted himself by maintaining that the "secret powers" of reason of state would be able to compensate for the "natural lacks" of democracy to the same extent they once had for those of the monarchy.[25] What is quite evident here is Meinecke's concern for the *state* as being the common denominator of German political life. The role of his own party was seen as one predetermined and defended by its efforts to adhere to reason of state.

As alluded to previously, Meinecke was making few moral claims on behalf of *raison d'état* at this time. The term was being used in an almost mechanical fashion. It meant assuring national unity. The roles of the political parties had to reinforce, or at least be subordinated to, this unity. This emphasis upon unity was presented with great clarity in a 1921 essay entitled "The Volk-Community" ("Volksgemeinschaft"). Here, Meinecke made a strong effort to root the Republic in the German past. He pointed out that its philosophical bases could be found as far back as the schemes of von Boyen. In this context, he exalted the hero

22. *Ibid.*
23. *Ibid.*, p. 322.
24. *Ibid.*, p. 324.
25. *Ibid.*, p. 341.

of his first major work as being the first "Prussian social reformer" who was concerned with the problems of the modern proletariat.[26] Meinecke reiterated his belief that the Republic was the form of government which divided the German people the least. Furthermore, he felt that it could serve as the means to the glorious end of the *Volksgemeinschaft,* but only if it functioned as the instrument to end the class struggle. The Republic had to be able to "beat the sword of class struggle into the sickle of *Volksgemeinschaft.*" [27] Again, we can see here the most important concern of Friedrich Meinecke during the Weimar period: national unity. A superpolitical, superclass *Volksstaat* dependent upon no one class or party had to be formed. The political parties had to eschew their roles as interest groups in favor of this national unity.

Meinecke was aware that one of the most dangerous threats to national unity came from the radical Right, in particular, from right-wing youth. It is interesting to note that he, in keeping with at least some elements of his Rankean heritage, had the strong tendency to look for the source of this right-wing radicalization of German youth in external pressures. On July 24, 1922, the Jewish foreign minister of Germany, Walther Rathenau, was murdered by youths from a right-wing group, the *Organization Consul*. In commenting upon the "psychological sources of the Rathenau murder," Meinecke remarked:

It is no wonder if ever new toxins are developing in the body; for this also France bears a responsibility and culpability for the events [that have taken place] among us; a very moral, not merely historical guilt.[28]

Leaving this rather one-sided explanation up in the air, Meinecke then went on to make the interesting observation that much of the increase of right-wing sympathies in Germany could be attributed to the less agreeable nature and disposition of left-wing youth. Right-wing youth was orderly, neat, and punctual. The left-wing offspring spawned by industrialism and the metropolis were not. In this regard, Meinecke remarked, "A colleague just recently made precisely the same observations; it is easier and smoother he said, to work with right-wing people than with the left-wing people." [29] It is thus both interesting and revealing that Meinecke attributed much of the responsibility for such events as the Rathenau murder of 1922 to: (1) irrational hatreds and pressures attributable to outside stimuli; and (2) an increase in sympathy

26. *Ibid.,* p. 342.
27. *Ibid.,* p. 339.
28. *Ibid.*
29. *Ibid.,* pp. 336–337.

for right-wing movements generated by the difficulties encountered by educators and politicians in dealing with left-wing youth.

It is certainly true that Meinecke was opposed to the violent activities of the youth of the radical Right. Indeed, he scorned those individuals who "lacked the capability and patience to attain the development of their ideals through systematic work." [30] Moreover, Meinecke was careful to differentiate between the student violence of 1819 and the contemporary actions of radical right-wing youths. The student of 1819 at least looked "forward" toward unification, while the radical right-wing student of 1922 looked "backward" toward the false ideal of a heroic imperial past.[31] Nevertheless, despite Meinecke's concern for the lack of "psychic balance" ("seelische Gleichgewicht") which he saw in modern German youth, his own emotional (as opposed to realpolitical) affinities lay with the youth of the Right. These affinities were not ones Meinecke chose to investigate very closely, and his attitude toward those right-wing thugs who were shooting down people from speeding automobiles with the same alacrity as was being displayed by their spiritual brothers in Chicago was not as severe as one would expect it to have been. His attitude was, perhaps, the result of something we observed in *After the Revolution*. Meinecke himself was beginning to toy with some of the same romantic concepts that traditionally had driven German youth in the direction of the Right. Of course, the extent of Meinecke's fascination with romantic ideas must remain somewhat in doubt. Nevertheless, certain previously examined elements prominent in his reaction to World War I would indicate at least a tendency in this direction. Furthermore, his assumption that much—if not most—of the right-wing violence of the 1920s resulted from outside pressures was questionable. This assumption allowed him to refrain from investigating the roots such activities had in Germany's past. It also permitted him to gloss over some of his own very real antirepublican sentiments. Meinecke, at least in his own eyes, was a *Vernunftsrepublikaner*. But *Vernunft* had yielded in part to emotion, albeit emotion born of defeat.

Meinecke's emphasizing of heart over mind resulted in part from some of the changes in his historiography. The 1920s saw Meinecke attempting to achieve a synthesis of irrational and rational historical "life-forces." Walther Hofer may have been correct in pointing out that this represented the final stage of Meinecke's historical thinking; however, in the realm of politics, it created quite a bit of trouble, especially when this new concern with the rationally irreducible elements in life

30. *Ibid.*, p. 334.   31. *Ibid.*, pp. 334–335.

was fused with Meinecke's traditional view of the state. Statism demanded order over pluralism. Emotionalism favored the German Right over the German Left. Neither statist nor emotional drives were satiated by vapid constitutional democracy.

Meinecke's acceptance of the irrational in politics was reflected even in the cool realm of foreign affairs. Of interest here is Meinecke's somewhat mystical justification for *Anschluss* with Austria. This appeared in the previously mentioned essay "Signs of Political Progress in Germany." In this piece he maintained that

the demand for the unification of the German Austrians with Germany belongs to that genre of rare and great political ideas in which the irrational and rational strengths of events are harmoniously and inextricably intertwined, and in which all richly sensitive parties, and even all the wings within the parties, could combine with us.[32]

In a sense, such an outlook was quite understandable. Almost all political goals have strains of the irrational within them or at least conditioning their conceptualization and implementation. Meinecke himself always had reacted, to some degree, in a quasi-romantic fashion to the harsh industrial age of the twentieth century (such feelings are brought out rather clearly in volume two of his memoirs). However, up to World War I, Meinecke's political thinking had pretty much excluded the irrational from participation either in policy formulation or in the implementation of these policies. He always had recognized the need to respond to internal and external problems in terms of classical *Realpolitik*. His very acceptance of the Weimar Republic would seem to point to just such an approach on his part.

From the end of the war and extending into the 1920s, there took place not only a philosophical but apparently a *political* acceptance of the irrational. Now, it was seen as being of salient importance in the decision-making process. It was no longer merely a factor to be taken into consideration, but also a positive ingredient essential to the formation of national goals.

It seems probable that Meinecke was aware of the feelings he shared with right-wing youths. This of course made him rather reluctant to investigate the romantic/organic elements that historically had existed as the most prominent conditioning factor for the German right wing.

As mentioned before, the question of *Realpolitik* was still an important one for Meinecke. Again and again, Meinecke called upon the German people to unite behind the Republic or to reject political

32. *Ibid.*, p. 336.

divisiveness or to reject Nazism in the name of *Realpolitik*. As we have noted in the previous chapter, *Realpolitik*, or *raison d'état*, had been given rather dark overtones in *Machiavellism*. Furthermore, Meinecke had begun to disavow his earlier statist position and was attempting, during the 1920s, to give history a *Kultur* orientation. Yet, the exclusion of statism from Meinecke's historiographical considerations did not effect his *political* approach to the state. Previously, the state had been the hallowed unit of historical individuality. Now, Meinecke recognized its perfidy and yet he rendered unto Caeser. In so doing, he reinforced that separation of spirit and power which had been prominent in German intellectual history since the Reformation.

Meinecke's great concern for state unity was reflected in a 1924 essay entitled "Before the Reichstag Elections" ("Vor den Reichstagwahlen," April 20, 1924). Here Meinecke described the dangers he felt would arise from an increase in the power of the reactionary German National People's party (DNVP) and of the Communists (KPD). He compared the situation of 1924 with the one that faced Prussia in 1813, pointing out that all Prussians, during that fateful year of liberation and sacrifice, were at least aware of the need for national unity. It was of immense significance, Meinecke thought, that the class-divided Prussian society of 1813 had been bound together by a "consciousness of an inner unity." [33] Unhappily, such was not true of Germany in 1924. Meinecke rather perceptively pointed out that elements of class conflict were just thinly glossed over in the platforms of the volkish right-wing parties—the Nazis and the DNVP—by their use of the catchwords "national socialism." An increase in the strength of these parties could lead only to an increasing fragmentation of German political life. This was particularly true inasmuch as "the more the bourgeoisie behaves [in a] *deutsch-völkischer* [manner], the more the working class will behave in a communist manner." [34] Meinecke was not really too critical of the volkish party platform as such. What really concerned him was the debilitating influence such a platform possibly could have had on national unity. Meinecke did go on to point out that "the German people is suffering from a blood-poisoning induced from the outside, which is very dangerous but not incurable." However, his critique was not devoted to an analysis of the origin and dangers of this phenomenon. It was concerned, rather, with the dangers Meinecke felt the volkish ideology posed to the unity of the German state. In this context, Meinecke once again reiterated the efforts the DDP was making to construct bridges between the two halves of the nation: the working class and the bourgeoisie.[35]

33. *Ibid.*, p. 365.   34. *Ibid.*, p. 366.   35. *Ibid.*, p. 367.

In this context, we should consider again the significance of *Realpolitik* for Meinecke in the 1920s. By the 1920s, *Realpolitik* had been divorced from its thin Rankean connections to teleology. Meinecke also had questioned its ability to function as the preservor of bourgeois *Kultur*. Despite Meinecke's demand that *raison d'état* be somehow "elevated," he was applying it only to the realm of national unity. In a strange fashion, then, Meinecke's separation of power considerations from those of *Kultur* served to strengthen the role of *Realpolitik* in the field of politics.

The precise ideological configurations of the various political parties, even of his own German Democratic party, were of little importance of Meinecke except to the degree that they affected *Realpolitik,* in other words, the desired *Volksgemeinschaft*. At this point, the line between Machiavellian *Realpolitik* and an organic Romanticism had become very thin. It is certainly true that Meinecke was not alone in adhering to real-political principles. In the context of German political history, however, *Realpolitik,* had been generally interpreted to mean the subordination of the parts to the whole. Meinecke was not concerned with imitating the American variety of republicanism when he opted for the strong executive which he correctly saw as an important part of the American political system. He was concerned mainly with saving the German *Volk* from the consequences of a too hastily introduced and mercenary parliamentarianism. These attitudes should be borne in mind, for it is thinking of this nature which puts Meinecke's dedication to republicanism in a rather questionable light.

In a 1925 essay entitled "Republic, Citizenship and Youth" ("Republik, Bürgertum und Jugend"), Meinecke made the understandable statement that "the life of the modern national state is too rich and complicated for it to be in any way smoothly absorbed within the form of one party." [36] This was a justifiable statement, but one that was rather portentous in view of Germany's rather spotty constitutional history. The statement also reflects that suspicion of political parties which had become an important part of Meinecke's political outlook. In this regard, it is well to recall that the Nazis did not really conceive of themselves as constituting a political party, but rather a *movement*. Furthermore, they saw their movement as one that in some rationally irreducible fashion transcended the narrow and nationally destructive parochialism of the individual parties. Minus the all-important element of racism, Meinecke's attitudes toward political parties bore an embarrassing resemblance to those displayed by the nationalistic New Conservatives of Moeller van den Bruck. All of these individuals and

---

36. *Ibid.*, p. 369.

groups seemed to feel that there was something intrinsically "dirty" about politics, while the nation-state existed above it all. Furthermore, parties were dangerous because they fragmented the *Volk*. They were divisive and worked against the conciliation of all elements of the population.

In this same essay, Meinecke described how he greeted the Conservative party's Tivoli Program of 1892 "because it appeared to bring social reform, and with it, the conciliation of classes." [37] The Tivoli Program had been significant for yet another reason, one not mentioned by Meinecke: the program was the first one of a major German political party which contained anti-Semitism. In his memoirs, Meinecke admitted to being something of an anti-Semite during his younger years; however, he did not go out of his way to reject the 1892 program in 1925. For our purposes, it is more important to note the role played in the Tivoli Program by the element of class conciliation. It is this element that stands out in Meinecke's political desires of the 1920s. "I would welcome the day," he remarked, "when it would be possible to build a government which stretched from the Social Democrats to the German Nationalists [DNVP]." [38] Meinecke pointed out the unifying principle that allowed him to come over to the German Democratic party from an essentially conservative position: his realization "that the state must be free and powerful and the nation must be unified and, within itself, brotherly-minded." [39] Meinecke was quite honest in admitting that he had become a democrat to save the state. Indeed, he was adamant in maintaining that the individual citizen should not approach politics from the point of view of class interests but from the dominant point of view of the interest of the state.[40] In this regard, he indicated his disapproval of any efforts to restore the Hohenzollern Dynasty. He felt that such a restoration would weaken the state and create a strong republican opposition. This opposition would be at least as strong as the current monarchical opposition to the Weimar Republic.[41] He also disapproved of those groups who utilized anti-Semitism in their criticisms of the Weimar democrats, for, after all "a good political cause certainly will not be made worse by the fact that it is also represented by Jews." [42]

In this essay, Meinecke again had carried over the principle of national unification into the question of political parties. He pressed his point a bit further by indicating that he thought the time had come for a new "republican-conservative" party. This party would embody the best aspects of both traditions and would be freed from the vitiating

37. *Ibid.*, p. 370.
38. *Ibid.*, p. 377.
39. *Ibid.*, p. 369.
40. *Ibid.*, p. 371.
41. *Ibid.*, p. 374.
42. *Ibid.*, p. 377.

class hatreds and interests that had enfeebled German parliamentarianism.[43] Since Meinecke viewed the parliamentary tradition "as an unavoidable transitional form" anyway, the proposed sacrificing of republican form to national content obviously troubled him very little.[44] In an all too real sense, the essence of republicanism had been shunted to one side by Meinecke; or perhaps he felt he had transcended it. At any rate, he displayed a petulant unwillingness to accept conflict of interests or its objectification in the pluralistic society.

It is in this context that the negative quality of Meinecke's support and defense of the Republic can be readily appreciated. It is true that Meinecke did try, or at least he thought that he had tried, to "root" the Republic in the German past. However, it is doubtful whether he ever really accepted the ramifications of republicanism. It is true that many of his pre-World War I writings had been concerned with the problems of integrating the masses into the state. However, such a process was based on the presupposition that an integration of all the elements in German society somehow could have been achieved within the framework of the monarchical system. During the Weimar period, Meinecke envisioned a mass integration into the state in order to preserve the state. Thus, despite his prewar support for a constitutional monarchy and his later defense of the Republic, it is difficult to imagine how one could be certain of himself in calling Meinecke a republican. Meinecke at first thought the Republic was the one form of government which would divide the German people the least. When this idea seemed to be contradicted to some degree by the course of events during the 1920s, traditional considerations of national unity—and those to some extent colored by a post-World War Romanticism—tended to supplant his rather conditional acceptance of the Republic as a *parliamentary republican entity*. All in all, Meinecke's acceptance of the Republic as a *Vernunftsrepublikaner* must be seen as being a highly qualified one, particularly since he was beginning to place great emphasis on *Herz*.

Students of the Weimar years can sympathize with Meinecke's distrust of political parties. After all, a "chaos of parties" often has been cited as one of the reasons for the fall of the Weimar Republic. Particularly in Germany, where parties tended to assume genuinely ideological stances, a proliferation of them certainly posed a palpable threat. Nevertheless, we must also realize that Meinecke was not merely attempting to overthrow party chaos, but rather was attempting to promote a superpolitical national unity. Indeed, as we have seen, he really did not view the DDP as a formal political party, but rather as providing a

---

43. *Ibid.*, p. 378.   44. *Ibid.*

political and cultural *bridge* between Left and Right. Moreover, Meinecke's own view of the necessary role of parties—that is, as being true *Staatsparteien*—pointed to that same inability to grasp the essence of political pluralism which was *reflected* in the party chaos of pre-1933 Germany. Meinecke may well have seen himself and his party as representing unifying forces in German political life. However, Meinecke was in reality not calling for political solutions to the problems that beset Weimar Germany, and he was at one with a broad stratum of Germany's *Bildungsbürgertum* in his oft-stated suspicion of both political parties and parliamentarianism. As before the war, that national unity necessary to assure the advancement of state interests remained the ultimate purpose of political activity. The political parties of Weimar Germany might well have been disruptive and unwieldy creatures, but the political immaturity that was evidenced in their activities, or lack of them, was also reflected in Meinecke's demands for nonpolitical parties and class conciliation, a demand echoed by more shrill calls from the radical Right.

Meinecke's emphasis upon class conciliation raises the possibility of comparing his ideas on the state with those ideas of the *Ständestaat* which we have grown to recognize as being central to German right-wing ideology. In an extraordinarily perceptive essay written in 1933, Isidor Ginsburg pictured the founders of the new *Reich* as envisioning a nation-state in which "there are to be no class antagonisms, but the friendly understandings and adjustments of a functional state (*Ständestaat*)."[45] It is true that the complete doctrine of Fascist corporations, such as it was extolled in Italy, was not formally a part of Nazi ideology. However, the concept of a superpolitical *Ständestaat*, at least in terms of economics, was certainly present in some measure. It is curious to note that, for all his political sagacity and powers of analysis, Meinecke never was able to perceive what the Nazis stood for ideologically. Rather, he tended to view the Nazi movement as being something that was intrinsically divisive and therefore inimical to the national order.[46] It is one of the strange paradoxes of German intellectual history that Meinecke was eager to preserve this national order by implementing an approach based on the same view of party politics as was that of the German Right. Meinecke was particularly close to the German New Conservatives who also deemed necessary the establishment of a functional state based on class conciliation.

45. Isidor Ginsburg, "National Symbolism," in Paul Kosok, *Modern Germany* (Chicago, 1933), p. 322.
46. Friedrich Meinecke, "Von Schleicher zu Hitler" (February 22, 1933), in *Politische Schriften und Reden, op. cit.*, p. 481.

The concept of *Ständestaat,* of course, was an old one. It clearly antidated the maximalist ideologies that have utilized it. In the twentieth century, however, particularly in the German context, the line between the functional state of class conciliation and the state of political Romanticism (which derived much of its impetus from a revolt against the industrial age) often has been rather thin. The New Conservatives were no doubt considerably further over this line than Meinecke. However, there can be little doubt that Meinecke himself had at least crossed over the more palpable line that separated the state of constitutional parliamentarianism from the functional state of class conciliation. He also shared many of the romantic biases that characterized the Conservative Revolution.

In this regard, it is of some importance to reconsider the distinction that Klemens von Klemper has established between the "young" generation of New Conservatives and the so-called "elders," which by and large represented traditional conservatism. Here, von Klemperer draws a fairly sharp line between such individuals as Max Weber, Friedrich Naumann, Ernst Troeltsch, and Friedrich Meinecke, and the "younger" conservatives of the 1920s, Moeller van den Bruck, Oswald Spengler, Ernst Jünger, the *Tat Kreis,* and the Strasser brothers.[47] Von Klemperer maintains that the younger generation of the 1920s tended in the direction of a dynamic, youth-oriented conservatism. This led them in turn toward antiparliamentarianism and an organic view of the *Staat* and *Volk*. The "elders" repudiated this antirepublicanism and sought to work within the framework of the Weimar Republic.[48]

There can be little doubt that the so-called elders, as a whole, did repudiate the antilibertarian and irrational elements they observed emanating from the postwar rebels. Indeed, von Klemperer quotes one of the young generation, Theodor Böttiger (writing under the pseudonym of Georg Quabbe), as saying that "Troeltsch and Meinecke were and are against us."[49] Von Klemperer maintains that the Young Conservatives had been "morally orphaned" by their rejection by Germany's more traditionalistic "elders."[50] It must be pointed out, however, that the "nonpartisan point of view" of Moeller von den Bruck, condemned as dangerous to political freedom by von Klemperer,[51] had its parallel in the thinking of Friedrich Meinecke. To make a comparison of the two figures, one must first examine the ideas of Moeller van den Bruck.

47. Klemens von Klemperer, *Germany's New Conservatism* (Princeton, N.J., 1957), p. 74.
48. *Ibid.,* p. 114.
49. *Ibid.,* p. 124.
50. *Ibid.,* p. 129.
51. *Ibid.,* pp. 162–163.

Throughout his rather well-known work, *The Third Reich* (*Das Dritte Reich*), Moeller van den Bruck emphasized the need for a superpolitical German unity. He demanded a spiritual coming together of the Left and Right. Both groups, Moeller van den Bruck maintained, were distrustful of political parties and were against parliamentarianism.[52] Much like Lassalle before him, Moeller van den Bruck envisioned a happy crushing of the republican-bourgeois middle between the two millstones of political extremes. All classes, including the alienated proletariat, had to be made to feel part of a broader *Volkstum*. Parliaments and parties were simply divisive organizations of interests and thus were not truly democratic. In their place a new form of German socialism had to be created, not to divide but to unify the nation.[53]

Basically, Moeller van den Bruck's concept of the Third Reich was that of a nation in which socialistic and nationalistic interests were fused in a final and satisfying unity.[54] To this extent, it was in the mainstream of the National Socialist tradition of Friedrich Naumann. Unlike Naumann, however, Moeller van den Bruck's repudiation of republicanism was clear and decisive. Furthermore, Moeller van den Bruck and other figures of the New Conservative revolution (e.g., Carl Schmitt) were adamant in differentiating between liberalism and democracy. The rejection of "indirect powers" (i.e., of republican parliamentarianism) was an important aspect of the political ideology of the Young Conservatives.[55] The emphasis upon a true "representation of the people" (*Volksvertretung*), as opposed to the remote and interest-enslaved parliamentarianism, was an important part of Moeller van den Bruck's vision of the Third Reich.[56]

Friedrich Meinecke, probably not relishing the thought of being ground up between Left and Right, envisioned national unification coming from the center, that is, from his own German Democratic party and, if and when it would see the light, from the DVP. However, Meinecke did not care for parties as they then existed. Some of his objections and ideas for the parties of the future, were enunciated in a May 6, 1925, essay entitled "Questions of *Kultur* and the Parties" ("Die Kulturfragen und die Parteien"). Here, he called for a new liberal *Grosspartei*. He also expressed concern for a party that would have more of a "state and social feeling for the whole," a party that would

---

52. Arthur Moeller van den Bruck, *Das dritte Reich* (3d ed.; Hamburg, 1931), p. 208.
53. *Ibid.*, p. 67.
54. Armin Mohler, *Die konservative Revolution in Deutschland: 1918–1932* (Stuttgart, 1950), p. 34.
55. *Ibid.*, pp. 75–76.
56. Moeller van den Bruck, *op. cit.*, pp. 116–117.

be able to bind Left and Right together and to thus "overthrow the simple partiality of the parties." [57] Meinecke was forthrightly demanding the formation of political parties that were not political parties, at least not in the pluralistic sense. What Meinecke felt the role of a political party should be can be seen in his view of *Kultur* reform. Meinecke felt it was necessary to modify the *Kulturideale* of the nation as a whole. The *Kulturideal* that had to be preserved was that uniquely German one that reconciled individualism and subordination to the whole, an element in German *Kultur* which saw "spiritual freedom of personality" as being "embedded with the living community of the *Kultur and Staatsnation*." [58]

Unlike Moeller van den Bruck and the other luminaries of German New Conservatism, Meinecke did not openly call for the total overthrow of political parties. Indeed, he obviously was concerned with utilizing the German Democratic party to construct the basis for a liberal, bourgeois *Grosspartei*. However, as Meinecke saw it, political parties as *parties* were inimical to the national interest. He had no use for the party to the degree that it embodied particular interests. A party was acceptable only if it was willing to participate in the broader interests of state. His own German Democratic party, even the great liberal coalition party he hoped would be built upon it, justified itself only to the degree that it served the cause of social and political ecumenism. Each party had to represent the interests and needs of all citizens of the state. Each party had to attempt to strengthen the state. The political party of Friedrich Meinecke was certainly not the political party of pluralistic republicanism. Indeed, as if in answer to the nationalistic demands of Moeller van den Bruck (and certainly, Meinecke himself probably felt little regard for him or scant need to respond to his demands), he had constructed a hypothetical *Staatspartei*.

Meinecke differed from Moeller van den Bruck in another way. He never formally rejected political liberalism. Also, those elements of racism that did exist among the New Conservatives were not to be found in the political thinking of Meinecke. He was, however, extraordinarily close to the position of Moeller van den Bruck in this way: Meinecke had an almost morbid disdain for parliamentarianism, and he tended to relegate it to the lowly position of being a bothersome, if significant, palliative. Meinecke also approached Moeller van den Bruck and the New Conservative movement he represented in his strong emphasis upon a *Volksvertretung*. For Meinecke, this emphasis took the form of demands for a powerful executive, above and beyond politics and parliamentary majorities. All of these similarities between Meinecke and

57. Meinecke, *Politische Schriften und Reden*, p. 386.
58. *Ibid.*, p. 388.

the New Conservatives can be placed under the rubric of one basic similarity: both Meinecke and the New Conservatives viewed the nation-state as being largely above politics. Volkish elements were largely absent from Meinecke's speculations, although his occasional use of such phrases as "will of the *Volk*" is suggestive of his post-World War I flirtations with Romanticism. Nevertheless, Meinecke had strong, if unconscious, emotional bonds with the Young Conservatives, even if his sense for *Realpolitik* prohibited him from associating himself with them. In this, he was hardly alone in Weimar Germany.

In criticizing the New Conservatives as being destructive to the Weimar Republic, von Klemperer wisely points out that "a republic cannot live on being condescendingly, and grudgingly, tolerated." [59] A criticism of Meinecke probably could be made using much the same language, for Meinecke *tolerated* the Republic, if barely so. Certainly, he cannot be blamed completely for his lack of enthusiasm. Meinecke the *Biedermeier*, Meinecke the student of Ranke, Meinecke the Idealist —all must have been revolted by parliamentary quarreling, the loss of German international prestige, and the atmosphere of cosmopolitan cynicism that pervaded the music halls and cabarets of 1920s Berlin. In this also, he was hardly alone in Weimar Germany. That is the sadness of it. Of course, Meinecke was not the only supposedly liberal-oriented individual who gradually disavowed the very basis on which the Weimer Republic was built in his frenetic efforts to "defend" it. Members of his own party and the party as a whole were or would be guilty of this.[60] However, neither such individuals as Gessler, Koch-Weser, and Hjalmar Schacht nor the party itself had had moral, if not intellectual, reputations based on their roles as defenders of the Republic. Meinecke's reputation has been based, to a great degree, upon such an assumed role.

The above is not to be understood as an attempt to represent Meinecke as a Fascist. Certainly, his lack of racism puts the possibility of his being an unconscious Nazi sympathizer completely out of the question. He was obviously much closer to Moeller van den Bruck's Third Reich than to the more spectacular one of the Nazis. What should concern critics of Meinecke are: (1) the strong elements of irrationalism and state-functionalism which had become a part of Meinecke's political out-

59. von Klemperer, *op. cit.*, p. 129.
60. As an example of a member of the German Democratic party who later rebelled against parliamentary republicanism, see: Erich Koch-Weser, *Und dennoch aufwärts!* (Berlin, 1933), especially pp. 96–108. Otto Gessler's autobiography, *Reichswehrpolitik in der Weimarer Zeit,* is also quite interesting in this regard. Of course, the actual platform of the *Staatspartei* (1930) is also of interest. See Wolfgang Treue's *Deutsche Parteiprogrämme: 1861–1954* (Göttingen, 1954), especially pp. 148–149.

look, elements which in part link him, ideologically speaking, to the New Conservatism of the Weimar period; and (2) his emphasis upon subordination of politics to *Realpolitik*. Even if one were to deny that Meinecke participated in any way in the German Conservative Revolution of the 1920s—and certainly his involvement, if any, was more unconscious than not—his very obvious distaste for *political conflict* was one of the elements most prominent among those who saw the Republic as being inimical to the unified *Volkstum*. It should be pointed out again that elements of corporatism, irrationalism, and antiparliamentarianism had become important in Meinecke's political thinking both because and in spite of his claimed adherence to doctrines of *Realpolitik*.

Here again can be seen the curious result of Meinecke's separation of power and *Kultur*. In the vulgar world of politics, he was quite willing to surrender himself (and Germany as well) to superpolitical demands of state. At the same time, he preserved for himself a superrational realm of *Kultur* in which he was spiritually free. He did not realize that various unwholesome elements of Germany's spiritual heritage had definite political corollaries and that these corollaries had found a place in his own thinking. Meinecke certainly was not calling for authoritarianism. However, he was never able to rid himself of that unhappy tendency in German political thinking to consider the state as a unit. Hence, the question of the political unification of all Germans was of utmost importance for Meinecke, both as romantic and *Realpolitiker*.

In "Questions of *Kultur* and the Parties," Meinecke expressed his concern for a great bourgeois party of unification: "But it would, for a long period of time, have to be able to work—conciliating, unifying—in a situation in which conciliation and unification of those elements estranged from each other will have become once again of the most penetrating *Staatsnotwendigkeit*." [61] Here again, the primary problem in Meinecke's relationship to the Weimar Republic is clearly stated. For Meinecke, republicanism apparently did not represent anything more than an almost superfluous (at least in terms of the primary issues) method of administration. It was something that had been dictated by the real-political demands of post-World War I vicissitudes. It was a temporary means of preserving a state threatened with extinction. Someday, this too would pass.

Meinecke felt that the Republic had to be preserved, it is true. However, this was not because he felt for it as a republican. Rather, since it was the form of government that apparently divided the German people the least, its existence as a first step in the direction of a higher unity

---

61. Meinecke, *op. cit.*, p. 386.

had to be assured. It had to be protected against those forces of fragmentation on the Right and on the Left which threatened this unification by threatening the Republic. Meinecke's speculations concerning a party of national unification which somehow would conciliate and unify all elements in the German political spectrum point to a deeper concern than that of simply assuring the existence of the Republic as an experiment in democracy.

In a report to a convention of German high-school teachers on April 23 and 24, 1926, entitled "The German Universities and the Contemporary State" ("Die deutschen Universitäten und der heutige Staat"), Meinecke pointed out that democracy should be defended more vigorously and its positive ethical qualities more openly exalted by academicians. Here, Meinecke praised those qualities of democracy which impressed him most of all: "the immanent ethical value of democracy, the recognition of human worth in each *Volk* comrade, the joint responsibility of each for the whole . . . ." [62] It was certainly true, Meinecke said, that republican democracy had led to unfortunate license in some instances. In fact, there was now a distinct and unfortunate disrespect shown the past by many Weimar liberals. He also criticized the left-wing press. Usually, it had "attempted to protect our true national interests," he admitted. However, it had shown from time to time, "a somewhat Jewish resentment." [63] Meinecke did not elaborate upon this rather provincial statement. One can only assume that some of the big city, cosmopolitan cynicism was disturbing his idealistic psyche. Nevertheless, the overall tone of this address was sympathetic to democracy, as Meinecke understood the term, if not to parliamentary republicanism. Furthermore, it is of interest to note that Meinecke, in this address of April 1926, seemed to have broken with the "nonpolitical tradition" so characteristic of his own stratum of *Bildungsbürgertum*. It is again necessary to point out, however, that the issue he saw as being of primary importance was that of *maintaining the state*. The citizen possessed human worth to the degree that he participated in the *Volk* and insofar as he took responsibility for the preservation of the whole. Meinecke was most clear in pointing out that the important demand of the hour was to achieve the greatest degree of coherence between *Staat* and *Volk*, this having been the "iron political necessity" that had led to the establishment of the democratic form of government in Germany.[64]

Meinecke did seem to be sensitive to the charge, emanating particularly from the Right, that democracy and the Democratic party that represented it were "unheroic." In an October 1926 article in the

62. *Ibid.*, p. 412.
63. *Ibid.*, p. 411.

64. *Ibid.*, p. 407.

Breslauer Zeitung entitled "Heroismus und Demokratie," Meinecke maintained that the outwardly unheroic Democrats were carried forward by the inwardly heroic sense of having to save the nation. Here, Meinecke contrasted the figures of Friedrich Ebert and Paul von Hindenburg, emphasizing that they were part of the same, heroic German spirit.[65] Again the issue of salient importance for Meinecke, was the creation of a totally unified *Volksstaat*. Divisiveness had to be avoided at all costs.

In this regard it seems all the more remarkable that Meinecke apparently did not recognize that antidivisiveness was one of the most important ideological demands of Nazism. Meinecke seems not to have appreciated the political capital Hitler was accruing because of, among other things, the Nazis' claim to represent a superclass party of national unification. For Meinecke, the Nazis represented divisiveness, pure and simple. Moreover, as has been pointed out, Meinecke tended to view right-wing aberrations, such as the murder of Walther Rathenau, as being induced from the outside. In terms of the immediate situation, this may have been in part true. However, it is rather remarkable that Meinecke, at least at this time, did not concern himself with discovering their origins within the context of German history.

Walther Hofer maintains that, in the 1920s, Meinecke's historiographical methodology tended toward a "vertical" rather than a "horizontal" orientation. What Hofer meant by this was that Meinecke was tending more and more to approach history in terms of investigations of such *zeitgebunden* problems as the relationship of *Kultur* and *Macht* in specific situations. He was substituting a narrower but deeper approach for the broader, statis-universalist one of Ranke.[66] However, it is extremely difficult to perceive this new "vertical" aspect of Meinecke's approach in his treatment of the problems arising out of, or revealed by, the period of the Weimar Republic. Meinecke devoted scarcely any time at all to ideological investigations of the several right-wing groups. Rather, he chose to examine them only in a most general and undifferentiated fashion. Previously, in some of his pre-World War I writings, there was at least a recognition on Meinecke's part of the existence of racist thinking among even the most cultivated elements of the bourgeoisie. Now, strangely enough, these concerns had been apparently jettisoned. It is true that Meinecke recognized the use made of anti-Semitism by such parties as the Nazis and the DNVP; however, he seemed to be unaware of the vast audiences such a doctrine could have

65. *Stiftung Preussischer Kulturbesitz, Geheimes Staatsarchiv*, Rep. 92, *Nachlass Meinecke*, Nr. 97, Breslauer Zeitung, October 26, 1926.
66. Walther Hofer, *Geschichtschreibung und Weltanschauung* (München, 1950), pp. 501–502.

in Germany. Even in his post-World War II writings, Meinecke spent little time discussing the origins of racism in Germany, or even its role in Nazi ideology. It is difficult to say whether or not this unwillingness or inability to deal with the question of racist ideology stemmed from Meinecke's Weimar flirtations with corporate and romantic solutions to Germany's problems. Nevertheless, it is obvious that we are confronted with a most interesting aspect of Meinecke's thought, one that apparently has not been treated too extensively. It is true that Louis Snyder, perhaps Meinecke's most unsympathetic critic, points out what he considers to be inconsistencies in Meinecke's liberalism. He attributes these inconsistencies to remnants of Prussian statism and Hegelian monism. Unfortunately, Synder is never too clear in pointing out the specific roles played by these admittedly important elements. Meinecke's approach to the state never had been Hegelian, although his attitude toward power tended to become so. However, there can be little doubt that he did preserve the statist tendency to view the state as a unit and not as an amalgam of interacting interests. This tendency was complemented and reinforced by Meinecke's turning toward more romantic solutions during the Weimar Period.

It is interesting to note that this unconscious synthesis of statism and neo-Romanticism was juxtapositioned with a traditional sort of cultural elitism. In referring to the participation of the workers in the proposed *Volksgemeinschaft*, which Meinecke had hoped would grow out of the Weimar Republic, he remarked that such a participation would be most beneficial to the workers. If they allowed the *Kultur* of this *Gemeinschaft* to influence them and to work upon them, the workers would become "human" in the sense of an enlightened individual.[67] In this statement, Meinecke seemed to be implying that *Kultur*, while a product of the collective experiences and desires of the whole *Volk*, had to be discovered and elaborated upon by some sort of cultural elite. These were the "humans" implicitly referred to in this statement, and it was this class that would function as purveyors of *Kultur* to Germany's lower strata. In view of his previous works, particularly *After the Revolution*, in which he condemned *both* the bourgeoisie and the proletariat for their materialism and political rapacity, it would appear that *Kultur* was an intuitive heritage of the *Volk*. Yet, it did not stem from any group, and did not seem to be vouchsafed even to those elements that would elevate the masses. This inconsistency in Meinecke's thinking both stemmed from and accentuated the growing separation between *Kultur* and *Macht* discussed previously. In the widening hiatus between the eternal spirit of *Kultur* and the machine gun and ballot box of

67. Friedrich Meinecke, *op. cit.*, p. 390.

political life, national unity remained as sacred to Meinecke the neo-romantic as it had been to Meinecke the statist. Yet, there was a subtle difference.

Concepts of national unity certainly had not been foreign to the Rankean statism to which Meinecke had adhered before World War I. Yet, the romantic as well as the corporate elements we have observed in his writings of the 1920s were missing from these schemes. Also, Meinecke did not then question the Rankean *dictum* that a true nationalism could be created only by the state. It can be argued that the *Volksgemeinschaft* was to have been created, in Meinecke's thinking, by the Weimar Republic. In fact, various statements of his would tend to support this point of view. Yet, Meinecke's demand for a superpolitical party to correspond to the "collective will" of the *Volk* would seem to indicate that he considered such a will as being antecedent to the state. From this assumption, one would presume that the state's role was to objectify this will. Here, Meinecke seemed uncertain. At times, the statism of old was dominant; at times, more mystical speculations. Both statist and quasi-volkish tendencies served to reinforce Meinecke's belief that liberalism could and should have been divorced from that parliamentarianism with which it is so often identified. In his 1927 essay "Several thoughts about Liberalism" ("Einige Gedanken über Liberalismus," January 1, 1927) Meinecke did declare that the only thing that would be possible for Germany if the democratic state were overthrown would be the "mighty, lordly systems of armed minorities" such as existed in Fascist Italy. However, he went on to state that Germany was in dire need of a strong liberal reform movement. This movement would have to make war on the most negative democratic contention: "the belief that pure parliamentarianism is the best guarantee for freedom." [68]

In an August 11, 1929, article, "A Day of Thinking" ("Ein Tag des Denkens"), Meinecke continued his analysis in much the same vein. Again, he attacked the excess of parliamentarianism which he claimed was weakening the German state. He also continued his strictures against the egoistical political parties. He saw them as tending to discredit the government and officialdom through partisan politics and patronage. Meinecke thought that this unfortunate situation could be resolved only through a *"transformation in being of the parties,"* in other words, a redefinition of party roles in terms of the national self-interest.[69] A party no longer should be ideologically oriented, as in Germany, and certainly not *interest* oriented as elsewhere. A party should serve the state. In this article, Meinecke also made a most interesting (and revealing)

---

68. *Ibid.*, p. 417.   69. *Ibid.*, p. 431; emphasis is Meinecke's.

attack on Fascism. Fascism, he said, represented a weakening influence on the German *Volk,* and this *Volk* must not copy foreign models of state and attempt to apply them to Germany.[70] Fascism was being condemned on the basis of a quasi-volkish conception of national uniqueness. Meinecke also emphasized the *divisive* effects that Fascism would have upon the nation.

In a later essay, which was published in the *Kölnische Zeitung* on December 2, 1929, Meinecke again picked up a most prominent theme in his political outlook: the necessity of creating a great, middle-of-the-road bourgeois political party, one that could function in terms of protecting the state interest. Here, Meinecke called for *"a great Staatspartei of the middle"* which stretched from the Democratic party all the way over to Lindeiner-Wildau who was in the left wing of the DNVP. Meinecke sagely cautioned prospective overenthusiastic supporters of the plan that it had to be implemented "along organic, not mechanical paths." [71] Meinecke was demanding a *Grosspartei* of the bourgeoisie, a party that still could serve the cherished function of constructing bridges of understanding between the Left and the Right. It is quite understandable that Meinecke chose to anchor the right wing of the newly proposed party in Lindeiner-Wildau. This individual was a member of the left wing of the DNVP, and was soon to join Westarp and Treviranus in bolting Hugenberg's party to form the *Volkskonservativen.* In a later essay, which appeared in August 1930, Meinecke praised the secession of Treviranus and Westarp from the DNVP. Party-ego interests were no doubt involved, but, thought Meinecke, *"vaterländischer"* motives could be detected also.[72] Here, Meinecke seemed to be overlooking a very interesting issue, or perhaps he did not think it to be worthy of consideration. It was true that, as representing the left wing of the DNVP, Westarp, Treviranus, and Lindeiner-Wildau perhaps would have been easier to work with than the more reactionary members of the party. However, Westarp, at least, was far more anti-Semitic and ideologically racist than was the communist-obsessed Hugenburg. During the early and middle 1920s, when Westarp had been formulating the program of the DNVP, extreme anti-Semitism had been an important element of the party's ideology.[73] Hugenberg, when he came to head the party in 1928, never formally rejected this anti-Semitism; however, he seemed to be concerned more with combating the great Bolshevik menace than with the more esoteric intricacies of racial politics. It would be inac-

70. *Ibid.,* pp. 429–430.
71. *Ibid.,* p. 433; emphasis is Meinecke's.
72. *Ibid.,* p. 437.
73. George L. Mosse, *The Crisis of German Ideology* (New York, 1964), p. 241.

curate to claim, on the basis of this, that Meinecke was an anti-Semite of Westarp's strip, although various statements made by Meinecke point to a pronounced social, if not racist, anti-Semitism. What is indicated here is Meinecke's lack of concern over the issue of anti-Semitism, particularly when he was confronted with the, to him, vastly more important issues of *Volk* and *Staat*.

Meinecke was greatly pleased by the secessions from the DNVP. For him, they indicated that there now existed the possibility of forming a "*great, conservative Staatspartei.*" [74] This conservative *Staatspartei* could well complement the existing "liberal" *Staatspartei*. This was of particular importance inasmuch as the actual *Staatspartei*, according to Meinecke, was built on too small a base. For Meinecke, the primary issue that confronted the *Staatspartei* was whether or not the party base could be broadened through inclusion of the right of center German People's party (DVP). Nevertheless, apparently he felt that there existed the strong possibility of establishing viable *Staatsparteien* at both poles of the German political spectrum. These *Staatsparteien* would be ones that recognized the need of subordinating their own interests to those of the state.[75]

From the above, we can perceive once again Meinecke's rather problematical position vis-à-vis parliamentary republicanism. The negative factors operative in this process were both remnants of the nineteenth-century Prussian Statism (although not those elements associated with Hegelian "state worship") and fairly recently developed (or at least recently expressed) antiparliamentary tendencies. The immediate reasons for their development are not uncertain: political violence and Meinecke's feeling that the Reichstag could not act positively on Germany's behalf. However, this antiparliamentarianism also can be traced back to the previously discussed syndrome of Romanticism which we observed in Meinecke's immediate post-World War I writings.

Meinecke appears to have been unable to perceive that his own call for unity in the name of *Volksgemeinschaft* was echoed by right-wing radicals throughout Germany. The plea for protection or furtherance of the *Volksgemeinschaft* traditionally has been the biggest drawing card of the German Right. Meinecke tended to dismiss such philosophies as being irrational and/or divisive, being apparently unable or unwilling to ascertain what he had in common with them. The solutions as offered were in reality no solutions that could have been applied within either the conceptual or practical framework of a parliamentary system. It is no doubt true that, as Hofer says, the Weimar period was the period of the greatest political involvement for Meinecke. However, it is ob-

74. Meinecke, *op. cit.*; emphasis is Meinecke's.   75. *Ibid.*, p. 439.

vious that his concerns led him in no other direction than that one which called for a defense of the Weimar Republic because it constituted a palliative—albeit a less than satisfactory one—dictated by the harsh demands of political necessity. In a sense, we could say that part of the philosophical basis for such an attitude was a carry-over from Meinecke's earlier Rankean period (e.g., those views expressed in *Cosmopolitanism and the National State*) but now colored by the organic terminology of romantic nationalism. It would be most inaccurate for us to maintain that Meinecke's position could be described as being volkish to the same degree as could those of the great German right-wing movements of the twentieth century. To call Meinecke a republican, however, necessitates such a distortion of the term as to render it virtually unrecognizable.

By 1930, Meinecke had become even more specific in his view of what he felt was the main problem confronting the Weimar Republic. In an essay entitled "Strengthening of the State Power" ("Starkung der Staatsgewalt," January 1, 1930), he said that the state "must be liberated from the ensnarements of party interest." [76] Also in this essay, and for the first time in any of his political writings, Meinecke pointed out that Fascism purported to do just this. However, even if it did liberate the state from party interests, it had a tendency to damage other vital parts of the body politic.[77] The specific variety of unification desired by *Meinecke* has been indicated previously. It was revealed again in the support he gave to Brüning's overthrow of parliamentarianism under Article 48 of the Weimar Constitution. Until the fall of the Schleicher government in January 1933, Meinecke never ceased voicing the demand that the mundane and transient interests of party politics be sacrificed in the name of *Staatsnotwendigkeit*. Of course, as we have seen, this point of view was complicated a bit by the ambiguous role Meinecke had assigned to the state by this time. On the one hand, he thought of it as being an embodiment of the collective will of the *Volk*, the administrative and juridical framework for the *Volksgemeinschaft*. On the other hand, it still possessed for him a *Notwendigkeit* inherent in its very being, a curious result of his rendering unto Caesar in the name of *Kultur*.

Strangely enough, neither of the above views made it possible for him to come to a real understanding of the dangers and alarming possibilities of Nazism. Meinecke's partial "conversion" to the interesting mixture of state functionalism and Romanticism considered above made it difficult for him to perceive the relevance of these doctrines within a maximalist context. However, the remnants of his more or less tradi-

76. *Ibid.* 77. *Ibid.*, p. 434.

tionalist view of the state tended to make him see the Nazis as being a traditional authoritarian movement, the reign of an armed minority over the supine mass of the population. In this regard, Meinecke compared the attraction of Nazism to that exercised by the Communists in the Soviet Union. Russia may well have been hungry, but the attraction of Communism subsisted in the fact that one million organized Communists lived a relatively happy and secure existence among the suffering millions of their countrymen.[78] Germany was not exactly in the same plight as the Soviet Union, at least not yet. However, the armed minority of Nazi storm troopers also led a relatively secure life in the present, while promising the same for everybody in the future. Meinecke felt that he was living in an intolerant era which was inimical to individualism. He referred to this era which compelled association as the "We-time" (*"Wir-Zeit,"* as compared to *"Ich-Zeit"*) of unstrictured individualism. Nazism and Communism epitomized the atavistic striving of the masses for "power and security" (*"nach Macht und Sicherheit"*).[79]

While such efforts to "place" contemporary mass hysterias metaphysically possibly might have been of some value heuristically, they served little purpose for Meinecke in that they were not linked to any further substantive efforts to come to an understanding of what the Nazi movement actually represented. To begin with, Nazism, while certainly divisive in fact, represented *hypothetically* a party of national unification. Nor was Nazism as such antidemocratic. An early theoretician of Nazi political science, Carl Schmitt, was always careful to delineate between democracy and the liberal (*rechtsstaatlich*) parliamentarianism which, for him, merely represented one of its historically conditioned forms. Thus, parliamentarianism could be overthrown without damaging democracy.[80]

In this context, it is important to point out that the relationship of Nazism to the state raised massive problems of historical analysis of which Meinecke seemed to have no cognizance. Certainly Nazism differed sharply from New Conservatism in its willingness to indulge in mass politics and in its one-sided emphasis upon radical, racist anti-Semitism (as opposed to many New Conservatives of the 1920s, such as Moeller van den Bruck, many members of the DNVP—probably excluding Westarp—and people like Walther Rathenau, who believed in a rather curious variety of spiritual anti-Semitism). However, the roots of Nazism were firmly embedded in the same volkish soil as were those

78. *Ibid.,* p. 444.
79. *Ibid.,* pp. 444–445.
80. Franz Neumann, *Behemoth: The Structure and Practice of National Socialism* (Harper Torchbook ed.; New York, 1966), p. 43.

of the New Conservatives. Looking at it from this angle, we can see that the Nazis were as logically consistent as the New Conservatives in that their party did not represent a party in the traditional use of the word. They did not think of themselves as an organization representing an amalgam of interests and ideas and desirous of rationalizing and/or utilizing the state in terms of those ideas. Rather, they thought of themselves as being a superparty and superstate movement (*Bewegung*) whose emphasis was on preservation of the *Volk* rather than the state.[81]

This Nazi attitude raised many problems as to the actual relationship between *Staat* and *Volk* in the ideology.[82] Franz Neumann justifiably deprecated the Nazis' claim that they had ended class conflict and liberated the Germans from atomization and the dominances of semi-authoritarian organizations.[83] Nevertheless, Nazi ideology qua ideology derived much of its drawing power from such claims. Meinecke's attacks upon Nazism indicate that he had little real appreciation of what the Nazi *ideology* actually was. Or perhaps he did unconsciously. In an article entitled "National Socialism and Citizenship" ("National-sozialismus und Bürgertum") which appeared in the *Kölnische Zeitung* on December 21, 1930, Meinecke did admit that he saw certain valuable elements in the ideology of the Nazi movement. He could particularly empathize with its "strong national will, the passionate feeling in regards to our political dependency and the ethical revolt against big city dirt." [84] The city dirt was no doubt a composite of all those elements that so shocked an Idealistic *Biedermeier:* cosmopolitan cabaret cynicism, materialistic proletarians, and that "resentful" left-wing Jewish press. In other words, Meinecke, perhaps without realizing that he was doing so, was in fact defending some of the essential points of the Nazi ideology! However, he concurrently attacked the Nazis because he felt they represented a danger to the state in real-political terms. This danger stemmed from the awkward position in which Nazism put the German state in its relations with other states, and from its divisiveness.[85]

It is one of the peculiar ironies of Meinecke's career that his own demands for a superparty solution and a strong national will, combined with his conservative revulsion against the big cities and their obnoxious newspapers and cosmopolitan cynicism, made it impossible for him to recognize the significance of these ideas in the context of an ideological system. In other words, it is quite probable that Meinecke's own emotional leanings toward some of the volkish and functional-statist ideas that were so vital both to the New Conservatives and to the Nazis made

81. *Ibid.*, pp. 62–64.
82. *Ibid.*, pp. 67–68, 82.
83. *Ibid.*, pp. 366–368.

84. Meinecke, *op. cit.*, p. 443.
85. *Ibid.*

it impossible for him to recognize the significance of these ideas in another, perhaps more consistent form. In his attempts to understand Nazism, Meinecke's efforts were vitiated by one glaring weakness: he was neither an ideologist nor was he capable to understanding an ideology. He was merely a rather conservative, very cultured, rather pleasant, and somewhat prejudiced German burgher.

His inability to come to an understanding of the content and power of the Nazi ideology resulted also from his inability to appreciate Nazism as a mass movement. Furthermore, he seemed to be unable to grasp the implications of mass totalitarianism, although some of his *Machiavellism* considerations possibly could have allowed him to do so. Despite his references to the *"Wir-Zeit"* as being a possible explanation for such a phenomenon, he was apparently unable or unwilling to appreciate Nazism except in terms of its representing traditional authoritarianism. He seemed to view it as an authoritarian movement made more pervasive and destructive of personality through application of the instruments of modern terror and coercion. In comparing Nazism to Communism, Meinecke appeared to make little effort to delineate differences in origin and application between the two systems. The rather common saying "extremes meet" often has considerable validity; however, it can be more of a hindrance than a help in investigating the *origins* of a particular ideology. In his appraisals of Nazism and of the dangers he felt were inherent in such a movement, Meinecke evidenced a tendency we noticed earlier in his considerations of *raison d'état*. He was unable to examine a historical phenomenon in terms of the specific historical and societal conditions that might have led to its development. Meinecke never considered Nazism as being a response to certain, very palpable needs and perversions which arose in the course of German political and social history. He regarded Nazism as being in essence a conspiracy. It embodied those same dull and oppressive qualities as the conspiracies of 1819, 1848, and 1867. Like these other previous triumphs of reaction, it also was attempting to block the road leading to complete integration of all elements of the German population into the state. Perhaps justifiably, Meinecke viewed the masses in rather negative terms. However, this apparently prevented him from appreciating Nazism as a *mass* phenomenon, and not merely as a conspiracy which deceived the masses in order to utilize them in fulfilling its nefarious ends. Meinecke the idealist was unable to recognize the perverse idealism of the Nazi movement. Meinecke, no doubt correctly, regarded Nazism as a class phenomenon like Communism. However, he missed the point when he maintained that Nazism called for one class to rule over all the others.[86]

86. *Ibid.*, p. 444.

Whether or not Nazism in fact represented the domination of the entire bourgeoisie or one element of the bourgeoisie over the rest of the population must remain a moot point in terms of this discussion. Of immense importance, however, is the role *Ständestaat* mentality played in Fascist and, admittedly to a lesser degree, in Nazi mentality. We already have examined Meinecke's thoughts along this line. It would appear that he never considered the Nazi movement in these terms. Rather, he tended to view it, like the Communist movement, as consisting of the rule of one class over all the others and thus as being a divisive force in German politics. Perhaps it was. But, as mentioned before, the agitational strength of the Nazi party was in part derived from its superclass and superpolitical claims.

As late as 1931, Meinecke still seemed to feel that outside pressures were prohibiting the German people from accepting the Weimar Republic. Speaking on this subject, he stated, "Our Weimar government will be able to become a heart-felt thing for all Germans only if, besides the internal freedom which it assures us, it is able to attain equality in the council of nations; the loosening of the chains which lie upon us." [87] In view of the Dawes Plan of 1924 and the Young Plan of 1929, which were meant to relieve some of the pressures of reparation payments, and of the withdrawal of the last Allied troops from the Rhineland area in 1930, it would appear that the chains were already in the process of dissolution. In fact, von Papen's abrupt withdrawal from the Laussane Reparations Conference in 1932 marked the end of a period of sustained German recovery, at least in terms of her international position. At any rate, it would appear that Meinecke's linking of the continued failure of the Weimar government to obtain a consensus to the stern demands placed upon Germany by outside forces leaves something to be desired in the establishment of a causal relationship.[88] Perhaps Meinecke felt that, as Allied inhibitive measures were relaxed, there was developing a revolution of "rising expectations." He was not too clear about it, at any rate.

The years of the Brüning ministry (1930–1932) witnessed the rule of Germany by decree in conformity with Article 48 of the Weimar Constitution. As might be expected, in view of his rather negative attitude toward parliamentarianism, Meinecke came to the defense of the

---

87. *Ibid.*, p. 454.
88. Though, in a letter to his married daughter Sabine Rabl, dated October 30, 1930, Meinecke maintained that the ". . . Nazi movement was both evil and good at the same time . . . [as] . . . it called attention to the outside that the boiler is threatening to explode if ventilation is not provided for it" and had pushed the SPD to support the Brüning government (Friedrich Meinecke, *Ausgewählter Briefwechsel*, ed. Ludwig Dehio [Stuttgart, 1962], p. 128).

Brüning government: "To call undemocratic the exceptional regime which economic and spiritual confusion have made necessary for us is tendentious hypocrisy." [89] In view of the darkening economic horizon, Meinecke's positive attitude toward the usurption of constitutional government was certainly understandable. It is an interesting fact, however, that while Meinecke came to the defense of Heinrich Brüning of the Center party, he had not even once come to the defense, at least in print, of his predecessor, the unfortunate Hermann Müller of the Social Democratic party. This man had come to grief over issues somewhat similar to those Brüning at least attempted to face through his use of Article 48. Furthermore, it is surprising that Meinecke never appears to have spoken out against continuation of government subsidies in support of the decaying if hoary landed estates of Prussia. This program (euphemistically called the *Osthilfe*) of supporting the insupportable helped to prevent the Weimar government from making any consolidated effort to expand the overburdened facilities for relief and unemployment compensation. All in all, a strange fusion of romantic and statist views seems to have paralyzed Meinecke's ability to comprehend either the rise to prominence of those forces inimical to the Republic, or the conditions that accelerated this process.

Throughout the Brüning period, Meinecke's solutions for the ills of the doomed Republic remained constant: the strengthening of the president, the limitation of party interests, and the limiting of parliamentarianism.[90] These views most clearly coalesced in his article written before the presidential election of 1932, "Vote Hindenburg!" ("Wählt Hindenburg!"). Here the basic antirepublicanism that pervaded Meinecke's political thinking can be seen most clearly. Meinecke thought that the German people should vote for Hindenburg partly, to be sure, because he and Defense Minister Groener, like the first president of the Republic, Ebert, recognized the need for the existence of the Weimar Republic. They were able to recognize this need because "they had a higher quality of national feeling, of a German sense which, at decisive moments, shatters all party-determined rubber-stamp formulas of national feeling and recognizes and loves the German in the Germans." [91] In other words, the German people should vote for Hindenburg because he, like Groener and Ebert, was able to transcend the political activities of the Weimar Republic in order to best defend this Republic. The old marshal "wants to be elected only as the super-party individual in whom

89. Meinecke, *Politische Schriften und Reden*, p. 455.
90. *Ibid.*, especially "Das Reich der Zukunft," pp. 447–448, and "Ein Wort zur Verfassungsreform," especially p. 474.
91. *Ibid.*, p. 461.

the nation places its trust" (*Vertrauensmann der Nation*).[92] Again, we see the appeal to powers higher than those generated by the seeming glycerine flow of day-to-day political life. Again, we must recognize the fact that republicanism was not enough for Meinecke.

Meinecke thought that the Republic had to be saved from itself. To preserve itself as a state, the Weimar Republic had to slough off the political and constitutional impedimenta that historically had been the lifeblood of republicanism. However, as noted above, Meinecke seemed to be more receptive to such measures of expediency when they were promulgated from the Right. At this point, it is a temptation to raise once again a question considered before: What was the *value* of the Republic for Meinecke in 1932? The answer to this question is a disappointing one: Even as the Republic was sliding palpably to its doom, Meinecke evidenced the same critical attitude, or at best, ambivalence, he had displayed in his early, post-World War I writings.

The goal Meinecke saw as important for his own *Staatspartei* (in reality, for all those parties that supported the Republic) remained constant: the preservation of the state. In an essay which appeared in the January 5, 1931, issue of the *Blätter der Staatspartei*, Meinecke enthused, "The German Democratic republic can reflect upon the men who created the German Empire with thankfulness and respect. For the *Reich* has remained to us."[93] Somewhat surprisingly, Meinecke fell back upon Hegel in describing a curious dialectic in German history: the Weimar Republic had been put together by those parties that had been opposed to the state during Bismarck's time. Now, though, these parties had saved the state, and thus contributed to the task of January 18, 1871, the day in which the German Empire had been proclaimed.[94]

In the last days of the Republic, Meinecke did seem to gain a brief cognizance both of some of the theoretical contents of Nazism and of the political realities attending its rise to power. Now, for the first and, for all intents and purposes, the last time, he pointed to the "misuse of the old romantic-organic thinking in the national socialist program."[95] Yet, in this 1932 essay (entitled "Staatsräson"), he did not admit to the presence of some of those very same doctrines in his own political philosophy, or perhaps he felt that he had not misused them. At any

92. *Ibid.*, p. 463.
93. *Stiftung Preussischer Kulturbesitz Geheimes Staatsarchiv*, Rep. 92, *Nachlass Meinecke*, no. 97, *Blätter der Staatspartei*, 1 Jahrgang, no. 1 (Berlin, January 5, 1931), p. 94.
94. *Ibid.*, p. 95.
95. Meinecke, *Politische Schriften und Reden*, p. 467.

rate, this was the last time Meinecke ever considered political Romanticism as a possible salient contributor to the Nazi ideology.

Meinecke also pointed out, in very specific terms, the mistake he thought Kurt von Schleicher had made in regard to the Nazis: he made an effort to canalize them. "He wanted, as we had presumed, to 'interrupt' a threatening revolution . . . ."[96] According to Meinecke, Schleicher had attempted to do the same thing to the Nazis that Groener and Ebert had done to the Communists and left-wing Independent Socialists in 1918–1919. While there is a strong degree of truth in this, Meinecke never went on to explain why Ebert and Scheidemann were successful and why Schleicher was not. Although, for a brief moment, Meinecke seemed to be striking around some of the contributing factors for the rise of Nazism, he seemed to have left his efforts hanging in midair. No attempts were made to follow up any of the ideas and issues raised by him in this essay. In a later essay, he did refer to the rising tide of right-wing radicalism as "an irrational Volk-movement [*Volksbewegung*]." Unfortunately, Meinecke made little further effort to examine this *"Volksbewegung"* either in terms of causes or even of contributing factors.

The difficulties Meinecke encountered in coming to grips with Nazism were largely the result of a curious sort of nonideological proximity he had in relation to the extreme Right. As pointed out, the racism salient to at least Nazism was probably lacking in Meinecke.[97] In a sense, this served merely to confuse the issue for him. There was involved also another factor of no mean importance. As we have seen in an earlier chapter, the 1920s marked Meinecke's rejection of power. This rejection tended to lead him toward tarring such movements as the Nazi variety with a sort of nihilistic brush. The Nazis were concerned with power and power alone. They seemed to be dominated by a terrifying machiavellian cynicism. Therefore, one could not understand them, or at least treat them historically. It is this approach that Meinecke would in part adopt after World War II. It is probable that it already was making itself felt in his rather insufficient political analyses of the Weimar period.

Perhaps most important of all, Meinecke the *Vernunftsrepublikaner*

96. *Ibid.*, p. 469.
97. Louis Snyder, in his work on *German Nationalism: The Tragedy of a People*, points to Meinecke's statement, in volume two of his memoirs, that he was a "rugged anti-Semite" during his early years. While this was no doubt true, his attitude toward Walter Lenel, whom he accepted as a friend of the family after his conversion from Judaism to Christianity and subsequent marriage to Admiral Borckenhagen's daughter, would appear to point out that while Meinecke was certainly a social anti-Semite, he could not possibly have been a racist.

never really existed; therefore, it would be unfair to expect from him either a thoroughgoing defense of the Republic in republican terms or an appreciation of the dangers to it. The attitude Meinecke described as being dangerous to his own rather artificial "republic" was the same one the Nazis claimed the Republic posed to national unity: divisiveness.

The logical culmination of Meinecke's approach can be seen in his essay of December 30, 1932, "No Desertion before the Battle!" ("Keine Fahenflucht vor der Schlacht!"). In this essay, he called upon the bourgeoisie to unite with the Social Democrats in a last-ditch effort to save the Republic and, besides this, to prevent social democracy from being even more radical. The Social Democrats would have to do this, Meinecke said, "to prevent at least their supporters from streaming to Communism."[98] He assured the German people that Nazism was on the wane and that it would pass "as soon as the dangers of monarchical restoration, in which many harmless souls do not wish to believe today, will become more clear."[99] In this extraordinary statement, Meinecke appears to have identified the right-wing danger posed by the Nazis as being coextensive with the dangers posed by a monarchical restoration! Even if "monarchical restoration" is not to be taken here in a literal sense—although there is no reason why it could not be—it must be clear that Meinecke had revealed his total lack of comprehension as to what Nazism in fact represented. For Meinecke some of the forces that had *contributed* to the rise of Nazism—reactionary groups such as the old Prussian nobility and antirepublican monarchicists—represented and embodied the Nazi program. Perhaps Meinecke intended a sort of self-criticism here, in that he possibly was aware that his own efforts to sublimate antirepublican feelings had fallen through. Nevertheless, Nazism was not simply monarchism writ large or in racial hieroglyphics. There can be little doubt that the Nazis, *as a political party,* derived some support from monarchical or quasi-monarchical elements. However, to identify their cause with the causes of these particular elements constituted a serious error in political and historical analysis. Yet, we can readily understand this error when we consider the development of Meinecke's political thinking during the years of the Weimar Republic.

After the "fall" of the Weimar Republic, Meinecke wrote an essay entitled "Von Schleicher zu Hitler." In it, he attributed the rise of the Nazis to power in a large measure to the "decision of the *Reichspräsident* [Hindenburg] to dismiss Schleicher."[100] Again, there was little effort made by Meinecke in the direction of a "vertical" analysis of the historical forces and trends contributing to the situation. The question pre-

98. Friedrich Meinecke, *Politische Schriften und Reden,* p. 478.
99. *Ibid.*
100. *Ibid.*

sented by the rise of the Nazis to power was discussed in temporally extremely limited terms. Schleicher's attempts to fuse the army and the working class were not mentioned, and his actual role in the rise of Hitler to power was never discussed, except insofar as Meinecke made the criticism that he failed to meet the challenge posed to him by history and to "step-by-step suppress the Nazi movement." [101] More interesting for our purposes is Meinecke's description of the Nazi Revolution as being a "revolution from above" which threatened to enslave one half of the German population through the other half which had gained power.[102] In view of Hitler's post-1923 slavish adherence to legal form in his rise to the position of chancellor, it is easy to see what Meinecke meant in describing this as a "revolution from above." Yet, Meinecke never discussed the painfully real popular basis for Hitler's coming to power except insofar as he made the statement that one half of the German people were enslaving the other half. In itself, this was a rather cryptic analysis of the situation.

For Meinecke, the coming to power of the Nazi movement simply represented the culmination of another authoritarian development. His confusion as to either the goals or the origins of Nazism was reflected in his attitude that its rise to power could be discussed in conventional authoritarian terms. Meinecke had been extremely critical of Hegel's approach to history. One of his most effective critiques of Hegelian monism was that it reduced human activity and human will and desire to being simply a "play" (*Schauspiel*), behind which lurked the cunning of reason. In a sense, Meinecke had reduced the rise of the Nazi movement to power to the most diluted form of *Schauspiel*. There seemed to be no real reasons for it; it just happened. It represented a nihilistic power drive whose rise was facilitated through certain administrative and political errors. By not attempting to place the Nazi movement in some sort of historical perspective, Meinecke had reduced the historical process to a barren stage occupied only by the most stereotyped forces of atavism and contingency.

More remarkable than the above was the fact that "Von Schleicher zu Hitler," written in comparative freedom, ended on a note of partial reconciliation. "We want to confront these men at the voting table without hate [!] for they are our Volk-comrades [*Volksgenossen*] and we hate only the basically damaging ideas by which they allowed themselves to be intoxicated." [103] Thus, the Nazis were viewed by Meinecke as being, after all, honorable fellow countrymen who had simply allowed themselves to be beguiled into unreasonableness by "basically damaging ideas!" Here, Meinecke had thrown his Rankean heritage to the wind,

---

101. *Ibid.*, p. 480.
102. *Ibid.*, p. 481.

103. *Ibid.*, p. 482.

and for no good effect. There was no effort made to analyze the Nazi movement as a "historical individual" which was somehow representative of general trends or forces. On the one hand, Meinecke viewed the Nazis as being more or less historical anomalies, decent men who had been somehow ensnared by ideas that had no firm root in the German past. The men and the ideas they believed in were seen as mere aberrations. However, in an earlier article, Meinecke again chose to recognize some positive aspects in Nazism. After all, several of its ideas (Meinecke did not say which) were "common heritages of a better German past." "However," he continued, *"it is daemonic to strive to develop them through splitting the Volk instead of through Volksgemeinschaft."* [104]

It is important to note, however, that, as Helmut Heiber points out in his somewhat massive work on the "Nazi historian" Walter Frank, Meinecke never allowed any form of right-wing ideology, including that of the Nazis, to influence his *professional* concerns. Throughout the Weimar period, when Meinecke was deeply involved in the establishment of the all-important *Historische Reichskommission,* he was very much concerned that the commission "be unconditionally *purely* scientific." [105] To be sure, when the Nazis came to power in 1933, Meinecke and the other prominent historians on the commission, for example, Walter Goetz, Fritz Hartung, Gustav Mayer, and Georg Schreiber, did attempt to temporize a bit by assuring the new order that the *Historische Reichskommission* would concern itself with such pivotal issues as the struggle to revise the Versailles Treaty and Germany's relations with neighboring countries. However, the commission indicated that this would be done "insofar as it is possible from the stand-point of scientific historiography." [106] Further on June 7, 1933, Meinecke, Ludwig Dehio, Hartung, and others wrote a letter to the Nazi Minister for Science, Art and *Volk*-education, requesting that the Jewish Professor Gustav Mayer be allowed to remain at the University of Berlin,[107] and on the *Historische Reichskommission*. Naturally, these efforts were in vain.

Indeed, between 1933 and 1935, Meinecke was adamant in defending the right of Jews in general to work with and contribute to the commission and the *Historische Zeitschrift* as well.[108] As a matter of fact, the Nazi historian Hermann Löffler took pains to point out, in 1939, that "the younger Meinecke school" had been "pure Jewish." [109]

104. *Ibid.,* p. 482; emphasis is Meinecke's.
105. Helmut Heiber, *Walter Frank und sein Reichsinstitut für Geschichte des neuen Deutschlands* (Stuttgart, 1966), p. 135. Emphasis is Meinecke's.
106. *Ibid.,* p. 168.
107. *Geheimes Staatsarchiv,* Rep. 92, *Nachlass Meinecke,* no. 15, pp. 398–399.
108. Heiber, *op. cit.,* p. 283.
109. *Ibid.,* p. 697.

In 1934, Meinecke had taken yet another step to offend the more tendentious representatives of the new order. The year 1934 was the hundredth anniversary of Heinrich von Treitschke's birth. Naturally, Treitschke's extreme nationalism, often intertwined with vaguely revolutionary pronouncements, combined with his virulent anti-Semitism, caused him to be vastly admired by the Nazis in general and by Nazi historians in particular. Walter Frank, who was soon to establish a Nazi-directed institute of his own, the *Reich* Institute for the History of the New Germany (*Reichinstitut für Geschichte des neuen Deutschlands*), was especially fond of Treitschke, as Meinecke well knew. Consequently, it took a considerable degree of intellectual courage for Meinecke to publish, in the first issue (April) of volume 150 of the *Historische Zeitschrift,* a memorial to Treitschke in which he emphasized the latter's defense of individualistic idealism as opposed to naturalism and collectivism.[110] To be sure, Meinecke was careful to point out that he agreed with Treitschke that the state was of primary importance in history (thus, again obfuscating the issue of historical individuality) and to add, "The national socialist revolution feels itself borne by strengths of blood and race which stem from the distant past." (Meinecke did not actually say whether or not he thought the Nazis correct in this regard.) [111] However, Meinecke did declare that Treitschke himself felt that the historian could only work in conditions of freedom —a "self-limiting freedom, to be sure," Meinecke hastened to add— and he also indicated his preference for the Rankean tendency to attempt to balance state and *Kultur* as opposed to the more statist concerns of Treitschke.[112]

What all of this reveals is that Meinecke did what he could to protect the discipline of history from that ideological tendentiousness that had to come with the emergence of a totalitarian political movement onto the scene. Yet, one must recognize that, while Meinecke was very much aware of the threat posed by the Nazis to "scientific" historical methodology, he was, as seen before, totally unaware of their significance as a product of German history. He was also unaware of his own attitudes and prejudices which, shared by an entire class, contributed in no small measure to the success of the Nazi party, or at least allowed it to rule with little or no resistance on the part of Germany's *Bildungsbürgertum*. Yet, a negative sort of support was not enough for the Nazis who, being

---

110. *Ibid.*, p. 194. Friedrich Meinecke, "Geleitwort zum 150. Bande der *Historischen Zeitschrift* und zum 100. Geburtstage Heinrich V. Treitschkes," in *Historische Zeitschrift,* Band 150, Heft 1 (April 1934), p. 2.

111. Meinecke, "Geleitwort zum 150. Bande der Historischen Zeitschrift und zum 100. Geburtstage Heinrich V. Treitschkes," pp. 4–9.

112. *Ibid.*, pp. 4–8.

totalitarian in nature (and thus, in many ways, beyond the understanding of Meinecke), required total integration of all elements of life into the state. For this reason, Meinecke was removed from the Historical Commission in 1935, and forced to resign as editor of the *Historische Zeitschrift* in that same year, being replaced by the party hack, Alexander von Müller.

To analyze Meinecke's attitude toward the Nazis, we must first examine his attitude toward the Jews. To some extent, Meinecke's attitude toward them seemed to depend on the degree of ideological proximity to his own position. Eugen Schiffer, who adhered to a basically conservative view of the state, was lauded by Meinecke as "looking Jewish while having German heart."[113] Furthermore, as we have seen previously, Meinecke seemed to be decidedly unracist in his approach to the "Jewish Question." However, it would appear that he was always aware of there being deep-seated and palpable distinctions between Jew and German and his tendency to be highly critical of that, to him, rather noisy "Jewish resentment" manifested during the Weimar years, marks him as, at best, being merely a social anti-Semite. Meinecke might well have been very willing to have Jewish friends and students, presumably, as long as each was possessed of a "German heart"; however, his attitude toward the Jews as a group was decidedly prejudiced, and Nazi persecution of them never seems to have bothered him very much.

The above discussion should suffice to point out the unfortunate fact that Meinecke's understanding of the nature of totalitarianism was virtually nonexistent. To him, Nazism was simply another authoritarian seizure of power from above. No doubt, it would be subject to the same limitations as had inhibited previous authoritarian regimes. It was true that Schleicher had failed, unfortunately, to meet the challenge of Nazism. Nevertheless, the struggle against this most divisive influence in Germany—the enslavement of one half of the population by the other—could and would be continued as before. There would be "voting tables," of course. Important in explaining Meinecke's failure to understand the implications of the rise of the Nazis to power was his inability to differentiate adequately between mere *ideas* and ideology. The well-intentioned *Volksgenossen,* to whom Meinecke apparently felt a brotherly if not intellectual bond, were not enslaved by any idea or even by a combination of ideas, but by a system so thoroughgoing and penetrating in theory and application as to reduce Meinecke's apprehensions of it to being almost caricatures of the real article.

Throughout the Weimar period there can be observed: (1) a sort of

113. Friedrich Meinecke, *Erinnerungen,* Vol. II, *Strassburg, Freiburg, Berlin, 1901–1919* (Stuttgart, 1949), p. 160.

merging of Meinecke's previous statist thinking with his somewhat romantic reaction against it, and (2) his inability to respond in a meaningful fashion to the Nazi menace, largely because of this merging. The collapse of Germany in World War I aroused both romantic and corporate elements in Meinecke. These were complemented by remnants of the statism of earlier days, a statism that survived Meinecke's attempts to exclude it from his historiography. As mentioned previously, the strikingly close intellectual proximity these attitudes bore to at least some of the hypothetical bases of extreme right-wing ideology tended to obscure, for Meinecke, the actual spiritual and historical origins and implications of Nazism. Meinecke thought that the Republic, or at least what he understood to be the Republic, could be preserved best by establishing a superpolitical bourgeois liberal party. This party could provide the foundation for a state of class reconciliation in which each element of society could be ensured its respective position. While admittedly not to the degree as did Italian Fascism, both the Nazis and Moeller van den Bruck's radicals of the extreme Right demanded at least an economic *Ständestaat*. The radical Right felt that such a unity could be obtained only through the destruction of the Weimar Republic. Meinecke did not want to destroy the Republic. Rather, he saw it as a first step on the road to a higher unity. However, both the radical Right and Meinecke envisioned the Republic as being merely ephemeral, and neither one of the two parties in question seemed to have placed much faith in parliamentarianism.

Meinecke's romantic and corporate reactions against the seeming coldness and ruthlessness of his earlier statism tended to deaden him against a full appreciation of the meaning and significance of Nazism. At the same time, vestigial elements of this earlier statism prevented him from ascertaining the precise relationship Nazism bore to the state and vice versa. This latter difficulty was manifested in Meinecke's tendency to analyze the Nazi revolution within an exceedingly narrow, almost day-to-day constitutional framework. He watched the revolution "take place," but made no effort to arrive at a historical, much less an ideological, understanding of Nazism. In a word, the Nazi revolution was seen almost as a "palace revolution," albeit one made somehow more horrible by the divisive effects that it certainly was having upon the German *Volk*.

In spite of all that has been said above, we must appreciate the fact that Walther Hofer was basically correct in maintaining that the period of the Weimar Republic was, for Meinecke, the period of greatest political involvement. However, we must also recognize the fact that Meinecke's pre-World War I adherence to the left wing of the National Liberal party showed a greater degree of correspondence to the political realities and needs of that time than did both his joining of the German Democratic party and his rather doubtful conversion to republicanism which supposedly took place after the great liberal dream of a constitutional monarchy was destroyed in November 1918. The 1920s marked Meinecke's conceptualization of power into the realm of metaphysics. This period also saw a transformation in Meinecke's political thinking. Before the war, his political ideas had been tinctured by an almost simplistic statism. In the 1920s, Meinecke's political thought consisted of a confused melange of political Romanticism, antiparliamentarianism, genuine fear of the modern power state, and remnants of his earlier statist position. This synthesis failed both Meinecke and, inasmuch as he was both a product and an exponent of it, the German Idealist tradition. The synthesis was almost inherently incapable of providing either a conceptual or a pragmatic frame of reference in terms of which understanding of the truly demonic forces in twentieth-century German history could be gained.

To a large extent, this failure was reflected in some of Meinecke's works and correspondence during the Nazi period. Although, for obvious reasons, Meinecke's scholarly endeavors during this time were limited to methodological or monographical studies, one of these studies, *Aphorisms and Sketches in History (Aphorismen und Skizzen zur Geschichte)*, and some of his personal letters are fairly revealing. In *Aphorisms and Sketches in History*, published in 1942, Meinecke carried forward some of the themes he had developed in "Causality and Values in History" and in *The Origin of Historicism*. He was, first of all, concerned with establishing the validity of the total human experience (*Lebensgeschichte*) as the basis of Historicism. Hence, he summarized the three basic points of departure from rationalistic and hidebound Enlightenment historiography. There was, of course, the religious point of departure as exemplified by the English pre-Romantics and again by the German Romantics; and finally, there were, of course, roots in the political and social thinking of such individuals as Herder and, a favorite of Meinecke's, Justus Möser. In fact, "A common new fundamental experience lies [at the basis] of all three paths—the mobilization of irrational strengths of soul in various directions." [114]

Again, Meinecke emphasized the "three chains of causality," this time, however, being somewhat more specific in defining them. Now, the biological chain was defined as the "typical," that which repeated itself in the development of a *Volk*, a state, or a *Kultur*.[115] Here, it would seem that Meinecke was in part contradicting some of his arguments

---

114. Friedrich Meinecke, *Aphorismen und Skizzen zur Geschichte* (Leipzig, 1942), p. 19.

115. *Ibid.*, p. 39.

put forth in the 1928 essay, "Causalities and Values in History," where the uniqueness and uncontingent nature of historical individuals, that is, eminences of *Kultur,* was opposed to causal chains altogether. Meinecke, however, still adhered to his definition of *Kultur* as that which broke through causal chains, and he repeated his emphasis on establishing a *"geistig-sittlichen"* chain of causality, independent from biological and mechanical chains of causality. There would seem to have been some ambiguity in his thinking at this point. However, Meinecke did not return to any consideration of the problem. The mechanical chain of causality was now seen, in *Aphorisms and Sketches,* as representing "the hard hand of fate," that is, those accidental forces in history that seemed to operate in terms of a superhistorical and therefore historically irreducible chain of causality.[116] The contradiction involved here, that is, the difficulty of reconciling temporally uncontingent events with a chain of causality (or indeed, even being able to *define* them as events in a conventional historical sense), was something that we saw earlier in his 1928 efforts to establish a *"geistig-sittlichen"* chain of causality. Again, this problem was left hanging in the air. From this ingenious but intellectually amorphous classification, Meinecke concluded that "world history [is], therefore, a puzzling web of Necessity—internal and external Necessity—and Freedom." [117] Indeed, as Meinecke had described it, such would appear to be so.

Nonetheless, he still emphasized the value of *Kultur,* both *an sich* and as a heuristic principle, in pointing out that strong *Kulturwillen* would prevent Historicism from degenerating into relativistic amorality.[118] In this context, Meinecke was of course once more raising the problem involved in reconciling an almost neo-Kantian definition of *Kultur* with historical analysis, a problem that was not in the least ameliorated by his continued adherence to the Rankean conception of the importance of individualism in history.[119] In this regard, we can see fairly clearly the role that Meinecke would assign *Kultur* in his post-World War II works, a role that would logically put it under the purview of the aesthetician rather than the historian.

Aphorisms and Sketches is also significant in that it contains the only concessions, albeit rather parenthetical ones, to racism found in any of Meinecke's works. In this regard, Meinecke pointed out—in illustration of the continual creation of history by the various *zeitgebunden* historians—the new importance of racial history and the previously unrecognized value of racial thought and its evolution.[120] It is questionable

116. *Ibid.*
117. *Ibid.*
118. *Ibid.,* pp. 66–67.
119. *Ibid.,* p. 108.
120. *Ibid.,* p. 116.

just how strongly Meinecke actually emphasized racial science in his own mind, although the matter is not made any clearer by his efforts to subordinate " . . . *Volkstum,* Race and *Reich* . . . to the laws of individual historical development . . . " *a la Ranke.*[121] Unless Meinecke was making a concession to the rigors of censorship, which is quite possible, it would appear that, by dignifying volkish thinking in this fashion, he was making something more out of it than a mere heuristic device. Moreover, his wartime correspondences also reveal some rather curious aberrations in his thinking at this time. Nonetheless, it would perhaps be doing Meinecke an injustice to overemphasize such statements.

Racism aside, the significance of *Aphorisms and Sketches* is that it reaffirmed and perhaps concretized the basic problems and contradictions arising from Meinecke's reorienting historiographical analysis in terms of *Kulturgeschichte.* It also pointed to a phenomenon that would become an integral part of his post-World War II *Weltanschauung:* his emphasis upon Fate, or better "accident" (*Zufall*), as being of primary importance in history, both heuristically and ontologically. For, by the time Meinecke wrote *Aphorismen und Skizzen zur Geshichte,* history had become, in his eyes, a tragedy, interlaced with the strivings and defeats of fated tragic heroes.[122] In view of his earlier statements on the subject, it is only fair to ask whether or not the primary actors in history, the "historical individuals," were products of chance or accident, or whether they transcended altogether, in Kantian fashion, even the superphenomenal causal chain that seemed to give history its half-demonic character. Suffice it to say, Meinecke's *Kulturgeschichte* was a rather confused and contradictory concept, and his adherence to it as fact and principle would raise many problems in historical interpretation for him. However, we should now give brief consideration to some of Meinecke's more interesting correspondences.

In a letter dated June 13, 1938, Meinecke expressed concern that Czechoslovakia might be utilized by the British and French to fulfill the same role as did Serbia in starting a world war! [123] Germany's role and the role of Henlein's terrorists are not mentioned. Indeed, it would appear that Meinecke considered the Czechoslovakian crisis much as he would have Serbian *irridentism* vis-à-vis Bosnia, no regard at all being given to the role of Germany as an aggressor forcing a confrontation upon Beneš and the West.

In this regard, one will be able to see a rather interesting tendency, in Meinecke's early letters, to focus upon German military successes;

121. *Ibid.,* p. 124.
122. *Ibid.,* p. 172.
123. Friedrich Meinecke, *Ausgewählter Briefwechsel,* p. 180.

later letters, particularly after the disaster of Stalingrad, becoming more philosophical in tone, concerning themselves more with such abstruse topics as the necessity of preserving the German spirit and German *Kultur* in the face of adversity. In a letter to Siegfried Kaehler dated September 26, 1939 (one day before the capitulation of Warsaw), Meinecke mentioned how delighted he was over the course of the campaign in Poland.[124] Similarly, in a letter dated July 7, 1940 (fifteen days after the French surrender), Meinecke admitted to feelings of pride and happiness over the performance of the army in France and expressed the hope that such victories as had been achieved in the West would allow for more freedom for the people on the home front.[125]

However, by 1943, after the tide had turned against Germany through the destruction of the Sixth Army at Stalingrad and the landing of Allied troops in North Africa, there was a noticeable shift in emphasis in Meinecke's writings. Now, in writing about the ferocity of Allied air attacks upon Germany, he remarked that he was preparing himself for possible destruction, but was yet "filled with thanks for that life that had been lived and its contents and for the hope, which is not yet exhausted, that the Germany spirit and the German *Volk* had not yet perished."[126] In a letter to W. Goetz, dated March 22, 1943, Meinecke expressed fears of a Bolshevik inundation of Germany. Besides this, however, he also expressed an interest—other than previous methodological ones—in Burckhardt, a development that will be of considerable significance for the future.

Apparently, the intensity of the Allied air attacks against Germany was starting to arouse Meinecke once more against the horrors of war because, in a letter to Kaehler dated June 2, 1944, he remarked, "The direction and conduct of the war by the Anglo-Saxons is becoming more and more . . . brutal. They are contributing basically to the decline of bourgeois culture and have no more grounds for holding morality over us."[127] Apparently, the Nazi conduct of the war made little impression upon him; neither did the hideousness of the war as a whole until it was brought home to Germany in the form of days and nights of bombing. Perhaps the greatest indictment that can be hurled against Meinecke both as a historian and as a supposedly cultured and sensitive human being is that, until the defeat of Germany became all but a foregone conclusion, both the war and the conduct of the war were matters that concerned him very little except insofar as he expressed satisfaction at the successes of German arms from September 1939, up to the first winter campaign in Russia.

Only with approaching disaster did Meinecke turn to the problem of

124. *Ibid.*, p. 357.
125. *Ibid.*, p. 364.
126. *Ibid.*, p. 415.
127. *Ibid.*, p. 453.

salvaging something of value from the war, and the problem of evil; for until the "reaping of the whirlwind" in German skies and on the continent of Europe, Meinecke's dislike of Nazism never developed to the point where he condemned it as *evil*. "Evil, Schelling already mentioned, belongs with the essence of God," he wrote in a September 18, 1944, letter to Kaehler. "All of us, positive Christian or Free Thinker, will not overcome this hiatus in the world through thought." In this context, Meinecke turned to the writings of St. Paul: "love and faith and finally also hope [will] bear us over the hiatus . . . love yet more than faith and hope." [128]

From the above examples, we can only assume that, as a German nationalist, Meinecke obviously was able to sublimate whatever feelings he had against the Nazis into at least mildly positive feelings in regard to German military successes. Only when the sea of conflict began to wash upon German soil and erode German hopes did he turn again to a concern—but, a very general one, never clearly focused upon the Nazis—with the persistence of evil in the world, in a way, picking up some of the strands dropped after *Machiavellism* and *The Origin of Historicism*. While much of this can be attributed, perhaps, to the exigencies of censorship, and the fear that most certainly must have been very real for him, the shift in tone and concern in his letters points to a very dubious side to his thinking, one that was perhaps both rationalized and reinforced by his previous inability to recognize Nazism as something more than a conventional militaristic authoritarian construct, somewhat in the classical European tradition of such phenomena. At least, looking back to this prewar tendency, we can treat him more charitably.

The Meinecke of the Weimar period was not Nazi in temperament or political orientation. There is little doubt that he was constitutionally incapable of approving of the bestial acts carried out by the regime of Adolf Hitler. Yet, Meinecke's understanding of Nazism was limited and, despite his removal from the editorship of the *Historische Zeitschrift* in 1935, he displayed a curious unwillingness to become bitter. Accusations of spiritual cowardice would miss the point, for Meinecke, within his own rather limited *Biedermeier* appreciation of things, was not a coward. Besides falling victim to the limitations of his own historiography, Meinecke was also a victim of his class and intellectual position.

Like most members of Germany's bourgeois intelligentsia, Meinecke was enslaved not by an idea, but by a nexus of ideas. His mind was ensnared and his political judgment enfeebled by that fascinating but

---

128. *Ibid.*, p. 464.

pernicious combination of machiavellian cynicism, heart-throbbing Romanticism, state worship, and revolt against modernity which was the bourgeois *Weltanschauung* of Weimar Germany. Such a combination allowed for a person to be against war in the abstract yet to tolerate victorious war in the concrete. This combination did not prohibit opposition to the Nazis; however, it did prohibit palpable action against them. The confused spiritual legacy that was bequeathed by World War I to Germany's lethargic liberals hardly provided that moral stiffening necessary to enable a person to oppose the most brutally efficient terror machine known to modern man. In this respect, Meinecke was not alone. His bitterness, confusion, hesitation, prejudices, and desire for escape into the realm of the eternal were symptomatic of the ills of a class that, perhaps even more than the General Staff, had staked its political life on victory in World War I. Now, the garden plot of Weimar republicanism had proved to be too limited a play area for individuals who once had attempted to synthesize dreadnaughts and voting reform. On the other hand, the endless realm provided by Nazi ideology was uncharted and therefore dangerous territory.

Meinecke was more intelligent and perceptive than most of his class. However, this merely allowed him to more persuasively rationalize his emotional unwillingness (or inability) to confront the ghastly facts of Nazism or to question the course of German cultural history. We must now turn to a consideration of Meinecke's post-World War II writings.

7

The Rejection of Power

THE IMPACT of World War II upon Friedrich Meinecke is fairly well known and has been well publicized through the translation of perhaps his most widely read work, *Die deutsche Katastrophe*. For H. Stuart Hughes, Richard Sterling, and Walther Hofer, this book marked the end of the trail for Meinecke, the final and unconditional rejection of all elements of state worship. It also pointed to his acceptance of the Goethean cosmopolitanism he had once scorned as being unhistorical. In a very real sense, they are correct, and much time has been devoted to tracing this process during and after World War I and during the Weimar period.

Yet, the significance of this supposed journey down the road from statism to cosmopolitanism—a march cadenced by the creped drum of disillusionment—has never been quite clear. Inasmuch as cosmopolitanism implies in an almost tautological fashion the rejection of more extreme forms of nationalism and/or state worship, the turning of Meinecke to this pole of thought has been considered of great ethical and historiographical significance. Such an attitude, however, is begging the question. In terms of what Meinecke himself probably hoped he was doing, there can be little doubt that his motives were of the highest quality throughout the long, drawn-out course of his eventual rejection of the self-assured statism we saw in *Cosmopolitanism and the National State*. However, if we are to consider Meinecke's role as a historian—moreover, one who had always been devoted to some form of political liberalism—we cannot judge in a facile fashion the purposes actually served by this development. We cannot allow ourselves to be beguiled by the archaic and perhaps not entirely genuine cosmopolitanism that Meinecke in part utilized to cover up flagrant errors of omission.

As mentioned before in the introduction, we must bear in mind that the writings of the post-World War II Meinecke were those of a man in his eighties and half-blind. However, also as mentioned before, we must realize that Meinecke's post-World War II writings were merely continuations of themes and attitudes easily observable in his earlier works.

As has been seen, several interesting developments occurred in Meinecke's thinking during the Weimar years, developments that *ipso facto* raised fairly penetrating questions regarding his role as a historian. Succinctly, these problems all revolved around Meinecke's changing attitude toward the state and toward the political process itself. As has been noted, his change in attitude toward the state was both resultant from and causal of certain pronounced changes in his attitude toward power. During Meinecke's statist period, the state had been nothing other than a vital synthesis of *Macht* and *Kultur,* each element serving the other in a dialectical process of spiritual growth. Meinecke had rejected both the Rankean and Hegelian teleologies. Nevertheless, he had never doubted that a spiritualization of state life could and would occur through this synthesis. The doubts came with World War I, and perhaps more important, with defeat. We have considered already the influence of statist, romantic, and corporatist elements in Meinecke's thinking, and how the often uncertain blending of these elements made his commitment to constitutionalism and to republicanism rather problematical. The political ramifications of this uncertain blend for his thought during the Weimar period have already been observed. It is hoped that thus far the connection of Meinecke's political thoughts to events during the period from 1907, the year *Weltbürgertum und Nationalstaat* was published, up to and including the years of the Weimar Republic have been reasonably clear. It is necessary to pick up where we left off, by considering his political thought, particularly as it was affected by the catastrophe of World War I. However, attention must first be paid to a strand of his thinking last considered in regard to his discussion of Ranke and Goethe in *The Origin of Historicism.* This is Meinecke's rejection of *raison d'état,* that is, *Macht,* and the concurrent opting for a purely cultural orientation for the German *Volk.*

Whether or not Meinecke's post-World War II rejection of Historicism signified, as Geoffrey Barraclough seems to think it did, his recognition that Historicism was *zeitgebunden* is rather difficult to prove. More important in this regard is something else Barraclough points to: "his switching his allegiance from Ranke to Burckhardt." [1] It is here that the end result of Meinecke's rejection of power through his conceptualization of it can best be observed and the subsequent results for his political thinking best appreciated.

1. Geoffrey Barraclough, "The Historian in a Changing World," in *The Philosophy of History in Our Time,* ed. Hans Meyerhoff (New York, 1959), p. 31.

The work that is perhaps most useful in gaining an appreciation of Meinecke's eventual rejection of power is his 1948 essay, *Ranke und Burckhardt*. It would not be overstating the case to declare that this essay most clearly points to the end product of his conceptualization of power, a process that, as we have seen, began with Meinecke's *Machiavellism* of 1924. Now, Meinecke was pointing to Burckhardt's concept of the *terribles simplificateurs*, the end result of a "mass assault against authority." [2] It was this "new and more forceful usurper of power," a phenomenon of which Ranke was unaware, that Burckhardt understood, at least emotionally. In a way, Meinecke's concern with the *terribles simplificateurs* of Burckhardt was in itself rather remarkable, particularly when we consider that the concept of "a mass assault on authority" was something to which he had never previously devoted any sustained attention. Certainly his treatment of it in *Machiavellism* was somewhat less than satisfactory. As we will see, however, this concession to the masses, which granted them recognition as bearing something of an active relationship to authority, made little real impression upon Meinecke, particularly in regard to his own solution to the German problem.

To a great extent, Meinecke's acceptance of Burckhardt's profound dictum, something that could have opened the door for him in gaining an understanding or at least an appreciation of the role of mass politics in twentieth-century Germany, was allowed in this essay to remain suspended. Most of the essay was devoted to a highly polished discussion of the unbridgeable dichotomy between Rankean statism and Burckhardt's definition of *Kultur* which necessitated a negative judgment upon the role of state influence. It is true that Meinecke pointed out the need for a new "composure" (*Fassung*), combining Ranke and Burckhardt; not an eclecticism, "but . . . a deep new feeling about the relationship of power and *Kultur*, of the elemental and the spiritual in history." [3] However, the dichotomy between Ranke, who, Meinecke admitted, tended to find a spiritual element in power itself, and Burckhardt who, although accepting power as necessary, nonetheless thought it evil, was never satisfactorily resolved. It was in fact deepened through the introduction again of the often-discussed qualitative differences between *Kultur* and Civilization. In setting up Burckhardt as an exponent of the former, Meinecke raised once again the problem of the precise relationship between *Macht* and *Kultur*. In this instance, the problem was resolved in a most curious fashion. Demonic *raison d'état* was held to make its appearance in the material and selfish Civilization.[4]

2. Friedrich Meinecke, *Ranke und Burckhardt* (Berlin, 1948), p. 9.
3. *Ibid.*, p. 22.
4. *Ibid.*, pp. 29–31.

Kultur occurred only when men wanted to create something beautiful about himself. In other words, the *Kulturmensch* stemmed naturally from *Kultur*, while the *Machtmensch* derived his perverted essence from that superfluous and pitiless *raison d'état* that stemmed from Civilization! Previously, in his work *The German Catastrophe*, Meinecke rather sharply differentiated between the *Kulturmenschen* and the *Machtmenschen* (*homo sapiens* and *homo faber*) and their respective roles in German history.[5] It would follow logically, although Meinecke never explicitly said so, that the *Machtmenschen* of German history, that is, those whose essence subsisted in a slavish adherence to ruthless *raison d'état*, partook of the more superfluous aspects of "Western" Civilization. The *Kulturmenschen* who, Meinecke seemed to feel were typical of Germany,[6] drew their nutriments from the wellsprings of Goethean cosmopolitanism. Thus again, the reader is faced with the problem created by Meinecke's divorcing of *Macht* from *Kultur*. Again it can be observed that he apparently was unwilling (or perhaps unable) to study *Macht* in terms of its role within a specific *Kultur*. Rather, he tended to relegate power to the realm of the surface and the ephemeral. He exiled it to the barren territory of material Civilization. Power had no roots in the realm of the spirit.

The problems raised by Meinecke's essay *Ranke and Burckhardt* arose from his continued revolt against the thesis of *Cosmopolitanism and the National State*. It was shown earlier that *Machiavellism* marked the beginning of Meinecke's conceptualization of power. Concurrently, it pointed to the abandonment of the state concept in terms of which his earlier historical thinking had been oriented. However, the logical conclusion of this process can be appreciated only in *Ranke und Burckhardt*. Although Meinecke evinced considerable perceptivity in applying Burckhardt's point of view to the problems arising from twentieth-century mass revolt against authority, his final divorcing of *Kultur* from *Macht* made any meaningful study of these problems almost impossible; for if the masses rebelled, they obviously had to be doing so within a particular historical context, within the framework of past hopes and present prejudices which in part constituted a given *Kultur*. To say that something as far-reaching and palpably meaningful as a mass re-

5. Friedrich Meinecke, *Die deutsche Katastrophe* (trans. by Sidney Fay as *The German Catastrophe;* Cambridge, Mass., 1950), pp. 27 and 28. Although Meinecke himself pointed out that, on page 20 of Fay's translation of *Die deutsche Katastrophe*, *Kulturmenschen* and *Machtmenschen* were clumsy classifications under which to categorize the attitudes of the German people during World War I, this *homo sapiens* and *homo faber* classification served virtually the same purpose, sharply differentiating between people of *Kultur* and people of *Civilization*.

6. *Ibid.*, p. 117–118.

bellion against authority derived its energies and rationalizations from the crass and superfluous netherworld Meinecke defined as "Civilization" avoided altogether the responsibilities of the historian. Meinecke at least recognized in this essay the problems involved in mass utilization of power and, more important, the problems arising from mass rebellion against authority, constituted or unconstituted. By the same token, however, he refused to pursue this theme any longer within the German context. With his final qualitative division between *Kultur* and *Macht*, symbolized by this setting up Ranke and Burckhardt as polarities, he seemed to jettison the historian's role and responsibility to investigate historical phenomena in the thoroughgoing fashion that was, hypothetically at least, the *raison d'être* of Historicism. Cultural history and political history were thus forever estranged from each other, never to be reunited except insofar as his desire to fuse Ranke and Burckhardt—how, exactly he did not quite say—could be taken as an abstract attempt to do so.

If the sources for *raison d'état* and its twentieth-century degeneration within the context of the mass society were not to be found in *Kultur*, the precise reasons for this degeneration become rather difficult to follow and become indeed quite obscure. At any rate, Meinecke's apparent recognition of the role of the masses in twentieth-century historical and social perversions was almost immediately lost in the final breakup between *Macht* and *Kultur*. Furthermore, his differentiation between *Kultur* and Civilization, and his strident identification of *Macht* with the latter, cast a pall over any future efforts to investigate the sources, particularly in the German context, of "German Fascism," and, perhaps more important, why this "Fascism" was so different, qualitatively and quantitatively, from all other varieties. Meinecke's dualistic approach led to rather meaningless, or at least extremely superfluous, statements in this regard in *The German Catastrophe*, where he explained why Italian Fascism had failed while Germany's Fascism, at least for awhile, had gone from success to success: the Italians were "not a soldiering people."[7] Meinecke had identified Fascism as representing a sort of nihilistic militarism. It is true that successful pursuit of militaristic goals represents a part of Fascist ideology. However, it was hardly the whole thing. By identifying Fascism with military atavism, Meinecke cut the heart out of any meaningful efforts to investigate Fascism in historical terms. For Meinecke, history had become in reality that process which described the evolution of a historical *Kultur*, as this was the one process possessed of any spiritual value which survived the barbarism of the twentieth century (the contradiction implicit here—particu-

---

7. *Ibid.*, p. 6.

larly in view of Meinecke's own definition of *Kultur*—is obvious). It is true, of course, that Meinecke's work, *The German Catastrophe*, was devoted largely, if not entirely, to an effort to investigate the root causes of Nazism, at least as Meinecke understood them. However, as we shall see, this effort never got off the ground, because an investigation of Nazism in terms of the total evolution of German *Kultur* was out of the question. Thus, at one point Meinecke went so far as to maintain that, for him, Nazism appeared to be something "foreign," an injustice that was more or less imposed upon Germany from the outside.[8]

In a sense, there is an immense irony here. Meinecke himself apparently did not recognize that, as a result of his attempts to save history from the barbaric meaninglessness inherent in its sacrifice to power, meaninglessness had entered into his own work in a most decisive fashion, for now, the root causes for Nazism had to remain forever secret, except to the degree that one can accept Meinecke's rather surface treatment of them as stemming from militarism and nihilistic lusting for power. If there was any rhyme or reason to Nazism or the causes of its coming into existence, they could not be discovered. In fact, it might be virtually undiscoverable as

The ideology . . . *völkischer Deutschtum* . . . the new religion of race, was in essence nothing other than a means to power for a thoroughly nihilistic tendency for which each ideology was correct only if it brought quick power.[9]

Thus Nazism, for Meinecke, was simply the apotheosis of nihilism. It was meaningful and understandable only insofar as every human being was possessed of atavistic urges for power. In the final analysis, moreover, the roots of the Nazism could not really be found in Germany, because its triumph in the 1930s represented an "un-German domination!"[10] Only the means for implementing an ideology, selected on the basis of grossest expedience, were important. Here, Meinecke emphasized only the most stereotyped causes for the rise of the Nazis: the role of Prussia, the clash between *homo sapiens* and *homo faber*, and the failure of the army. The ideology itself was apparently not of particular importance. Such a conclusion saved Meinecke from having to undertake an embarrassing investigation into Germany's spiritual heritage: *Kultur*.

---

8. Friedrich Meinecke, "Zusammenarbeit" (November 5, 1945), in *Politsche Schriften und Reden*, ed. Georg Kotowski (Darmstadt, 1958), p. 489.
9. *Ibid.*, p. 488.
10. *Ibid.*, p. 489.

The final estrangement of *Kultur* from *Macht* thus bore bitter fruit. It is true that the old, overly optimistic statism of earlier days had been jettisoned; however, the price had been inordinately high. Meinecke's successful effort (at least in his own eyes) to divorce considerations of power from the spatiotemporal matrix within which they developed led almost irrevocably to his final capitulation to forces he could not understand. Morever, his almost self-conscious bifurcation between *Kultur* and *Civilization* pointed back to the romantic currents we recognized as being so prominent after World War I and during the period of the Weimar Republic. In a broader sense, Meinecke, through his separation of the polarities whose integration constituted at least a viable framework for investigating the historical evolution and maturation of states, put himself in the position of being unable to recognize or even to have the vaguest appreciation for the true meaning of his descent into obscurantism in the name of *Kultur*.

8

The Rejection of Politics

MEINECKE'S FINAL CAPITULATION to the massive irrationalities of German history is evidenced in his ultimate rejection of politics, an action which followed World War II. This is not to say that he discarded politics altogether, either as a valid historical category or as a tool for the investigation of Germany's past. However, his final division between *Macht* and *Kultur*, as signified in his polarization of *homo sapiens* and *homo faber* in *The German Catastrophe*, made any holistic investigation of the roots of twentieth-century German political and social problems impossible. Furthermore, the solution Meinecke proposed for Germany herself (not for Germany as part of a Western Alliance) raises a rather serious problem. It indicates that Meinecke either could or would not recognize politics as being the product of the same spiritual forces that produced the *Kulturmenschen*, with whom he chose to identify that which was unique to Germany. Succinctly, in more or less discarding considerations of power and politics in positing solutions for Germany's problems, Meinecke in reality sacrificed a large segment of German culture to a formalistic concept of the word. *Kultur* was not really Spirit any longer. It was certainly not the entire spiritual heritage of the nation. It was, rather, one *portion* of this heritage, a portion that could be neither questioned nor rationally investigated.

The often bewildering results of this process have, in part, already been considered. We have seen how, in his 1945 essay "Cooperation" ("Zusammenarbeit"), Meinecke maintained that the ideology of Nazism was really only of minor importance in that "the new religion of race was, in essence, nothing other than a means to power for a thoroughly nihilistic tendency for which ideology was correct only if it brought quick power."[1] His assertion, in this same essay, that the triumph of

---

1. Friedrich Meinecke, *Politische Schriften und Reden*, ed. Georg Kotowski (Darmstadt, 1958), p. 488.

Nazism represented an "un-German" inner *"Fremdherrschaft"* was later repeated in *The German Catastrophe* where he makes the somewhat interesting statement that Hitler's National Socialism was not constituted of purely German forces, "but had also certain analogies and precedents in the authoritarian systems of neighboring countries."[2] In this statement, Meinecke revealed that he was, to a large extent, unaware of the many qualitative differences between Nazi totalitarianism and, as revealed in his statement regarding the failure of Italian Fascism, even other varieties of Fascism, to say nothing of the older forms of authoritarianism. Which "neighboring countries" he actually had in mind is rather unclear, although he might conceivably have been referring to Karl Lueger's precedent in regard to anti-Semitism and to the authoritarian Fascist rule of Dollfuss in Austria, as well as to France at the time of the Dreyfus trial.

Of course, Meinecke's motive for attempting to make the source of Nazism more European, rather than strictly German, is obvious: he was still attempting to preserve as much of the time-hallowed—indeed, in Meinecke's eyes, eternal—German *Kultur* as possible. In fact, Meinecke's commitment to cosmopolitanism was qualified somewhat by his emphasis upon the "dialectical" relationship between the individual nation-state and mankind in general. After all, Meinecke pointed out in *The German Catastrophe*, that the musical tradition of Bach to Brahms, the concerns manifested in Goethe's *Faust*—these were all uniquely *German* phenomena. Better an adherence to the peculiarly German permutation of universality than adherence to a "pale, empty, abstract cosmopolitanism."[3]

Outside of attributing the rise of National Socialism in Germany to the fusion of the uninhibited forces of nationalism and socialism which grew out of the nineteenth century,[4] Meinecke was really never specifically concerned with the ultimate causes of the German catastrophe. He never really considered racism, a problem he probably recognized before World War I, in any detail other than to point out that the development of anti-Semitism was one of the first steps on the road to National Socialism and, curiously enough, to maintain that the Jewish problem was never considered or treated adequately. He thus implied that he thought a "Jewish problem" existed.[5] As a matter of fact, what Meinecke actually did say about this problem would indicate he thought the Jews were somewhat responsible for the catastrophe that broke over

---

2. Friedrich Meinecke, *Die deutsche Katastrophe* (trans. by Sidney Fay as *The German Catastrophe;* Cambridge, Mass., 1950), p. 1.
3. *Ibid.*, p. 119.
4. *Ibid.*, pp. 2–3.
5. *Ibid.*, p. 58.

them after 1933. At one point Meinecke accused the Jews of being inclined "to enjoy indiscreetly the favorable economic situation" in which they found themselves after emancipation. In behaving this way, Meinecke indicated, the Jews "contributed much to that gradual deprecation and discrediting of the liberal world of ideas that set in after the end of the nineteenth century."[6] Of course, Meinecke's stolid sense of fair play compelled him to admit that the Jews had made positive contributions as well to the cultural and economic life of this country. However, that well-mannered anti-Semitism so characteristic of his class did come through, even while the stench of the death camps hung over Europe. The issue was blurred even further by Meinecke's statement in the preface of the book that he would "pass over in silence, for instance, all Hitler's political successes in the years before the outbreak of the Second World War. They have all vanished away into nothingness."[7] In other words, the causes behind both Hitler's rise to power and World War II were superfluous and not even of tangential concern to Meinecke because these successes were ephemeral. Only the war itself, the actual German Catastrophe, was important. Furthermore, in a June 16, 1945, essay entitled "Zur Selbstbesinnung" ("Toward Self-awareness"), he remarked that after Hitler's breaking of the Munich Agreement in March of 1939, Germany and the world could have finally realized the dangers inherent in his philosophy because "he showed that he did not recognize limits on the extension of power [and] that it was not to be expected that he held to treaties."[8] In other words, the formal breaking of a treaty revealed the dangers inherent in Nazism. By implication, the reasons behind this action, the forces and relationships that led Hitler to the point of the march into Prague, were factors with which Europe did not have to concern itself. A year or so later, in his *German Catastrophe*, Meinecke revealed little that would indicate a change from this position.

In *The German Catastrophe*, the German problem was summed up in this fashion: "The work of Bismarck's era has been destroyed through our own fault and we must now go back beyond its ruins to seek out the ways of Goethe's era."[9] In a word, the irrational fusion of nationalism and socialism had destroyed the old Bismarckian system (one supposes that he is referring either to his alliance system, or to his internal policies directed toward mollification of the proletariat, or to both). Hence Germany had to turn back to an era in which the state concept was altogether lacking. In this regard, Meinecke made his famous

6. *Ibid.*, p. 15.
7. *Ibid.*, xi.
8. Meinecke, *Politische Schriften und Reden*, p. 485.
9. Meinecke, *Die deutsche Katastrophe*, p. 115.

call for the establishment of the Goethe Circles and, concurrently, for a new variety of "ecumenical Christianity." [10] The corporatism we saw as being rather prominent during the Weimar period was gone. However, a final concession had been made to the strange blend of anachronistic Germany cosmopolitanism and quasi-Romanticism we saw as also being rather prominent during the years of the Weimar Republic. The *zeitgebunden* nature of Goethe's superpolitical world, something that was both a cardinal principle and probably a valid one of Historicism, was not considered, nor was its relative uselessness in a world of mass movements and mass perversions. One feels that Hofer was quite correct when he pointed to Meinecke's desires for a revival of Goethe as indicating his contempt or disregard for mass politics and mass movements.[11]

The brittle and almost impressively artificial nature of Meinecke's solutions to postwar Germany's problems was not redeemed by his 1948 essay entitled "1848, a Centenary Observation" ("1848, Eine Säkularbetrachtung"), in which he pointed to the years 1819 and 1848 as being of primary importance in exemplifying the failure of that liberalism which might conceivably have turned Germany away from the path of National Socialism. His concern here was with formal Prussianism and the failure to establish in Germany the machinery for liberal constitutionalism. He was not really concerned with the forces that both underlaid this failure and contributed to later developments that took place both because and inspite of the events of 1848. Therefore, the relevancy that Meinecke was attempting to create between 1848 and later events in Germany was never established with particular clarity, except insofar as he implicitly suggested the same oft-repeated general relationships between Prussian authoritarianism and militarism and the rise of Nazism.

Even accepting the validity of Meinecke's political observations regarding 1848, what relevance and purpose it had in regard both to post-World War II Germany and to his own political thinking was lost in the twilight zone consisting of Naumann's national socialism and apolitical romantic cosmopolitanism. Meinecke really had rejected politics as the framework within which solutions to the German problem of the twentieth century had to be sought. This rejection was not displaced by his final call for European unity and German and French reconciliation. This reconciliation was necessary, Meinecke thought, in

10. *Ibid.*, p. 120.
11. Walther Hofer, *Geschichtschreibung und Weltanschauung* (München, 1950), p. 148.

order to eliminate the "deadly blood-poisoning" threatened by modern war and to defend the free values of the West against Eastern menaces.[12] In espousing these ideas, he again begged the question, something that was almost certain to result from his artificial separation of *Macht* from *Kultur*. Would Germany's political and cultural traditions *allow* it to be integrated into a "Western system" in any sense of the term beyond the immediate concern for common defense? This question was never answered by Meinecke, nor was it ever asked. All that was certain for him was that *Kultur* and *Weltbürgertum* had to be synthesized to the exclusion of *Macht*. Weimar had to triumph over Potsdam; *Kultur* over Civilization. When this synthesis had been accomplished— and the anachronistic and chimerical nature of such an achievement seems never to have occurred to him—Germany could comfort herself upon turning its back to past forces and inclinations which Meinecke himself implicitly seems never to have understood.

It is perhaps of great significance for our analysis that, in his last major public address in 1951, Meinecke advised his countrymen that there was yet hope for the future of Germany, for "the deep cleft between Jesuit and Freemason still remains deep; but not so deep as previously." [13] Succinctly, in his last days, Meinecke appears to have been opting for a religiously based humanism founded within the cosmopolitan atmosphere of Goethe. In closing the address and, in effect, his career, the old historian quoted a phrase from Goethe that might well have been used to sum up his final position vis-à-vis Germany's past and future: "If only the eternal of each moment remains present with us, we are not suffering from past times." [14]

An almost aesthetic prestate cosmopolitanism complemented and reinforced by vague concepts of a united Western Europe—such was Meinecke's final solution for the German problem. In such a fashion did the great historian depart. He left half a dozen questions unanswered and perhaps unasked. The solutions he provided for a Germany ravaged in body (although this would not last for long) and in spirit must appear to us as being almost quaintly anachronistic ones. One of them, his desire for a united Europe, was really beside the point. Politics had been rejected. He had not rejected it as a field for historical investigation, for his essay on 1848 proved that it was still of some concern to him. He most certainly had rejected it spiritually. He did so by calling for Germans to turn back to their *Kultur*, a *Kultur* that had been divorced artificially from concerns of state and power. As we have noted

12. Friedrich Meinecke, "Ein Ernstes Wort" (December 31, 1949), in *Politische Schriften und Reden*, pp. 493–495.
13. Friedrich Meinecke, *ibid.*, p. 496.   14. *Ibid.*, p. 497.

before, Meinecke's separation of *Macht* from *Kultur*—in fact, of politics from culture—an effort that was meant to preserve the latter from the egotistical and nihilistic depredations of the former, succeeded only in making a substantive political investigation of Germany's past impossible. In Meinecke's eyes, power was power the world over. Every person or nation had been tainted with a primeval lusting for it. Once this demonic activity was recognized for what it was, the battle was over, if not won.

Meinecke's inability to provide for us an at least meaningful approach for the investigation of Germany's past must be seen as representing the sum of his intellectual experiences. To put it rather unromantically, the whole of his intellectual development was most certainly equal to the sum of its parts. Vestiges of nineteenth-century statism remained —this is to be seen in Meinecke's almost simplistic view of the role of Hitler *vis-à-vis* the state—and these were blended with the thirty-year process of his reactions against this statism. The product was a curiously nationalistic Goethean cosmopolite adrift in a world of mass chiliasm and mass politics, with only enough of the statist left in him to prohibit an understanding of the fundamental nature of the Nazi revolution and its relationship to that time-hallowed state he at first worshipped and later attempted to reject.

9

Summary

IT WOULD NOT BE overstating or overdramatizing the case to say that there is tragedy inherent in the course of Meinecke's evolution toward that final goal of political abnegation and facile cosmopolitanism which has been considered in this essay. It is also, one feels, almost extraordinarily simple to discern the roots of this tragedy. It is not, as Louis Snyder seems to think, that Meinecke's "liberalism" was counterfeit or posed.[1] Nor is it even in the fact, also suggested by Snyder, that Meinecke might at heart have been possessed both of Hegelian monism and anti-Semitism.[2]

The tragedy of Friedrich Meinecke subsisted in his inability to come to terms with the course of twentieth-century German history, or better, with the ascendancy of mass politics within this history, in reality the motive power of it. It is not that Meinecke failed to recognize the fact of the emergence of the masses onto the political scene, for it was, to a great degree, in fear of their emergence that he turned to the solutions of Friedrich Naumann. Rather, it is that he tended throughout his works to treat this phenomenon as if it could somehow be strictured or at least reoriented within the state framework that had come to him as an inheritance from the halcyon Wilhelmenian days. Before World War I, he attempted to wed the masses to the state, at least conceptually, through his support both of the National Liberal party and of much of the program envisioned by Naumann. His doing so is easily excusable insofar as the challenges posed by mass slaughter and the perversion (or perhaps, logical outcome) of mass politics, at least in the German context, had not yet been clearly outlined. However, his later ideas on the subject are far less easy to defend, for the quasi-romantic,

1. Louis L. Snyder, *German Nationalism: The Tragedy of a People* (Harrisburg, Pa., 1952), p. 287.
2. *Ibid.*, pp. 283 and 278.

quasi-corporatist state he seemed to favor during the Weimar period, while in part a reaction against the arid statism of prewar years, still envisioned the secure enclosure of the masses within an admittedly widened state framework. This framework was to have been first created in response to mass pressures and later, after a brief period of time, was to have inhibited these same pressures in the name of *Staatsnotwendigkeit*. Meinecke's apparent readiness to sacrifice parliamentary constitutionalism in the name of a sort of neo-Conservative state functionalism only served to point out that he did not understand the latter, at least in the German context, very well.

Even in these avowedly political ideas, Meinecke was well on the way to the "apolitical," a solution he proposed after the second German catastrophe, a tragedy that, for him, seemed to be qualitatively little different from the catastrophe of World War I. It is in the post-World War II solution that we can see the most palpable evidence of the historian's inability, or perhaps unwillingness, to come to terms with the issue that had been so clearly outlined so much earlier by Isidor Ginsburg in his 1933 essay on mass symbolism and certainly by José Ortega y Gasset: the problem posed by the devolution of power, or usurpation of it, by the masses.[3] Now, after the second blood bath, one that was even more clearly incited and carried through by mass emotionalism than was the first, Meinecke offered the solace that a return to prestatist Goethean Idealism, a return facilitated through the development of intellectually directed Goethe Circles (this of course to be linked to a revival of the ecumenical Christian spirit), would somehow succeed in either temporizing mass passions, or at least directing them into newer and more fruitful channels. *Machtmenschen* had to be sacrificed to *Kulturmenschen* and all would go well. It is here that another problem arose.

Machiavellism marked the intrusion of a rather important and far-reaching tendency into Meinecke's thinking: his attempt to conceptually separate *Macht* from *Kultur* in order to preserve the latter from apocalyptic intrusions of mass Machiavellism. As we have seen, this process was replete with rather serious consequences for Meinecke's historical outlook. Perhaps the most serious of these, and one whose presence has been implicit in all that has been covered in this treatment of Meinecke, was the intensifying of his previously discussed difficulty in coming to terms with mass politics. While the polarization of *Macht* and *Kultur* was perhaps a desirable thing from an ethical point of view, it made a holistic treatment or even consideration of the role of German mass power politics and its emergence from and relation to German

3. José Ortega y Gasset, *The Revolt of the Masses* (London, 1961).

Kultur almost impossible; for in the polarization of *Kultur* and *Macht*, we must recognize a polarization of cause and effect that served to make meaningful study of the development of mass ideology and its implementation into practice very difficult.

In criticizing Dilthey's positivistic recourse to psychological introspection in investigating the historical process, R. G. Collingwood notes, "The living past of history lives in the present; but it lives not in the immediate experience of the present, but only in the self-knowledge of the present." [4] Throughout his writings on twentieth-century German politics, it would appear that Meinecke was unable to perceive the limited nature of his *Weltanschauung,* a perception that might have at least allowed him to arrive at the synthesis of past and present pointed out by Collingwood as necessary in laying the methodological groundwork for historical investigation. Both in his inability to comprehend the qualitative revolution inherent in the politicalization of the masses and in his polarization of the *salient elements of public life* we must recognize Meinecke's fragmentation of the historical process, a perpetual avoiding of responsibility. In a very real sense, the course and tenor of his post-World War I reaction against *Weltbürgertum und Nationalstaat* prevented him from discerning his own rather problematical intellectual position in the mainstream of twentieth-century German political developments. This recognition on his part might well have been the first step on the road to an understanding of the forces against which he reacted, at first, only in fear, and later, when these forces had at least crystallized, in an almost desperate overlooking of their roles and significance in the German catastrophe.

The above constituted the tragedy of Meinecke the historian. The tragedy of Meinecke the good, bourgeois German intellectual raises a somewhat more disturbing question. Meinecke's post-World War II solutions to the "German problem" were solutions that proved to be quite palatable to the non-Nazi German of this class, for somehow, Meinecke, in his explanations of the spiritual disaster that had overtaken Germany in 1933, really did not blame anybody very much. The main villains for Meinecke were general European developments, that is, mass militaristic nationalism and the nihilistic craving for power. Admittedly, the German people, particularly its bourgeoisie, were guilty of sharing in these developments in great measure. Furthermore the national-social synthesis of Friedrich Naumann might have provided a way out. Perhaps, nationalist and socialist demands could have been synthesized in a satisfactory manner before the national-socialistic solution of Hitler first was offered. Yet, Meinecke essentially placed the blame for World War II and its attendant atrocities upon nihilistic power cravings,

4. R. G. Collingwood, *The Idea of History* (New York, 1956), p. 174.

historical accident, and fate. Such an approach is similar to placing the blame upon Original Sin. Certainly, it boils down to about the same thing. Perhaps such a conclusion is in the end correct. However, questions of cause, guilt, blameworthiness, or blamelessness then would be placed in the hands of the theologian rather than of the historian. Perhaps this is what Meinecke wanted all along. Certainly his specious division between spirituality and power led him in this direction. The tragedy of Germany is that so many have been enticed to travel on the same path.

Postscript

IN TERMS OF OUR WORK, it is of some interest and importance to consider German reaction to Meinecke, particularly after World War II, as well as some of the reactions of German historiography to the Nazi period, for the receptivity, or lack of it, displayed by German intellectuals and litterateurs toward Meinecke's work in general and toward his explorations of the sources of the German catastrophe are rather revealing as to their own outlooks on the subject, while the course of German historiography after World War II is obviously of some general interest.

Immediate reaction to *Die deutsche Katastrophe*, which first appeared in 1946, were rather mixed. Hans Ulrich Instinsky's review of it, in the October 29, 1946, issue of *Die Welt,* was perhaps the most questioning and reserved. Instinsky praised Meinecke for "making visible the interpenetrations of the general and the particular, his strong ability to depict intellectual developments . . . and, above all, . . . allow [ing us] to feel the breath of an atmosphere which derives its flavor from the personality of the writer as [well as] from the general essence of his time." [1] However, Instinsky went on to attack Meinecke's emphasis of the role of "chance" or "accident" in history, in particular in the rise of Hitler to power. "Chance," Instinsky pointed out, was merely the conceptualizaiton of a "transient moment," and it neither explained it nor precluded the role of general forces at work, forces that served to bring the Nazis to power.[2] Instinsky also attacked Meinecke's admittedly half-hearted "praise" for Hitler in unifying what the former thought to be the two foremost trends in German history: the rise to power, at least ideologically, of a nationally oriented bourgeoisie and the rise of internationalistic socialism. The very concept, Instinsky pointed out, of generic "national ideas" was a dangerous one and had been responsible for prohibiting the German bourgeoisie from playing a mature role in determining the fate of the nation. In emphasizing the

1. Hans Ulrich Instinsky in *Die Welt* (Hamburg), October 29, 1946.
2. *Ibid.*

synthesizing role of national socialism, Meinecke had yielded to it.[3] Instinsky was also healthfully skeptical of Meinecke's cosmopolitan solutions for Germany's spiritual ills. Commenting upon the *Goethe-Kreise* ideal, Instinsky remarked, "If it succeeds in fulfilling itself, it would be much, but not enough." [4] Throughout his review, Instinsky seemed to have maintained a position of analytical reserve, one largely free of emotionalism and Pollyanna-ish efforts to expunge recent horrors by retreating to the inviting glens of apolitical cosmopolitanism. However, this rather critical view of Meinecke was not shared by the majority of those German intellectuals who, after World War II, began to concern themselves with analyzing some of Meinecke's comments upon the origins and significance of Nazi bestiality.

In the November 1946 volume of the *Frankfurter Hefte*, Eugen Kogon, whose personal suffering under the Nazis was and is a matter of record (see his *Der SS Staat*, München, 1946, translated by Heinz Norden as *The Theory and Practice of Hell*, London, 1951), reviewed *Die deutsche Katastrophe*. In his review, he called into question two salient aspects of the work: the division of Germany into *homo faber* (*Machtmenschen*) and *homo sapiens* (*Kulturmenschen*), and, like Instinsky, the role Meinecke assigned to "accident" (*Zufall*) in history.[5] Germany, he maintained, could not possibly have been built and led by *homo sapiens* no matter what. Moreover, assigning a significant role to accident answered no questions and was, in any event, far-fetched insofar as methodology was concerned. Yet, Kogon praised the book as a whole, calling it important and hopeful for Germany's future.[6] Implicitly, he indicated that he shared Meinecke's hope for Germany's future.

Gisbert Beyerhaus's review ("Notwendigkeit und Freiheit in der deutschen Katastrophe: Gedanken zu Friedrich Meinecke's jüngsten Buch"), which appeared in volume 169 (1949) of the *Historische Zeitschrift*, was, on the other hand, both more detailed and more outspoken in its praise for Meinecke's work. The restoration (as Beyerhaus saw it) of *Zufall* into history reintroduced volition into historical methodology.[7] Moreover, Meinecke's ability to combine this with an

---

3. *Ibid.*
4. *Ibid.*
5. Eugen Kogon, "Review of *Die deutsche Katastrophe*," *Frankfurter Hefte*, vol. 1 (November 1946), pp. 776–779. Specific material quoted is from pp. 778–779.
6. *Ibid.*, p. 779.
7. Gisbert Beyerhaus, "Notwendigkeit und Freiheit in der deutschen Katastrophe: Gedanken zu Friedrich Meinecke juengstem Buch," *Historische*

uninhibited attack on Hitler's anti-Christian stance served both to stand the former in good stead as representing the "noblest liberalism" and to liberate German historiography from the Hegelianism that saw all acts in history as self-justifying. Beyerhaus also singled out as praiseworthy Meinecke's perception of Hitler in particular and Nazism in general as representing a *"fremdartigen Faktor"* in German history.[8] Actually, Beyerhaus maintained, the Hitlerian concept of "National hate" was more "Balkan" [!] than German (or Hapsburgian) in tenor and effect.[9] Overall, Beyerhaus was far more unstinting in his praise of *Die deutsche Katastrophe* than was Eugen Kogon, and certainly more than Instinsky.

Karl Dietrich Erdmann's article, "Anmerkungen zu Friedrich Meinecke's 'Irrwege in unserer Geschichte?' und *Die deutsche Katastrophe*," went even further than Beyerhaus's in defending Meinecke's emphasis upon chance in history. According to Erdmann, Meinecke was doing historiography a real turn by emphasizing the role of *Schicksal*, not from any complex of irrational motives, but out of his appreciation for it as a geopolitical and heuristic principle.[10] Moreover, Erdmann implicitly supported Meinecke's analysis of the origins and role of Nazism by: (1) adhering to Meinecke's bifurcation of *Kultur* and *Macht*, and (2) seeing Nazism in the same sort of syncretic light as did Meinecke (in this regard, Erdmann went so far as to identify the Weimar Republic with the socialist strand).[11] Erdmann, perhaps out of some inner uneasiness, went on to justify Meinecke's relatively mild accusations of his countrymen by pointing out that they came from one who loved his country, and thus out of deep misery and heartbreak.[12]

Walter Goetz, in his "Friedrich Meinecke: Leben und Persönlichkeit," was even more adamant in elevating Meinecke's moral role in German historiography. After all, had not Meinecke been a charter member of the "spiritual resistance movement" against Hitler?[13] Had he not

Zeitschrift, vol. 169, Heft 1 (1949), 73–87. Specific material quoted is from p. 75.

8. *Ibid.*
9. *Ibid.*, pp. 75–76.
10. Karl Dietrich Erdmann, "Anmerkungen zu Friedrich Meinecke's 'Irrwege in unserer Geschichte?' und Die deutsche Katastrophe," *Geschichte in Wissenschaft und Unterricht*, Band 2 (1951), p. 85. For a more critical evaluation of "Irrwege in unserer Geschichte?" see Hajo Holborn/G. Barraclough, "Noch einmal—'Irrwege in unserer Geschichte?' zwei ausländische Historiker kommentieren Friedrich Meineckes Aufsatz," *Der Monat*, 2 Jahrgang, no. 17 (February 1950).
11. *Ibid.*, p. 88.
12. *Ibid.*, pp. 89–90.
13. Walter Goetz, "Friedrich Meinecke: Leben und Persönlichkeit," *Historische Zeitschrift*, Band 174, Heft 2 (1952), p. 245.

attained a high point in historiography by fusing together *Wissenschaft* and *Leben*—in the form of Goethe—in *Die Entstehung des Historismus*?[14] Ignoring the rather unhappy realization that Meinecke did not actually accomplish the latter and probably gave but lip service to the former, we can certainly appreciate the depth of Goetz's feelings for Meinecke as a historian and as a human being.

By 1954, the year of Meinecke's death, much of the morbid questioning occasioned by military defeat and the attendant destruction had largely died away in German intellectual circles, and the death of Meinecke, on February 7, 1954, brought forth a flood of unqualified praise for him, both as a historian and as a lonely Cassandra, decrying the spiritual doom he saw inherent in Nazism. *Die Welt,* whose pages had contained, in 1946, the only really critical German analysis of Meinecke's thoughts on Nazism, now praised him for appreciating that *Geist* and *Macht* were qualitatively irreconcilable. Meinecke's emphasis on the role of *Zufall* was now accepted as representing a most cogent historical insight, while his concern with the twin developments of national and social streams was also praised.[15] In the words of the *Kölnische Rundschau,* Meinecke had been a "fighter for a true democracy"; while the *Frankfurter Allgemeine Zeitung für Deutschland* maintained that Meinecke had "recognized the dangers of National Socialism quite early and, in his writings, he attempted to warn and to enlighten the German public."[16] Hans Rothfels, in his *Trauerrede,* saw Meinecke as being rooted in a position between Burckhardt and Ranke, and partaking of the best features of both.[17]

All of the euphoric commentary upon the greatest German historian of the twentieth century was of course justified and correct. At the same time, all of it was equally indefensible and totally wrong. It would be superfluous, at this point, to repeat the salient criticisms of this work and to compress them into a rejoinder directed at the tendentious and poorly qualified praise German intellectuals saw fit to heap upon the admitted genius of Friedrich Meinecke. Meinecke's greatness as one of the foremost representatives of *Ideengeschichte* of our times deserved and deserves to be recognized. Yet, his inadequacies and weaknesses, intellectual and spiritual, must also be recognized.

Despite this apparent worship of Meinecke, it is well to point out that since the early 1950s, German historiography has made an ad-

14. *Ibid.,* p. 249.
15. Georg Schröder in *Die Welt* (Hamburg), February 9, 1954.
16. *Frankfurter Allgemeine Zeitung für Deutschland,* February 8, 1954; *Kölnische Rundschau,* February 8, 1954.
17. Hans Rothfels, *Friedrich Meinecke, Ein Rückblick auf sein wissenschaftliches Lebenswerk* (Berlin, 1954).

mirable effort to come to grips with the sources of the German catastrophe, or at least to describe it in substantive terms. It is doubtful that German historians have consciously reacted *against* Meinecke and his tendency to view the Nazi period as a nihilistic aberration and thus as relatively opaque to historical investigation. Nevertheless, there have been published numerous works on the Nazi period in particular, and on the "German problem" in general. The venerable historian Gerhard Ritter has contributed to the discussion in his *Das deutsche Problem* (München, 1962), and in his important contribution to *The Third Reich* (Baumont, Fried, Vermeil, et al., New York, 1955). Whether or not Ritter's tendency to view German developments in the twentieth century as being part and parcel of a Western tendency toward mass degeneration and totalitarianism has any more than heuristic value is questionable. Nevertheless, it must be admitted that while he is viewing Nazism from an angle considered by Meinecke, he seems to be more aware of the unique qualities of totalitarianism. Both Friedrich Glum, in his *Der National sozialismus, Werden und Vergehen* (München, 1962) and Hans Buchheim, in *Das Dritte Reich* (München, 1960), offer the reader comprehensive histories of the Nazi party and of the totalitarian state and attendant terrors that were its legacies. Both the Fischer Verlag and the rororo paperback series present an assortment of works treating the origins and the reign of Nazism in both documentary and analytical terms.[18] The most massive collection of documents regarding the Third Reich available in book form is *Das Dritte Reich, 1933–1945* (ed. Heinz Huber, Arthur Müller, and Waldemar Besson, München, 1966, 2 vols.). This book of well over eight hundred pages represents a significant contribution to the historiography of the period. Of course, Ernst Nolte's work, *Der Faschismus in seiner Epoche* (München, 1963) represents a notable contribution to the historiography of Fascism, and its translation into English

---

18. In the Fischer Bücherei series, see *Der Nationalsozialismus, Dokumente 1933–1945*, edited and with commentary by Walther Hofer, Band 172, and *Die Zerstörung der deutschen Politik, Dokumente, 1871–1933*, edited and with commentary by Harry Pross, Band 264. Walther Hofer also edited Band 323, *Entfesselung des 2. Weltkrieges*. The rororo paperback firm has published a series *Kunst und Kultur im Dritten Reich*, edited and with commentary by Joseph Wulf. The series consists of five books: *Presse and Funk im Dritten Reich, Literatur und Dichtung im Dritten Reich, Theater und Film im Dritten Reich, Musik im Dritten Reich*, and *Die Bildenden Künste im Dritten Reich*. Mr. Wulf has also published works on: *Das Dritte Reich und die Juden, Das Dritte Reich und seine Diener*, and *Das Dritte Reich und seine Denker*. He has written numerous other works on the wartime experiences of Polish Jewry and received the Leo Baeck prize in 1961.

(*The Three Faces of Fascism; Action Française, Italian Fascism and Nazism*) should make it readily available to a wide audience. Nolte, however, is not so much interested in Germany per se, but in synthesizing salient aspects of international Fascism, and this is perhaps a rather debatable approach.

Several other important works, written by German authors, have been translated into English. Joachim C. Fest's *Das Gesicht des dritten Reich* (München, 1963), has been translated by Michael Bullock as *The Face of the Third Reich* (Brattleboro, Vt., 1970). This work consists of a series of portraits of the more important Nazi leaders. Karl Dietrich Bracher's comprehensive study of Nazi rule in Germany, *Die deutsche Diktatur* (Köln, 1969), is now available in English. It has been translated by Jean Steinberg as *German Dictatorship: Origins, Structure and Effects of National Socialism* (New York, 1970). This is the most comprehensive history of the Nazi movement available in any language, and provides both a needed adjunct and corrective for Franz Neumann's massive *Behemoth*. The translation of Albert Speer's *Erinnerungen* (Berlin, 1969) by Richard and Clara Winton provides an interesting view of the inner workings of the Nazi government. As a study of Nazism as a movement, however, it is somewhat disappointing. The title of this work in English is *Inside the Third Reich: Memoirs of Albert Speer* (New York, 1970). Probably one of the best-known works on the Nazi concentration camps, Eugen Kogon's *Der SS Staat* (München, 1946) has been available in English since 1951. In that year, it was published in London as *The Theory and Practice of Hell* and, since 1959, the book has been available in the United States in paperback form. A most interesting textbook by Hannah Vogt, *Schuld oder Verhängis? Zwölf Fragen an Deutschlands jüngste Vergangenheit* (Frankfurt, 1961), has been translated by Herbert Strauss as *The Burden of Guilt: A Short History of Germany, 1914–1945* (New York, 1964). This book, designed as a textbook for secondary schools in Germany, is a courageous attempt to make at least young Germans aware of the hideous atrocities committed by their countrymen while under Nazi rule.

All of the above works testify to a willingness on the part of Germans to confront the tortured history of their country. To this extent, they represent an improvement upon the approach of Friedrich Meinecke who, conditioned emotionally as well as historiographically by the brittle culture and tenacious prejudices of his class, was hardly able to offer valid commentary upon a phenomenon too close to home for comfort.

Obviously, the response of German historiography to Germany's role in the twentieth century has been quite varied. On the one hand,

Ludwig Dehio has approached the problem from an almost quasi-Rankean viewpoint, that is, in analyzing the Nazi drive for hegemony in traditional power-political terms.[19] On the other, Kurt Sontheimer, in his *Antidemokratisches Denken in der Weimarer Republic* (München, 1962), has gone to great lengths to point out and to explicate the existence of volkish and antirepublican tendencies in organizations and parties *other than* those of the Nazis, thus tending more toward that "vertical" approach attributed by Hofer to Meinecke.[20] The *Vierteljahrshefte für Zeitgeschichte,* established by Hans Rothfels and Theodor Eschenburg in 1953, has printed numerous articles on all aspects of Nazism, from church policy to the Nazi attitude toward aesthetics. Moreover, an extremely interesting and significant article by Alexander Bein, differentiating between traditional forms of anti-Semitism and racial anti-Semitism ("Moderner Antisemitismus," *Vierteljahrshefte für Zeitgeschichte,* October, 1958, pp. 340–360) has appeared in this journal. The October issue of the journal carries a complete bibliography of literature on the Nazi movement published during the year.

Literature coming out of Germany on the National Socialist Movement and on the spiritual sources for the German catastrophe is both varied and voluminous. Obviously, I have not read all of it and have mentioned a few examples that appear to be more or less representative of those approaches with which I am familiar.

However, despite the obvious concern of German historiography with the sources of the German tragedy of the twentieth century, it is equally obvious that most of the major analytical works on this topic have come from outside Germany. Most of the books that represent attempts to approach the "German problem" from the point of view of a broad cultural standpoint, that is, the works that are concerned with the volkish mystique, the significance of the politicalization of Romanticism, and the roles of these phenomena in the rise of National Socialism, have flowed from the pens of non-Germans or individuals who were victims of Nazi persecution. Here, the reader is referred to Peter Viereck's *Metapolitics: The Roots of the Nazi Mind,* R. O. Butler's *The Roots of National Socialism,* Fritz Stern's *The Politics of Cultural Despair,* George L. Mosse's *The Crisis of German Ideology,* Klemens von

19. In particular, see Dehio's *Deutschland und die Weltpolitik im 20. Jahrhundert* (translated by Dieter Pevsner as *Germany and World Politics in the Twentieth Century;* New York, 1959), and his *Gleichgewicht oder Hegemonie* (translated by Charles Fullman as *The Precarious Balance;* New York, 1962), chap. iv, particularly pp. 247–265.

20. In this book, Sontheimer is largely concerned with forces that von Klemperer and, to some extent, Mohler would classify under the rubric of neo-Conservatism. Sontheimer has contributed articles to the *Vierteljahrshefte für Zeitgeschichte.*

Klemperer's *Germany's New Conservatism*, Walter Laqueur's *Young Germany*, and Mosse's recent anthology, *Nazi Culture*. Perhaps, in their efforts to examine the sources of Nazism from a sociocultural point of view, these works can be considered one-sided. But, even so, they must be seen as representing a needed corrective to the *Macht-Kultur* dichotomy, a phenomenon that is a legacy of Meinecke's rebellion against statism. In this regard, Germany historiography would do well to address itself to the task of reexamining the writings and ideas of Friedrich Meinecke.

Since Meinecke's death in 1954, his influence on German historiography was diminished, however his *position in* historiography has been virtually unchallenged at least in Germany. As we have seen, Waldemar Besson, in the April 1959 issue of the *Vierteljahrshefte für Zeitgeschichte*, called attention to Meinecke's inability to break away from his earlier egoistical view of the state and to accept the uncertainties and party egoisms of republicanism.[21] However, this article is significant because of its unusually critical approach. Moreover, Meinecke's tendency toward various aspects of neo-Conservative thinking (besides his slavish adherence to the older, statist conservatism) is not considered. Furthermore, Ernst Schulin, in an article, "Das Problem der Individualität," which appeared in the August 1963 issue of the *Historische Zeitschrift*, did point out that Meinecke's concern for the historical individual tended to preclude an investigation of the various collective phenomena of history.[22] Also, he pointed out that historiography should be on guard against the various irrational elements in Meinecke's thinking.[23] However, in this discussion (concerned largely with *Die Entstehung des Historismus*), Schulin did not link the *Individualitätsgedanke* of Meinecke to his conception of *Kultur*. He thus tended to overlook some of the basic historiographical implications of such thinking, implications that were sadly concretized in Meinecke's view of the German catastrophe. Nevertheless, Schulin's article must be seen as being indicative of a more critical attitude toward Meinecke and thus as being a useful point of departure for further endeavors. By and large, however, the darker aspects of Meinecke's thinking have been left alone by German historiography and by historiography in general, with the notable exceptions of a chapter in Iggers's fine work and in Maarten Brand's excellent work, *Historisme als Ideologie* (Aswen, 1965), which, unfortunately,

---

21. Waldemar Besson, "Friedrich Meinecke und die Weimarer Republik," *Vierteljahrshefte für Zeitgeschichte*, 7 Jahrgang, 1 Heft (April 1959), p. 124.

22. Ernst Schulin, "Das Problem der Individualität," *Historische Zeitschrift*, Band 197, Heft 1 (1963).

23. *Ibid.*, p. 132.

has appeared only in Dutch, and Snyder's rather incomplete analysis. Unfortunately, at least from my point of view, Sergio Pistone has come out with a somewhat laudatory work on Meinecke, *Frederico Meinecke e la Crisi dello-Stata nazionale tedesco* (Turin, 1969). Apparently, Mr. Pistone agrees with Sterling's evaluation without, unfortunately, having actually read Sterling or any of the other major secondary works concerning Meinecke.

An understanding of Nazism and the reasons for it successes cannot be gained through a one-sided analysis of its more spectacular and morbidly fascinating aspects. Attention must also be paid to the writings and ideas of the quiet, cultured, probably decent men who on the surface fought Nazism but were yet unaware of their own spiritual allegiances, or at least proximity, to traditions that contributed to the spiritual milieu in which Nazism was spawned and in which it prospered. In this regard, a reexamination of the role and significance of Friedrich Meinecke in German cultural and political history would appear to be in order.

Bibliography

Stiftung Preussischer Kulturbesitz Geheimes Staatsarchiv, Rep. 92, *Nachlass Meinecke*.

ARTICLES

Meinecke, Friedrich. "Geleitwort zum 150. Bande der *Historische Zeitschrift*, und aum 100. Geburtstage. Heinrich v. Treitschkes," *Historische Zeitschrift*, vol. 150, Heft 1 (April 1934).

———. "Irrwege in unserer Geschichte," *Der Monat*, 2 Jahrgang, no. 13 (1949).

———. "Johann Gustav Droysen," "*Historische Zeitschrift*, Band 141, Heft 2 (1930).

———. "Kausälitaten and Werte in der Geschichte," *Historische Zeitschrift*, Band 134, Heft 1 (1928).

———. "Preussen und Deutschland im 19. Jahrhundert," *Historische Zeitschrift*, Band 97, Heft 1 (1906).

BOOKS

Meinecke, Friedrich. *Aphorismen und Skizzen zur Geschichte*. Leipzig, 1942.

———. *Ausgewählter Briefwechsel*. Ed. Ludwig Dehio. Stuttgart, 1962.

———. *Die Deutsche Erhebung von 1914*. Stuttgart, 1914.

———. *Die deutsche Katastrophe*. Trans. Sidney Fay as *The German Catastrophe*. Cambridge, Mass., 1950.

———. *Die Entstehung des Historismus*. München, 1936. 2 vols.

———. *Die Idee der Staaträson*. Trans. Douglas Scott as *Machiavellism*. London, 1957.

———. *Für Welche Güter zog Deutschland 1914 sein Schwert?* Berlin, 1918.

———. *Geschichte des deutsch-englischen Bündnisproblems 1890–1901*. München, 1927.

———. *Leben des Generalfeldmarschalls Hermann von Boyen*, Stuttgart, 1896–1899. 2 vols.

———. *Nach der Revolution*. München, 1919.

———. *Politische Schriften und Reden*. Ed. George Kotowski. Darmstadt, 1958.

———. *Ranke und Burckhardt*. Berlin, 1948.

———. *1848, Ein Säkularbetrachtung*. Berlin, 1948.

———. *Schaffender Spiegel*. Stuttgart, 1948.

———. *Staat und Persönlichkeit*. Berlin, 1933.

———. *Strassburg, Freiburg, Berlin, 1901–1919.* Vol. II of *Erinnerungen.* Stuttgart, 1949.
———. *Weltbürgertum und Nationalstaat.* München, 1908.

Secondary Sources

BOOKS

Antoni, Carlo. *Dallo storicismo alla sociologia.* Trans. Hayden V. White as *From History to Sociology.* Detroit, 1959.
Barraclough, Geoffrey. "The Historian in a Changing World," in *The Philosophy of History in Our Time,* ed. Hans Meyerhoff. New York, 1959.
Berthold, Werner. . . . *Grosshungern und Gehorchen.* Berlin, 1960.
Beilchowsky, Albert. *Goethe, Sein Leben und seine Werke.* München, 1908.
Burckhardt, Jacob. *Force and Freedom: Reflections on History.* Ed. James Hastings Nichols. Boston, 1943.
———. *The Civilization of the Renaissance in Italy.* Trans. S. G. C. Middlemore. Harper Torchbook ed. New York, 1958. 2 vols.
Collingwood, R. G. *The Idea of History.* New York, 1956.
Craig, Gordon A. *The Politics of the Prussian Army 1640–1945.* Oxford, 1955.
Croce, Benedetto. *History as the Story of Liberty.* Trans. Sylvia Sprigge. New York, 1941.
———. *History: Its Theory and Practice.* Trans. Douglas Ainslie. New York, 1960.
———. *Logic as the Science of the Pure Concept.* Trans. by Douglas Ainslie. London, 1917.
———. *Philosophy of the Practical.* Trans. Douglas Ainslie. London, 1913.
Daniels, H. G. *The Rise of the German Republic.* London, 1927.
Dehio, Ludwig. *Friedrich Meinecke, der Historiker in der Krise.* Berlin, 1952.
———. *Deutschland und die Weltpolitik im 20. Jahrhundert.* Trans. Dieter Pevsner as *Germany and World Politics in the Twentieth Century.* New York, 1959.
———. *Gleichgewicht oder Hegemonie.* Trans. Charles Fullman as *The Precarious Balance.* New York, 1962.
Fife, Robert H. *The German Empire Between Two Wars.* New York, 1916.
Friedensburg, Ferdinand. *Die Weimarer Republik.* Berlin, 1946.
Gessler, Otto. *Reichswehrpolitik in der Weimarer Zeit.* Stuttgart, 1958.
Ginsburg, Isidor. "National Symbolism," in Paul Kosok, *Modern Germany.* Chicago, 1933.
Goethe, Johann Wolfgang von. *Wilhelm Meisters Lehrjahre* [Wilhem Goldmann Verlag]. München, 1964.
Gooch, G. P. *History and Historians in the Nineteenth Century.* Boston, 1959.
Heiber, Helmut. *Walter Frank und sein Reichsinstitut für Geschichte des neuen Deutschlands.* Stuttgart, 1966.
Heuss, Theodor. *Erinnerungen, 1905–1933.* Tübingen, 1963.
———. *Friedrich Naumann: der Mann, das Werk, die Zeit.* Stuttgart, 1937.
Hofer, Walther. *Geschichtschreibung und Weltanschauung.* München, 1950.
———. *Geschichte zwischen Philosophie und Politik.* Basel, 1956.
Holborn, Hajo. *The Political Collapse of Europe.* New York, 1962.

BIBLIOGRAPHY 159

Hughes, H. Stuart. *Consciousness and Society.* New York, 1961.
———. *Contemporary Europe: A History.* New Jersey, 1961.
Hunt, Richard N. *German Social Democracy: 1918–1933.* New Haven, Conn., 1964.
Iggers, Georg G. *The German Conception of History: The National Tradition of Historical Thought from Herder to the Present.* Middletown, Conn., 1968.
Klemperer, Klemens von. *Germany's New Conservatism.* Princeton, N.J., 1957.
Koch-Weser, Erich. *Und dennoch aufwärts!* Berlin, 1933.
Kohn, Hans. *German History: Some New Views.* Boston, 1954.
———. *The Mind of Germany, The Education of a Nation.* New York, 1960.
Krieger, Leonard. *The German Idea of Freedom.* Boston, 1957.
Matthias, Eric, and Rudolph Morsey, eds. *Das Ende der Parteien 1933.* Düsseldorf, 1960.
Mazlish, Bruce. *The Riddle of History.* New York, 1966.
Meyer, Henry C. *Mitteleuropa in German Thought and Action, 1815–1945.* The Hague, 1955.
Moeller van den Bruck, Arthur. *Das dritte Reich.* 3rd ed. Hamburg, 1931.
Mohler, Armin. *Die konservative Revolution in Deutschland: 1918–1932.* Stuttgart, 1950.
Mommsen, Wolfgang J. *Max Weber und die deutsche Politik: 1890–1920.* Tübingen, 1959.
———. *The Crisis of German Ideology.* New York, 1964.
Mosse, George L. *The Culture of Western Europe.* New York, 1961.
Naumann, Friedrich. *Das Blaue Buch von Vaterland und Freiheit.* Leipzig, 1913.
———. *Mitteleuropa.* Trans. Christabel M. Meredith as *Central Europe.* New York, 1917.
———. *Demokratie und Kaisertum.* 3rd ed., enlg. Berlin, 1904.
———. *Der Weg zum Volksstaat.* Berlin, 1918.
Neumann, Franz. *Behemoth: The Structure and Practice of National Socialism.* Harper Torchbook ed. New York, 1966.
Ortega y Gasset, José. *The Revolt of the Masses.* London, 1961.
Pinson, Koppel S. *Modern Germany: Its History and Civilization.* New York, 1954.
Ranke, Leopold von. *Das Politische Gespräch.* Introduction by Friedrich Meinecke. München and Leipzig, 1924.
———. *Die grossen Mächte in Zeitbilder und Charakteristiken.* Berlin, 1834.
Rathenau, Walther. *Briefe.* Dresden, 1926. 2 vols.
———. *Politische Briefe* Dresden, 1929.
Rosenberg, Arthur. *Imperial Germany: The Birth of the German Republic 1871–1918.* Boston, 1964.
Rothfels, Hans. *Friedrich Meinecke, Ein Rückblick auf sein wissenschaftliches Lebenswerk.* Berlin, 1954.
Saloman, Felix. *Die deutsche Parteiprogrämme,* Heft 3. *Die Anfange des Deutschen Reich als Republik 1918–1925.* Leipzig, 1926.
Schorske, Carl E. *German Social Democracy.* Cambridge, Mass., 1955.
Snyder, Louis L. *German Nationalism: The Tragedy of a People.* Harrisburg, Pa., 1952.

Sontheimer, Kurt. *Antidemokratisches Denken in der Weimarer Republik*. München, 1962.
Sterling, Richard W. *Ethics in a World of Power: The Political Ideas of Friedrich Meinecke*. Princeton, N.J., 1958.
Taylor, A. J. P. *The Course of German History*. New York, 1961.
Treue, Wolfgang. *Deutsche Parteiprogrämme: 1861–1954*. Göttingen, 1954.
von Klemperer, Klemens. *Germany's New Conservatism*. Princeton, N.J., 1957.
Weber, Max. *Gesammelte Politische Schriften*. 2d ed., ed. Johannes Winckelmann. Tübingen, 1958.
Wheeler-Bennett, John W. *The Nemesis of Power: The German Army in Politics, 1918–1945*. New York 1967.
Wolff, Theodor. *Through Two Decades*. Trans. E. W. Dickes. London, 1936.

NEWSPAPERS

Das Berliner Tageblatt, January 1, 1918–December 31, 1919.
Die Welt (Hamburg), October 29, 1946, February 9, 1954.
Frankfurter Allgemeine Zeitung Für Deutschland, February 8, 1954.
Kölnische Rundschau, February 8, 1954.

PERIODICALS

Beard, Charles A., and Alfred Vagts. "Currents of Thought in Historiography," *American Historical Review*, vol. 42, no. 3 (1936–1937).
Besson, Waldemar. "Friedrich Meinecke und die Weimarer Republik," *Vierteljahrshefte für Zeitgeschichte*, 7 Jahrgang, 1 Heft (April 1959).
Beyerhaus, Gisbert. "Notwendigkeit und Freiheit in der deutschen Katastrophe: Gedanken zu Friedrich Meineckes juengstem Buch," *Historische Zeitschrift*, vol. 169, Heft 1 (1949).
Erdmann, Karl Dietrich. "Anmerkungen zu Friedrich Meinecke's "Irrwege in unserer Geschichte?' und *Die deutsche Katastrophe*," *Geschichte in Wissenschaft und Unterricht*, Band 2 (1951).
Goetz, Walter. "Friedrich Meinecke: Leben und Persönlichkeit," *Historische Zeitschrift*, Band 174, Heft 2 (1952).
Gooch, George P. "Some Conceptions of History," *The Sociological Review*, vol. 31, no. 3 (1939).
Hajo Holborn/G. Barraclough. "Noch Einmal—'Irrwege in unserer Geschichte?' zwei ausländische Historiker kommentieren Friedrich Meineckes Aufsatz," *Der Monat*, 2 Jahrgang, no. 17 (February, 1950).
Iggers, Georg G. "The Decline of the Classical National Tradition of German Historiography," *History and Theory*, vol. VI, no. 3 (1967).
Kogon, Eugen. "Review of *Die deutsche Katastrophe*," *Frankfurter Hefte* vol. 1 (November 1946).
Neumann, Sigmund. "Decision in Germany?" *The Yale Review*, vol. XXXIX (Summer 1950).
Nürnberger, Richard. "Imperialismus, Sozialismus und Christentum bei Friedrich Naumann," *Historische Zeitschrift*, Band 170, Heft 3 (1950).
Schulin, Ernst. "Das Problem der Individualität, *Historische Zeitschrift*, Band 197, Heft 1 (1963).
Wolfson, Philip J. "Friedrich Meinecke, 1862–1954," *Journal of the History of Ideas*, vol. 17, no. 3 (1956).

Index

Africa, 69
America, 21, 22, 43, 45, 96
Anschluss, 94
Anti-Semitism, 2, 17, 39n, 91, 97, 106, 109–110, 112, 118n, 122, 123, 139, 140, 144, 154. *See also* Jews
Antoni, Carlo, 73, 81
Aschoff, Ludwig, 17
Austria, 94
Austria-Hungary, 44

Baden, Max von, 28
Barraclough, Geoffrey, 132
Bassermann, Ernst, 17
Bein, Alexander, 154
Belgium, 20
Below, Georg von, 16, 30n
Beneš, Eduard, 127
Besson, Waldemar, 86–87, 152, 155
Bethmann-Hollweg, Theobald von, 21
Beyerhaus, Gisbert, 149–150
Biedermeier, Meinecke as, 9, 23, 25, 38, 113, 129
Bismarck, Otto von, 12, 19, 23, 36, 38, 52, 82, 140
Bolshevism, 27
Borckenhagen, Ludwig, 118n
Bosnia, 127
Böttiger, Theodor, 100
Boxer Rebellion, 69
Boyen, Hermann von, 12, 13, 37, 38, 52, 91, 92
Bracher, Karl, 153
Brand, Maarten, 155
Brüning, Heinrich, 111, 115, 116, 134
Buchheim, Hans, 152
Bülow, Bernhard von, 68, 69
Bülow, Karl von, 32
Burckhardt, Jacob, 51, 53, 71, 74, 84, 128, 132, 133, 134, 135, 151
Butler, R. O., 154

Campanella, Thomas, 56, 58
Carrara, 51

Carthage, 43
Cassirer, Hugo, 33
Catholicism, Meinecke's attitude toward, 17
Center party, 16, 91, 116
Chamberlain, Joseph, 68
China, 69
Collingwood, R. G., 146; "historical imagination" of, 146
Communism, 112, 114, 115, 118, 119
Communist party (KPD), 95
Conservative party, 16, 17
Courland, 20
Croce, Benedetto, critique of Meinecke, 59–60, 66, 68, 72, 73
Czechoslovakia, 127

Dahlmann, Friedrich, 12
Darwinism, 18
Dawes Plan, 115
Dehio, Ludwig, 121, 154
Dilthey, Wilhelm, 68, 146
Dolchstosslegende, 41n
Dollfuss, Engelbert, 139
Dove, Alfred, 20
Dreiklassenwahlrecht, 16, 21
Dreyfus Affair, 139
Droysen, Johann Gustav, 12, 66

Ebert, Friedrich, 106, 116, 118
England. *See* Great Britain
English Pre-Romantics, 72, 125
Enlightenment, 13, 125
Erdmann, Karl, 150
Erfurt Program, 22
Eschenburg, Theodor, 154

Fascism, 99, 103, 108–109, 111, 115, 124, 131, 139
Fashoda Crisis, 69
Fest, Joachim, 153
Fichte, Johann Gottlieb, 14, 32, 64
France, 36, 43, 44, 45, 69, 92, 127, 128, 139, 141

Frank, Walter, 121, 122
Frederick II (Frederick the Great), 55, 56, 58
Freiburg, Meinecke as National Liberal delegate from, 17
Freiburg, University of, 5

German Democratic party (DDP), 3, 28, 29, 30, 31, 32, 33, 35, 42, 47, 89, 90, 91, 95, 96, 97, 98, 101, 102, 103n, 105, 109, 125. See also *Staatspartei*
German National People's party (DNVP), 2, 95, 97, 106, 108, 109, 110
German People's party (DVP), 2, 91, 101, 110
Gessler, Otto, 103
Gibbon, Edward, 72
Ginsburg, Isidor, 99, 145
Gneisenau, Neithardt von, 14, 37
Goethe Circles (*Goethe Kreise*), 42, 145, 149
Goethe, Johann Wolfgang von, 59, 68, 77–78, 79, 81, 84, 132, 134, 142, 143, 151; definition of *Kultur*, 74–76; Meinecke's admiration of, 2, 74, 140–141
Goetz, Walter, 121, 128, 150, 151
Great Britain, 21, 36, 43, 45, 69, 70, 127
Groener, Wilhelm, 116, 117, 118
Guizot, François, 46

Hammerstein, Kurt von, 34n
Hartung, Fritz, 121
Hatzfeld, Paul von, 68
Haussmann, Conrad, 62–63n
Hegel, Georg Wilhelm Friedrich, 58, 59, 64, 66, 72, 73, 81, 83, 110, 117, 120, 144, 150; Meinecke's criticism of, 12, 56, 120, 132
Heiber, Helmut, 121
Henlein, Konrad, 127
Herder, Johann Gottfried, 125
Heuss, Theodor, 62–63n, 90n
Hindenburg, Paul von, 106, 116, 119
Historicism, 60, 72, 76, 79, 125, 132, 134, 135, 141
Historische Zeitschrift, Meinecke as editor of, 121, 122, 123, 129
Hitler, Adolf, 87, 106, 119, 120, 129, 139, 140, 143, 146, 148, 149, 150
Hofer, Walther, 1, 3, 57, 60, 63, 64, 72, 86, 87, 98, 106, 110, 124, 131, 141, 152n
Hohenzollern Dynasty, 6, 97
Holstein, Friedrich von, 36, 68, 69, 70

Homo sapiens/homo faber, 134, 136, 138, 149
Huber, Heinz, 152
Hubertusburg, Peace of, 20, 21, 36
Hugenberg, Alfred, 109
Hughes, H. Stuart, 1, 59, 131
Humboldt, Wilhelm von, 38

Iggers, Georg, 87, 155
Independent Socialists (USPD), 28, 29, 118
Instinsky, Hans, 148, 149, 150
Italy, 36, 43, 44, 45, 51, 99, 108, 135, 139

Japan, 45, 70
Jews, 26, 97; Meinecke's attitude toward, 105, 113, 118, 123, 139–140. See also Anti-Semitism.
Jungdeutsche Orden, 29
Jünger, Ernst, 100

Kaehler, Siegfried, 128
Kant, Immanuel, 32, 80–81, 126, 127
Kapp Putsch, 32
Kaunitz, Wenzel von, 55
Klemperer, Klemens von, 100, 154–155
Koch-Weser, Erich, 103, 103n
Kogon, Eugen, 149–150, 153
Kotowski, Georg, 29

Landsdowne, Henry, 68
Laqueur, Walter, 155
Lassalle, Ferdinand, 101
Lausanne Reparations Conference, 115
League for the Renewal of the *Reich* (*Bund für die Erneurung des Reichs*), 90n
Leibniz, Gottfried von, 72
Lenel, Walther, 118n
Lindeiner-Wildau, Hans, 109
Lithuania, 20
Löffler, Hermann, 121
Ludendorff, Erich von, 41
Lüger, Karl, 139
Luther, Hans, 90n

Machiavelli, Niccolò, 54, 56, 58
Majority Socialists, 28, 29
Mann, Thomas, 3
Mayer, Gustav, 121
Mazlish, Bruce, 80
Medici, 71
Mediterranean, 44
Meinecke, Friedrich: adherence to Naumann's ideas, 2, 4–5, 10, 25, 81, 82, 141, 144, 146; attitude toward Jews

INDEX

(see Anti-Semitism, Jews); attitude toward Ranke, 9, 14, 15, 25, 34, 45, 46, 50, 52, 56, 57, 64, 70, 77, 78, 81, 83, 92, 103, 108, 111, 120, 122, 126, 127, 132, 133–135; attitude toward Weimar Republic, 1, 28, 29, 33, 44, 48, 88, 92, 94, 97–98, 104–108, 110–111, 115, 117, 124; German response to, 148–151; involvement with German Democratic party, 3, 28, 29, 30, 33, 89, 90, 91, 95, 97–98, 101, 102, 105, 106, 125; position toward Nazis, 1, 3, 11, 57, 95, 99, 106, 111–113, 114–115, 117, 118, 119–120, 121–124, 128, 129, 136, 138, 139, 143, 146, 150, 151; problem of defining *Kultur*, 49–50, 65–67, 73, 80, 125–126, 142; problem of determining role of state, 12–20, 23–26, 34, 45–46, 53–54, 56, 57, 62, 63, 76, 79, 82, 83, 95, 123–124, 133; reaction to World War I, 3, 10, 17, 18, 19, 24, 26, 27, 35, 37, 41, 42, 46–48, 52, 53, 83, 88, 94, 103, 110, 117, 124, 130, 131, 132, 137, 145–146; reaction to World War II, 3, 35, 42, 68, 107, 118, 128–129, 130, 131, 132, 140, 145–146; sympathy for Goethe (*see* Goethe, Johann Wolfgang von). See also *Mitteleuropa*

Metternich, Klemens von, 68
Mitteleuropa, Meinecke's ideas on, 20; Naumann's attitude toward, 8, 9, 20
Moeller van den Bruck, Arthur, 96, 100–101, 102, 103, 112, 124
Mosse, George, 154, 155
Möser, Justus, 125
Müller, Alexander von, 123
Müller, Arthur, 152
Müller, Hermann, 116
Munich Agreement, 140

National Liberal party, 4, 15, 16, 17, 124, 144
National Social Union, 5
Naumann, Friedrich, 2, 10, 13, 15, 16, 20, 23, 25, 29, 30, 32, 33, 81, 82, 83, 100, 141, 144; attitudes toward anti-Semitism, 5; *Mitteleuropa* (see *Mitteleuropa*); national socialist tradition of, 5, 100, 146; on social reform and the state 6, 7, 8, 9. *See also* Meinecke, Friedrich
Nazism, 71, 96, 103, 106, 107, 112, 113, 124, 125, 130, 141, 148, 149, 150, 151, 152, 153, 154, 155, 156. *See also* Meinecke, Friedrich

Neumann, Franz, 113, 151
New Conservatism, 38, 96, 99, 100, 101, 102, 103, 104, 112, 113
Nietzschean thinking, 18
Nolte, Ernst, 152, 153
North Africa, 128
Nürnberger, Richard, 8

Organization Consul, 92
Ortega y Gasset, José, 145
Osthilfe, 116

Pan-Germans, 18, 20, 39
Papen, Franz von, 115
People's League for Freedom and Fatherland (*Volksbund für Freiheit und Vaterland*), 18
Philip V (of Macedonia), 43
Pinson, Koppel, 29
Pistone, Sergio, 156
Poland, 128
Potsdam, 142
Prague, 140
Preuss, Hugo, 29, 30
Progressive party, 4, 16, 33
Pross, Harry, 152n
Pydna, Battle of, 43

Rabl, Sabine, 115n
Ranke, Leopold von, 3, 6, 12, 43, 45, 46, 48, 52, 59, 63, 65, 66, 67, 70, 76, 79, 82, 96, 106, 108, 111, 120, 122, 126, 127, 132, 151, 154. See also Meinecke, Friedrich
Rathenau, Walther, 10, 29, 33, 92, 106, 112
Reformation, 95
Reich Institute for the History of the New Germany (*Reichinstitut für Geschichte des neuen Deutschlands*), 122
Reichspartei, 17
Reichswehr, 34
Richelieu, Duc de, 58, 59
Riga, 30
Ritter, Gerhard, 152
Rohan, Duke Henri du, 62n
Romans, 43
Rothfels, Hans, 151, 154
Russia, 36, 69, 70, 112, 128

St. Germain, Treaty of, 31
St. Paul, 129
Salisbury, Robert, 68, 69
Schacht, Hjalmar, 29, 31, 103
Scharnhorst, Gerhard von, 14
Scheidemann, Philip, 118

Schelling, Friedrich Wilhelm Joseph von, 129
Schiffer, Eugen, 123
Schleicher, Kurt von, 111, 118, 119, 120, 123
Schmitt, Carl, 101, 112
Schreiber, Georg, 121
Schulin, Ernst, 155
Seleucids, 43
Serbia, 127
Seven Years' War, 20
Sforza, 51, 71
Shaftesbury, Earl of (Anthony Ashley Cooper), 72
Shimonoseki, Treaty of, 69
Snyder, Louis, 107, 118, 144, 156
Social Democratic party (SPD), 16, 17, 18, 22, 24, 28, 31, 40, 91, 97, 115, 116, 119
Sontheimer, Kurt, 154
Soviet Union. See Russia.
Spartacists, 31
Speer, Albert, 153
Spengler, Oswald, 100
Staatspartei, 26, 35, 103n, 110, 117. See also German Democratic party.
Stalingrad, 128
Stein, Karl vom, 14, 37, 52
Sterling, Richard, 1, 3, 53, 57, 59, 64, 84, 86, 87, 156
Stern, Fritz, 154
Stöcker, Adolf, 5
Strasser brothers, 100
Sybel, Heinrich von, 12

Talleyrand, Charles Maurice de, 27, 33, 43
Tat Kreis, die, 100
Tivoli Program, 96
Treitschke, Heinrich von, 122
Treviranus, Gottfried, 109
Triple Alliance, 36
Troeltsch, Ernst, 100

U-boat warfare, 40
Union of German Students (*Verein Deutsch Studenten*), 5
United States. See America

Vaterlandspartei, 18, 21, 39
Versailles, Treaty of, 31, 91, 121
Vico, Giambattista, 72, 76
Viereck, Peter, 154
Vierteljahrshefte für Zeitgeschichte, 86–87, 154
Vogt, Hannah, 153
Volkskonservativen, 109
Voltaire, François Marie Arouet de, 72

Wagner, Adolf, 17
Warsaw, 128
Weber, Alfred, 29
Weber, Max, 4, 5, 7, 9, 22, 23, 24, 29, 46, 89, 100
Weimar Constitutional Assembly, 47
Weimar Republic, 2, 3, 28, 62, 100, 103, 116, 118, 121, 123, 124, 130, 131, 132, 137, 141, 145, 150. See also Meinecke, Friedrich
Westarp, Kuno von, 109, 110, 112
Wilhelm II, 6, 23, 36, 68, 69, 144
Wolff, Theodor, 30, 31, 33
World War I, 15, 54, 71, 98, 104, 106, 124, 130, 139, 144. See also Meinecke, Friedrich
World War II, 15, 126, 148, 149. See also Meinecke, Friedrich

Young Plan, 115
Yugoslavia, 44

Zama, Battle of, 43

www.ingramcontent.com/pod-product-compliance
Lightning Source LLC
Chambersburg PA
CBHW021710230426

43668CB00008B/785